"PUT THE SON OF A BITCH
ON THE PHONE!"

Justin Thomas grabbed the phone away from Kim LeBlanc. "Look would you quit calling over here and arguing," he yelled into it at Regina Hartwell. "Quit your goddamned yelling. Quit your goddamned screaming, you know what I'm saying. It's pointless for y'all to fight and argue if y'all can't talk right."

"I can get you screwed," said Hartwell.

Thomas laughed. LeBlanc was terrified as she listened in on the extension. But Justin had dealt with real threats before, drug-family threats. Regina was just talking out of the side of her mouth. And he knew that.

"Just leave it alone, bitch," he shouted.

"If you hurt Kim," Hartwell screamed, "I'll have you—"

"Don't call if you're going to argue and threaten me." Justin hung up.

Kim stayed on the line.

"I can have the son of a bitch thrown in prison," Regina yelled to her.

The screaming voices raced through Kim's head and she felt caught. She hung up only to hear Justin yelling at her, too.

"I ain't letting nobody send me to prison. Especially not some coke-snorting lesbian bitch. Ain't nobody sending me to prison! And I'm going to make damn sure of that, with or without you."

WASTED

SUZY SPENCER

PINNACLE BOOKS
Kensington Publishing Corp.
http://www.kensingtonbooks.com

Some names have been changed to protect the privacy of individuals connected to this story.

PINNACLE BOOKS are published by

Kensington Publishing Corp.
850 Third Avenue
New York, NY 10022

All Kensington Titles, Imprints, and Distributed Lines are available at special quantity discounts for bulk purchases for sales promotions, premiums, fund-raising, and educational or institutional use. Special book excerpts or customized printings can also be created to fit specific needs. For details, write or phone the office of the Kensington special sales manager: Kensington Publishing Corp., 850 Third Avenue, New York, NY 10022, attn: Special Sales Department, Phone: 1-800-221-2647.

Pinnacle and the P logo Reg. U.S. Pat. & TM Off.

ISBN-13: 978-0-7860-2008-9
ISBN-10: 0-7860-2008-3

First Printing: December 1998

10 9 8 7 6 5 4 3

Printed in the United States of America

To my many friends and family who have the serenity to accept the things they cannot change and the courage to change the things they can.

PROLOGUE

Thursday, June 29, 1995, intermittent thunderstorms steadied the temperature near 80 degrees. Ninety percent humidity, though, provoked an easy, morning sweat. This was Texas.

In fact, it was Austin, Texas, home of high-tech millionaires and teenaged slackers, show-biz liberals, poor Hispanics, proud rednecks, environmentalists, and Fundamentalists.

It was a state capital full of bumper stickers reading, "On Earth as it is in Austin" and "Impeach Billary." Both stickers were plastered to the rusted fenders of old hippie vans, to the shiny rears of new Chevy Suburbans, to the scratched bumpers of dual-wheeled pickup trucks, even a Mercedes or two.

In the heat of the day, they all whizzed down Lamar Boulevard, a hectic street that wound from far north Austin to deep south Austin. Lamar cut past the Yellow Rose stripper bar, the State School for the Blind, through downtown, and across Town Lake—a vein of the Colorado River.

There, oak trees that looked like wise Indian chiefs, grew beside fast-food restaurants frequented by cops and prosecutors. Tanned, homeless men and women and vendors of tie-dyed T-shirts stood on corners near print shops, car washes, and nondescript apartment buildings.

One of those nondescript buildings on South Lamar was the Château. A three-story complex rising high on a hill, the Château was hidden behind a long, tall, plain, concrete wall. The wall looked ripe for gang graffiti, but rarely was graffiti there.

Occasionally a dead body was found down by the lake, over by the train tracks, but it was usually the body of a transient. Crime was less rampant in this neighborhood than one might have thought.

During the daytime, the Château was a quiet complex. It had one obscure driveway off Lamar, and two narrow back drives that exited onto the tiny residential street behind. Around noon, there were three, maybe four or five cars in the parking lot. Rarely, at that time of day, was anyone seen.

So no one noticed as a 6'4", handsome drug dealer and addict climbed the backstairs of the Château, a building known to police as a gay and lesbian residence. He strolled into an apartment on the second floor, easily. The doorway was shielded from the walkway by hallways, and the door was unlocked. It usually was. He knew that. He'd been there many times. Just a few weeks before, he'd stayed there while its twenty-five-year-old tenant, Regina Hartwell, vacationed in Cancun, Mexico.

He glanced at Regina's greyhound-whippet mutt Spirit and her mangy cat Ebenezer, the one with the bare-haired tail. They greeted him, and they smelled the enemy. He pushed them aside and walked on into the living room. The scent of Regina filled the place. Her scent was a bit musky: a lot of perfume—Bijan, her favorite—the dog, the cat. He glanced around.

Empty Marlboro cigarette packs and empty beer bottles

covered the black-and-white-checkered coffee table. So did photos of Kim LeBlanc. Kim alone. Kim and Regina hugging. His hazel-green eyes lingered on the photos. He felt his adrenaline start to pump. He looked down at Regina.

She lay on the living room couch, groggy. Only three or four hours had passed since her last drink. Even fewer had passed since her last Valium. She wore a purple T-shirt, just like he did. She had on Garfield boxer shorts with red hearts and "Eat Your Heart Out" printed on the fabric.

Her white, crepe paper-skinned legs from too-much, too-fast weight loss shone. She was only 5'1" tall and 110 pounds, having dropped thirty pounds in a mere three weeks. The tattoo on her ankle seemed smudged.

She had on dark blue, cotton panties and was having her period. She raised up and said matter of factly, "What up, Jay?"

"Hi, Reg," he said.

But Regina's hazel eyes betrayed her.

He sat down by the couch. His adrenaline pumped harder.

She knew she was about to die.

He lifted a single-edged knife.

Regina went numb with fear. She fought.

He hadn't expected that.

Hard, fast, she fought him. Fear made her strong, and fear made her feel no pain. It always had. She knocked the knife out of his fist, grabbed it, and sliced the webbing of his right hand.

The adrenaline coursed through his body as the blood squirted out of his hand. He was infuriated. He wasn't going to settle for this. Not this martial arts expert. Not this infantryman. He wrestled the weapon back from her.

He hammered the knife into the front of Regina's neck, one swift, precise blow, five, six inches deep. He severed her vein, then an artery, then the upper lobe of her right lung. Finally, the knife stopped deep between the fourth and fifth ribs of Regina's back.

He waited.

Two to three minutes later, she was unconscious.

He rested.

Five minutes more and Regina Hartwell was dead, drowned in her own blood.

CHAPTER 1

Terry Duval, fire chief of the Bluebonnet Volunteer Fire Department in rural Bastrop County, Texas, was putting his crew through their usual Thursday night drills. That night, it was truck training. There were fifteen to twenty volunteers, many of them teenaged, junior firefighters, working in a light, summer rain.

At 9:38 p.m., Duval received a page—vehicle fire on Farm to Market Road 1209. Immediately, an assistant fire chief left for the call in his private vehicle. Duval stayed behind to coordinate the crew, adults and teens alike. One minute later, he had a brush truck on its way. Another minute later, a larger pump truck left.

About the same time, Sharon Duval, Terry's wife and a labor-and-delivery nurse, received a medical call for the fire. She too left for the scene. The night would be hot, and the men would need fluids to drink—perhaps, but hopefully not, medical attention, too.

For half the run, the volunteers studied the fire—its orange glow lighting the night sky a mile away. Seven, eight minutes later, all the firefighters stood along the tiny road and stared into the blazing, green, grassy area.

A whirling, tornado-like column of flames roared twenty-five feet toward the charcoal heavens and clouded the men's view. Sun yellow tips of fire licked the trees' emerald leaves into amber brown. Sweat dripped down the firefighters' faces.

Duval set up the pumper and radio communication and got everyone in position. The assistant chief led a crew of four down the 170-foot trail to the fire. In the dark, one of them accidentally kicked over a nearly knee-high metal canister as he tried to stretch the 150-foot hose to 170 feet. Quickly, he uprighted the can and sat down on it as he fought the fire.

At 10:10 p.m., Duval called the sheriff's department and reported a probable stolen vehicle. He knew it wasn't uncommon for stolen cars and trucks to be dumped in this farmland just a half-hour drive from Austin. He then directed several men onto traffic control. Drizzle coated his body. Smoke was thick and heavy in the humid, night air.

Two firefighters returned from the fire to put on air packs. Five minutes later, the blaze was almost out, and Duval was down at the vehicle. He walked around the perimeter of the 40-foot-wide clearing, staring at a burned-out Jeep with no license plates and no tires.

The tires had melted so that the vehicle rested on its belly. Duval could not see in the dark that one license plate, its right half scorched black, lay on the ground—RHV 33H, the 33H barely readable. A burned compact disc lay a mere half inch or less from the plate. It, too, blended invisibly into the night.

Duval could see that the once green trees above the Jeep were brown from the heat. A trail of rain-dampened grass, burned black, ran from an upside down, five-gallon gas can to the Jeep. It was the same canister the firefighter had overturned earlier.

Near the can was a round, green spot of unburned grass that perfectly matched the circumference of the can. The opened top of the can was burned. The smell of gasoline permeated the wet air, and Duval knew that an accelerant had been used.

He directed two men to stay on the hand line. He was worried there might be a second explosion. The odor of gas was as dense as the wet air. Gas, burned rubber, melted metal—it was a sickening combination of smells.

Duval then took a closer inspection of the vehicle, starting at the burned Jeep's right-rear corner. Glass crunched under his feet. Duval stopped, having noticed something in the back seat. He ordered the junior firefighters away from the scene and everyone else back forty feet. Only the two men on the hand line were allowed to stay.

Duval had spotted bones, then a skull. He realized a blackened corpse lay in the back seat; it looked like a monkey carved out of cold, hard, black lava. The Jeep, in contrast, was ashen white.

"We have a crime scene here," Duval said as he called the sheriff's department a second time. "Step up the response."

"Want to go down and see the body?" said Duval to his wife.

"No," said Sharon. She looked around. Everyone seemed to be nervously smoking cigarettes, lots of cigarettes.

Patrol Sergeant John Barton of the Bastrop County Sheriff's Department arrived and met with Duval. The two men then walked down the trail to the Jeep, a flashlight in Barton's hand. Barton aimed his light beam and saw the body.

It lay in fetal position, the soft tissue of the head burned completely off. Its shrunken, cooked eyes were at the bottom of the orbital cavities. Its ears were missing. Its arms and legs were jagged stumps. Its chest was distorted, but the full curve of a woman's breasts was clearly visible.

The men sealed off the area, and Barton phoned the sheriff's office. "You need to call the Criminal Investigation Division investigator that handles homicide," he said.

The office called CID investigator Sergeant Don Nelson.

In response to Duval's first abandoned-vehicle call, two more

Bastrop County Sheriff's officers arrived. Then the sheriff and justice of the peace Katherine K. Hanna arrived. Within twenty to thirty minutes, Nelson was on the scene, and Barton turned the crime over to him.

But in the dark of night, even with lights set up, no one saw the burned, black license plate. Barton located the Jeep's Vehicle Identification Number—1J4FY49S5SP240535—and called the office via cell phone once again. "Run this number for me."

Nelson took measurements with Barton, then collected evidence with patrol Deputy Robert Gremillion. Nelson personally filled out an evidence tag for the burned fuel can. He took photographs of the Jeep and the body.

"I need to photograph the underneath," he said.

They rolled the body over and found tucked beneath the small of its back something that looked to Gremillion like toilet paper. It was scorched cotton cloth, the color blue. Wrapped in the cloth was a single-edged lockblade knife. The knife was unburned, except for one small, scorched, black spot on the wooden handle.

Nelson and two funeral-home workers then tried to remove the body from the back seat, but the crispened corpse crumbled like toast. They were forced to body bag the entire seat, which was only a frame and springs, and the blackened–like–lava corpse. Still, they left a few body parts behind.

Ten a.m., Friday, June 30, 1995, Travis County Chief Medical Examiner Roberto J. Bayardo, M.D. began the post-mortem examination under the written authorization of Katherine K. Hanna, Justice of the Peace, Precinct 3, Bastrop County, Texas.

The partially cremated remains had an estimated height of sixty inches and a residual weight of approximately seventy pounds. The external genitalia were identified as those of a female. The right foot and the lower portion of the right leg were missing. The right hand was completely separated. The back was also extensively charred.

Body X-rays revealed no bullets or broken knives.

There was a one-inch wide stab wound from the soft, front portion of the neck, just above the clavicle, to the fifth rib of the back. The stab track traced a thirty-degree angle, five to six inches deep. It cut through an artery, then a vein, then through the upper lobe of the right lung.

The wound cut the same vessels an undertaker cuts to clean a corpse.

There was a fixed, stainless steel retainer with stainless steel sleeves over the first bicuspid teeth. The retainer was placed in a special envelope, labeled, signed, and saved.

Vaginal smears were negative for sperm.

Dr. Bayardo slit the corpse from the chin to the pubis. In the rib cage, there was the end of the stab wound track. The right pleural cavity was filled with approximately three pints of liquid and clotted blood.

The left leaf of the diaphragm had a one-and-a-half-inch laceration that appeared to be heat-related. Through this laceration the burned base of the diaphragm was protruding.

Only a scanty amount of blood remained in the cardiovascular system.

Both lungs were collapsed. The lower lobe of the left lung was charred and markedly shrunken. The tracheobronchial tree contained a small amount of vomit, as did the upper trachea and larynx.

The woman had been menstruating. A recent corpus luteum was present in the right ovary.

The tip of her tongue was burned.

Her brain had coagulated from the heat, turning into jelly-like mush. The blood in her head had drained to the right side.

Alcohol and Valium were present in her blood, and alcohol and cocaine in her bile.

The cause of death, determined Dr. Bayardo, was a stab wound of the neck into the right chest.

Unable to identify the body through fingerprints or any

other visual means, the Travis County Morgue sent the corpse
to the Bastrop County funeral home.

Jeremy Barnes walked into Regina Hartwell's apartment to
get a pot she had borrowed so that he could cook spaghetti. He
also wanted to see how messy the apartment was and how long
it would take him to clean it. Barnes, a friend and neighbor of
Hartwell's, often cleaned her apartment to earn extra money.

The place was filthy—beer bottles, empty Marlboro packs,
ashtrays overflowing their rims, dirty bathroom, dirty bedroom. What he thought were tampons were on the floor. He
didn't pay much attention to them, though. He knew that
Hartwell was having her period and figured her mutt Spirit
had pulled them out of the trash.

In the living room, Barnes saw a dark stain on the carpet.
Tea, coffee, smeared dog do, he guessed. Regina was a slob.
He'd cleaned her apartment enough times to know that. No-
ticing that Spirit didn't have any food or water, he filled a
soup bowl with water and left.

Anita Morales closed out her last day on the job as an
intern for the Austin Police Department. As she drove home
on the hot, final Friday of June 1995, she passed Regina
Hartwell's apartment and stared. She and Regina had planned
to talk the day before, but they'd never connected despite several pages from Regina and returned calls from Anita. Morales was worried, but she drove on home.

Saturday, July 1, 1995 was a day of more warm tempera-
tures and bright, sunny skies. But Morales and her roommate,
Carla Reid, were indoors painting their new apartment, and

Carla knew that Anita was distracted. "Regina hasn't called you back, has she?"

Morales shook her head no.

"Have you tried . . . ?" Reid named a litany of friends, all of whom Morales had phoned, none of whom had heard from Hartwell.

Reid dropped her paintbrush and grabbed Morales by the hand. "We're going over there, now."

They entered Regina Hartwell's apartment through a window they both knew had been broken for months. Why they didn't go through the door, they don't remember. It was unlocked.

In the doorway, they spotted bloody tissues on the floor. Like Jeremy Barnes, they, too, thought the tissues were tampons Spirit had dragged from the trash. But they didn't pay much attention to them. They were busy looking for Regina, hoping she hadn't overdosed or passed out and hit herself on the head.

They glanced at Spirit. The sweet, abandoned mutt didn't run up to them like she usually did. She cowered in the bedroom.

They went into the living room and flipped on the light. It didn't work, so they didn't see the bloodstain on the floor.

Carla Reid went in to Hartwell's pink and white bathroom. Regina's makeup and hairbrush were laid out on the counter. She never went anywhere without her makeup and brush.

They walked into the bedroom. All of Hartwell's clothes were there. All of her shoes were there, except her favorite Doc Martens boots. Her purse was on her bed. It, too, had makeup in it.

"I'm going to check with Jeremy," said Anita.

She walked over to his apartment and knocked on the door. "Have you seen Regina?"

"No. She called on Thursday and asked me to clean her apartment by Monday."

Reid was looking through Hartwell's bills as Morales walked back in, a not-so-faint look of worry across her face.

"Jeremy says Regina told him to clean her apartment by Monday. Maybe she went out of town." But Anita knew that didn't ring true, not with Regina's makeup and purse there.

"But everything's here," said Carla.

"Write down every single number that's on her caller ID," Morales answered. "Then we'll start at the top and go all the way down the list and call every number."

On the list were the numbers of Kim LeBlanc, Kim's parents, Sean Murphy, Liz Brickman, Hope Rockwell and a Bastrop number. But also on the list were tons of names that Anita and Carla didn't recognize. It was almost as though Regina had a whole, other life secret from them.

Morales shook her head and pulled out a cigarette (she did that when she was nervous) and socked her hands into her pockets just like her friend Regina did.

Reid phoned Kim LeBlanc. Her number was busy.

She called Liz. Liz said Regina had stood her up Thursday night.

She phoned Sean Murphy. He was out of town.

Anita and Carla dialed Kim's number again and again. Finally, they went home and back to painting. There seemed to be nothing else to do.

Jeremy Barnes walked over to clean Hartwell's apartment. He started in the bathroom. He spotted tiny splatters of blood by the commode, tiny splatters of blood on the three walls of the shower—fine, thin splatters as if the blood had been slung on the wall.

But, again, Barnes didn't think much of it. He knew Hartwell was whacked out on coke these days, that she had blackouts, nosebleeds. He thought about how Regina joked that she did so much cocaine that she could stick her finger up her nose and hit nothing—it'd be hollow.

He thought about how each morning, Regina began her day by hacking and snorting to try to clear the cocaine from her sinuses. Barnes wouldn't have been surprised if Hartwell had just picked her nose and flicked her bloody mucous on the walls.

He wiped away some of the small specks of blood on the white wall across from the toilet. He scrubbed away more small specks of blood just above the toilet-paper holder. He scrubbed the bathroom counter. He tucked neatly into a drawer her makeup and her favorite towel—the one she used when she put on her makeup. She loved that towel like a toddler does her teddy. It was filthy with eyeliner and mascara. And it was always the first thing Regina pulled out after Jeremy cleaned.

He moved through the hallway and missed the slips of blood on the cream-colored walls, blood splatters that were so thin and short that they were about the size of runny insect droppings. Except they were red droppings, blood.

Barnes walked into the living room and started cleaning there. He noticed more blood splatters on the wall, blood on one of the marble spheres on Hartwell's beloved black-and-white-checkered coffee table. He scrubbed the walls of blood, but missed a few specks. He cleaned the cigarettes and beer from the coffee table. He wiped away the blood drops. He straightened Regina's four remote controls and bloodstained marble spheres.

He glared at the huge stain under the black, leather recliner. The recliner was in reclining position with the stain slightly camouflaged by the footstool.

"You little evil wench," he muttered to himself. "You knew I was coming in to clean. The least you could have done was clean up a little bit before I got here." Barnes moved the chair.

But he didn't think much of that either. He always had to move things when cleaning her apartment—Regina had a habit of hiding things. He scrubbed the hell out of the spots on the floor. Still, he missed some.

That night, as Anita Morales walked between Oil Can Harry's and Club 404, two gay clubs in Austin's downtown warehouse and party district, Anita ran into Kim LeBlanc's ex-roommate, Tim Gray. "Have you seen Regina?"

"She's probably dead somewhere," he said.

"That's not funny."

"Hey, I was only kidding."

Sunday afternoon, Jeremy Barnes returned to Hartwell's and he began to really worry. Once again, there was no food or water in the bowl for Regina's pets. That wasn't like Regina, he knew.

If she were just two hours late getting home to take care of Spirit and Ebenezer, she'd phone Jeremy to take care of them. And two days in a row, Spirit and Ebenezer had been without food and water. And for two days Barnes hadn't heard from Regina. That was a heck of a lot longer than two hours.

But Barnes really knew something was wrong when he looked in the bathroom. Its counter was too clean. That filthy, favorite towel of Regina's wasn't spread out on the counter with her makeup on top of it. Regina always pulled out that towel.

He opened the bathroom drawer. There was the dirty towel and all of her makeup.

He called Morales. "Anita, there's something really weird going on. Have you seen Reg, because she's left Spirit alone. And she needs to come pay me for cleaning the apartment."

* * *

"There's something really weird about this," Barnes repeated later.

Morales picked up Hartwell's favorite black, leather back-pack purse and held it in her hands. She fingered Regina's makeup in that favorite bag. She stared at Regina's favorite shoes. She and Carla had dropped by Hartwell's one more time to check once again on their friend.

"Maybe she got coked up and just said, 'to hell with it, I'm going to see my dad,'" Morales tried to rationalize, tried to convince herself. "Maybe she decided to go to Pasadena because of her threat to turn Justin in."

But Anita didn't buy even her own line.

By Monday, July 3, Anita Morales's anxiety over Regina Hartwell had escalated. She made more phone calls in search of her friend. Not one living soul had heard from Regina.

CHAPTER 2

Tuesday, the Fourth of July, it was hot and clear when the phone rang at Carla and Anita's. It was Jeremy calling.

"Have you heard from Reg?"

"I'm going through her caller ID numbers to find who she's with. I found blood in here when I was cleaning . . . in the bathroom, the shower, a little bit in the living room, on one of her statues."

"Have you cleaned it?" said Anita.

"Yeah."

"Damn, Jeremy."

"That's what she told me to do. She's in her period. It could be that. Or it could be a nosebleed."

Morales hung up and called the hospitals and jails. She called Regina's friend Kim LeBlanc and got her answering machine, which relayed Kim's pager number. She paged Kim.

Fifteen minutes later, Kim returned the page.

Carla answered the phone. "Have you seen or heard from Regina?"

"No," answered LeBlanc.

Reid passed the phone to Morales, who heard Kim say, "I'm on my way," before Kim hung up.

Anita dialed *69 to get Kim LeBlanc back on the line and a man answered. She supposed it was Justin Thomas, Kim's boyfriend. "Let me talk to Kim."

LeBlanc picked up the phone.

"Do you know where Regina is?" asked Morales.

"No," Kim answered. "We had an argument last Wednesday. We agreed we need some space from each other, and I haven't seen her since. Is her makeup there?"

"Yes."

"Spirit?"

"Yes."

"Her purse?"

"Yes. Kim," said Anita, "did Regina and Justin have a fight?"

"No," Kim LeBlanc answered, innocently. "She's only mad at me. She's mad because I took Justin over to Diva's."

Diva was Regina Hartwell's drag queen drug dealer.

"Kim," Anita was urgent by then, "Jeremy found blood in Regina's apartment."

"I'm coming into town," LeBlanc said, sounding very upset. "I'll call you when I get there."

Kim LeBlanc was frightened. She got into her Jeep and drove the half hour from Bastrop County to Austin and Hartwell's apartment. A blood bath, that's what she'd been told. She expected to see blood on the walls, blood on the carpet, blood everywhere.

The door was unlocked; she walked in.

LeBlanc went into the bathroom, thinking that would be the bloodiest room of them all. Looking around, she didn't see anything. She picked up a cheap, silver-toned dish that a former girlfriend had given Regina. Underneath that dish, Kim spotted a red, coin-sized spot. She began to shake.

She got a bottle of Sunlight liquid dishwashing soap out from under the sink and started scrubbing the red spot with a brush. LeBlanc cried, hysterically, like a child. Seeing what she thought was blood, scrubbing what she thought was Regina's blood, Kimberley Alex LeBlanc finally realized that Regina Stephanie Hartwell, her friend and former lover, was dead.

Jeremy Barnes got home from work around two p.m. He went again to Hartwell's, planning on feeding Spirit, but the door was locked. He heard someone crying. He cocked his head to listen. The wails came from inside the apartment.

"Reg, Reg," he screamed. "What are you doing? Are you okay, honey?"

All he could hear was murmuring.

Barnes slipped his torso through the broken window, knocked over a plant in his rush, and ran down Regina's hallway. The shadow of a figure stopped him as he passed the bathroom.

It was Kim LeBlanc—still crying hysterically, still scrubbing that coin-sized, rust stain.

"What's the matter?" said Jeremy. He looked at the stain. He had scrubbed on it many times himself. Bleached it. Done everything in the world to it. "What are you doing?"

"I'm trying to get this blood off. I'm trying to get this blood off," she repeated and wept uncontrollably.

"Honey, that's not blood. It's a rust stain. I haven't been able to get it up forever."

Kim fell to the ground, curled into a fetal position, and screamed. "I should have called her! I shouldn't have argued with her! I shouldn't have told her I wanted her out of my life! I should have come over!"

Suddenly, Jeremy Barnes was scared, really scared. Something had happened, he knew, and he freaked inside.

* * *

He was afraid that Kim was about to have a stroke. Jeremy reached down to her and hugged her, hoping to stop her shaking. She was thin and frail. Barnes was heavy and cuddly.

"Honey, don't worry about nothing." He led her into the living room and sat her down on the couch. "Whatever's happened, we can take care of this."

Jeremy knew Reg and Kim always worked things out. He knew that too well.

LeBlanc lit a cigarette and phoned Anita Morales. "I told Regina that I was going to move back to my parents' house," Kim cried. "And Regina wasn't going to pay my rent anymore. I thought she was giving me an ultimatum—Justin goes or Regina goes. I told her she couldn't make me choose like that. I thought she was asking me to get back with her. But Anita, I'm not a lesbian. I've tried to be, but I'm not. I love Regina like a sister."

"I'm on my way over," said Anita.

Anita glanced at Kim, then at Jeremy. Kim was still crying, and Jeremy was still trying to comfort her. "Anita, there is something really fucked up here. There's something just really, really wrong," said Jeremy.

They searched for Hartwell's computerized daytimer so they could call her father in Pasadena, Texas. They couldn't find the daytimer.

They checked Regina's caller ID and phoned everyone on it, everyone they hadn't phoned in days previous.

Kim LeBlanc phoned Ynema Mangum, a long-time friend of Hartwell's. "Ynema, this is Kim." Her voice was soft, but shaking.

"Kim?" Ynema didn't remember who Kim was.

"I'm Regina's girlfriend."

"Oh, yeah." She was shocked that Kim would call her, especially since Ynema and Regina hadn't been very close in a very long time.

"Have you seen Regina?"

"No, I've been out of town." Mangum was shocked that LeBlanc had her phone number, her home phone number. She and Kim barely knew each other.

"Regina hasn't been home in several days," said LeBlanc, sounding worried.

Ynema, a protector, felt the need to calm her. "Regina goes home every now and then, and she doesn't always tell people. Did you guys have a fight?"

"Yeah."

"She's probably just trying to get attention."

Kim didn't sound comforted.

"Hey, I'll take care of it," said Mangum. "I'm gonna come over to the apartment right now." Ynema hung up the phone and went straight over to Regina's.

Anita Morales reached for the phone and spotted an empty cocaine baggie. She glanced around. To Morales, the place looked like a freaking crack house. It disgusted her. She turned to Kim. "Get this shit out of here."

LeBlanc moved quickly. There was a lot of shit she wanted out of there—blood, death, herself.

"I'm calling the police," said Anita. She figured Hartwell had done something bad or wrong or illegal and had flown the coop by her own choice, by her own volatile temper. Certainly not death, not Regina's death.

She expected Hartwell to walk through the door any minute, smiling that great big smile of hers, then, upon seeing a cop in her apartment, yelling, "What the hell is going on here?"

Anita, Jeremy, and Kim tossed sex toys and drug paraphernalia into a garbage bag. Kim reached under the couch and pulled out more drug paraphernalia—mirrors, straws, spoons. She threw those in.

Morales shook her head—it wasn't any of her business what Regina did in her own apartment. "You know, Kim, Justin will probably come up as a suspect," she said.

LeBlanc searched Regina's desk drawer. God, she hoped she'd find some coke that she could sneak into her pocket. She searched the bathroom and stared at, and still worried about, that bloody-looking rust stain.

Barnes grabbed the garbage, walked down stairs, and heaved the toys and paraphernalia into the Château's dumpster.

Anita Morales called the cops.

Officer Timothy Pruett received the call at 5:27 p.m. Soon he arrived at the apartment on South Lamar. Officer Pruett took out his pen and looked around the room. He watched Kim LeBlanc. She smoked like an out-of-control fire, one Marlboro right after another. But she didn't say much.

He looked at Anita Morales and Jeremy Barnes. They, too, shakily smoked cigarettes. "What is your relationship with Ms. Hartwell? When did you last see her?"

Ynema Mangum and her girlfriend walked in. "I'm on Regina's bank account," said Mangum.

"I am, too," said Kim. She kept her head bowed low. "Regina gave me a Pulse card."

The friends told Officer Pruett that Hartwell had recently inherited $3 million.

"Is that blood?" said Pruett. He pointed his pen at a rust-colored smear on the marble sphere. The sphere covered several checks closest to the black, leather recliner.

Kim stared at the table's black checks and white checks.

"It's just a stain on the statue," said Morales, not able to see the blood from where she sat. "It was already there. But Jeremy did find blood when he was cleaning the apartment."

Pruett didn't notice any other blood. "Just calm down. You're probably overreacting."

Act regular. Black checks, white checks, smoke a cigarette. Don't look geeked out. LeBlanc's body seemed to be staring out the window, her back to everyone else.

"But her dog's been left unattended for days," said Anita. "And her makeup's still here. She never goes anywhere without her makeup. She even brings her bag with deodorant over to my house."

"Why can't she just go out and buy new things, if she has all that money?" asked Pruett.

"That's not the way she is," said Anita. "She doesn't go out and buy stuff for herself. And she calls me a lot, but no one's heard from her since Thursday." Anita stared at Kim.

Kim LeBlanc told Officer Pruett that she and Regina had been playing phone tag for days.

Anita still stared at Kim. "Kim, didn't you and Regina get into a fight?"

"Yeah, but that wasn't a big deal." She sucked harder on her Marlboro, her face still away from the others.

"What did she say to you?"

"Everything will be just fine," said Officer Pruett.

Jeremy Barnes was ticked. He thought the cop had a flighty attitude. Morales thought Pruett acted as though this were a waste of his time. Kim lit another cigarette and wept.

Barnes squashed out his cigarette. Between LeBlanc—her crying, her smoking—and the cop pissing him off, Jeremy was a nervous wreck, "I'll be at my place if you hear anything." Barnes got up and left.

"I'll check Regina's bank account," said Mangum. "I'll see if there's any unusual activity."

"Are you gonna at least take down our names?" said Morales to Officer Pruett.

He did. An hour to an hour and a half after he had arrived,
Officer Timothy Pruett left the scene of the murder of Regina
Hartwell.

During that hour, hour and a half, Kim LeBlanc polished
off an entire pack of Marlboros.

Kim pulled out another cigarette. "Oh, what if something
happened to her?" She cried hysterically.

Anita stared straight into Kim's brown eyes. "I know y'all
got into a fight. Regina told me."

"Yeah, but that was nothing," said LeBlanc, still not looking Morales in the eyes.

"You know," said Mangum, "there's money missing from
her bank account."

Anita watched Kim.

"Yeah," she said. Kim hugged her knees. "I've been taking
two or three hundred dollars a day from it." She rocked herself.

"Why do you need three hundred dollars a day?"

"Well, Regina said I could just take whatever I need."

"Regina made me steward of her bank account," said
Ynema, her voice firm. "I'm responsible. Stop doing that."

"I should have called her," LeBlanc cried. "I should have
called her."

Ynema Mangum and her girlfriend left.

Kim sat alone on the couch. She looked like a skinny, sad,
frightened friend, Regina's frightened friend.

Anita Morales walked over and sat down beside her. She
put her arm around Kim. "Everything's going to be okay.
We're going to find her. She's going to be okay." She patted
and rubbed Kim's back.

Kim LeBlanc shuddered and slipped herself off of the

couch and onto the floor. She curled herself into an upright, fetal position and rocked.

Anita thought, *Oh, my God.*

Memories of Cancun flooded her mind. Anita, Kim, Regina—they'd all gone on the trip. There, Kim and Regina had both cried uncontrollably as the two had fought and fought and fought some more. There, Anita had bounced from Regina to Kim and back again, comforting each. There, Kim had accepted Anita's comfort.

Today, she didn't.

With that one move away, Anita Morales knew something was wrong. And she suspected Kim LeBlanc.

Kim knows how much Regina means to me. That was all Anita could think.

LeBlanc got up and left. She went to the Dairy Queen to get something to eat. Then she went back to Bastrop County and her boyfriend, Justin Thomas. She wasn't worried one bit. Anita had been nice and understanding.

That's what she told Justin.

CHAPTER 3

"Oh, my, God, she's in jail."

It was early in the morning on Wednesday, July 5. Jeremy Barnes was on his way to work when he dropped by Regina Hartwell's apartment to feed Spirit. He glanced over at her caller ID and noticed several new calls on it, two of them from the Bastrop County Sheriff's Department. That was when he gasped, "Oh, my, God, she's in jail." Then he sighed with relief. "She's alive."

His heart pounded as he quickly picked up Hartwell's phone and called Bastrop County. "I know this is going to sound really stupid." He tried to joke away his anxiousness. "But I have a friend who may be in jail, and somebody has called her home, twice. Her name is Regina Hartwell. I want to find out if she's in jail, and how much it's going to take to get her out of jail."

Barnes was near breathlessness as he was placed on hold. He started to shake as he was transferred two, three times. Finally, investigator Don Nelson got on the line. "Who are you?" said Nelson.

"Jeremy Barnes. I'm one of Regina's best friends."

"Well, uh," said Nelson, "we have a Jeep that has been burned. And there has been a female body found in the Jeep.

We cannot say who it is for sure because we don't have any dental records. Where are you?"

"Actually, I'm in Regina's apartment." Barnes rubbed his hands along the kitchen countertop that he'd scrubbed spotless just days before.

"Whatever you do, don't touch anything."

"Well, uh, I've, uh, already cleaned it. I've already done everything."

"Don't touch anything else."

"I have Regina's dog."

"Take the dog, leave the apartment immediately, lock the door, and go back to your apartment. What is your phone number?"

Before Barnes reached his apartment, he heard his phone ringing. He ran in and answered it, practically numb. "Are you saying what I think you're saying?"

"Well, we have linked the Jeep to Regina Hartwell."

Jeremy freaked. He felt, but he didn't feel. Not at all. That's the way the shock was.

At nine-thirty a.m., Austin Police Department Detective David Carter was in the field, conducting a follow-up on an old murder case when he received a page from APD homicide supervisor Sergeant Hector Reveles.

Over cellular phone, Reveles advised Carter, who was up as primary investigator on the next homicide in the capital city, that the Bastrop County Sheriff's Department had discovered the body of a white female, burned in a Jeep in Bastrop County some days earlier.

Carter, a tall, lean, handsome, blue-eyed man who could easily play a television detective, returned to APD headquarters. There, he was further informed that APD had taken a missing-person report on Regina Hartwell the previous day

and that people were currently at her apartment, which may
or not be a crime scene.

Carter immediately spoke to Patrol Sergeant Tom Owens and
made arrangements for those at Regina Hartwell's apartment to
be transported to homicide detail for interviews. He also made
arrangements with Owens for the apartment to be secured.

Jeremy Barnes phoned Anita Morales. "Come over." He
wept as he circled his apartment, unable to sit, unable to be
still with death. "They think Regina is dead."

Morales hung up the phone. Shaking, she grabbed her bag.
Her roommate Carla Reid watched. "Well, you're not going by
yourself."

They didn't speak a word as they drove to the Château.

Jeremy Barnes phoned Ynema Mangum at work, and she
phoned the sheriff in Bastrop. "I want to see the body."

"No, you can't," said the deputy.

"I want desperately, desperately to see the body," begged
Ynema. "I can tell if it's Regina."

"No, you can't," he said again. "There's not that much left."
The deputy didn't tell Mangum that the left side of Hartwell's
body was burned away, that her brain had been cooked into
Jell-O.

A bone, a hair—Ynema felt she could recognize Regina
from those. "I know I can."

"We need dental records to identify the body."

At 10:30 a.m., APD Detective Douglas Dukes was also informed by Sergeant Reveles about the Bastrop County body

and Jeep, that Bastrop Deputy Don Nelson had spoken with a male at the phone number of the apartment listed for the Jeep's Vehicle Identification Number, and that Nelson was en route to APD.

Since two different counties were involved in the homicide, Dukes phoned the Texas Rangers—Texas Ranger L. R. "Rocky" Wardlow. Wardlow was known to work closely with the Bastrop Sheriff's Department.

Upon Wardlow's and Nelson's arrivals in Austin, Nelson briefed the APD detectives and Texas Ranger.

Ynema Mangum phoned Officer Timothy Pruett. "A lot of money's missing from Regina's account," she said. "Just last February she had $3 million dollars. Look, Officer Pruett, we don't like the way Kim was acting yesterday. This is all really suspicious."

"I checked Reg's messages," said Barnes to Morales and Reid. "I saw a Bastrop number and called it. It was the sheriff's department. They told me that Reg's car had been found, and there was a burned body in it."

"No!" Anita cried.

Jeremy reached out to hug her, but she shoved him away.

The police officers arrived, and Morales believed there was no time for sorrow. She had to talk to the police. She had to remember what had happened during the past few days. She had to call Regina's friends. There was just too much to do to cry. Not then. She wouldn't let herself.

APD cordoned off the area, stringing yellow tape. Between cops and friends, approximately twenty people were wedged into Jeremy Barnes's apartment.

Carla Reid stared at the production, the hysteria, the show. "Well, Regina," she said, "you did it again. You just had to do it your way. No one else's way." Regina Hartwell always wanted to be the star of the show.

Texas Ranger Rocky Wardlow prepared a search warrant for the Hartwell apartment, and District Judge Jon Wisser signed the warrant. It was 3:42 p.m. Wardlow and Detective Dukes met the Texas Department of Public Safety Crime Lab team at the South Lamar apartment. Dukes, in his own words, spent much of the time "holding up a wall" while the Crime Lab team collected evidence.

Ynema Mangum closed Hartwell's bank account so that no more transactions could be made. There was only $8,000 left in the account.

Wardlow wrote down the approximately sixty phone calls on Hartwell's caller ID. There were two calls from Bastrop County—the first at 11:28 p.m. on June 30th, the second at 8:13 a.m. on July 5th. There was also one on July 5th from the residence of James Thomas.

Continually, Wardlow heard the names Kim LeBlanc and Justin Thomas. He obtained LeBlanc's pager number, dialed it, and tapped in the phone number of Regina Hartwell. When the phone rang at Regina's, the number that came up on the caller ID was that of James Thomas.

Sgt. Reveles crisscrossed the name and number and got an address on Whirlaway Drive in Garfield, Texas in Bastrop County.

* * *

APD had transported Anita Morales, Carla Reid, Jeremy Barnes, and Brad Wilson, another Château resident, to headquarters, and Detective Carter interviewed Barnes for, what seemed to Jeremy, like hours. He was scared to death. Since he had scoured clean the apartment, he was terrified that the police would think he was involved.

"Jeremy, we know you're not involved. We don't suspect you."

But Barnes was intimidated as hell. His thought was, *You're not a suspect, but* . . . . Barnes had a police record.

"We know, Jeremy, that you're not involved. We don't suspect you of anything, but . . . ."

There was that "but . . ." he feared. Barnes sighed. He'd worked so hard to get his life together since his arrest.

"I threw some things out of the apartment. Drugs. Paraphernalia. I cleaned up blood. It was everywhere."

Detective Carter noted Barnes' sincerity and that he was cooperating. He knew, as Jeremy relayed his story, that there was clear evidence of foul play at Regina Hartwell's apartment.

"Tell me about Regina . . . her history."

"Reg is in love with this girl named Kim LeBlanc. But Kim dates this guy named Justin. Justin deals drugs, runs guns. Regina's fronted him money. He's nothing but trash. Kim and Regina had a fight the other night about Justin."

Carter knew he needed to talk to Kim LeBlanc.

After the police finished interviewing Anita Morales, they drove her home. They checked all of her locks on her doors; then the officer asked her to do him a favor. "Would you page Kim and ask her to meet you at Regina's?"

Anita paged Kim from the police car. "We found out some stuff about Regina," she said. "Can you please meet me at Regina's?"

* * *

"Mom?" Kim LeBlanc said into the phone. Her heart raced so that she felt like it was going to beat right out of her chest. It was like a horse after it had run the Kentucky Derby and then dropped dead after crossing the finish line, bathed in a white lather of sweat, foaming at the mouth. That's the way Kim felt—like she was about to drop dead with a heart attack.

"Can you meet me at the Circle K, like at 6:30?" The horse fell on Kim's chest. It was lying there now. She couldn't see. Everything was dark. It was as though she were dead. God, she was scared. She started crying. She knew that if her mother saw her, she'd know she was messed up and would help.

"Yes," said Cathy LeBlanc.

Kim hung up the phone, then phoned Anita back. "My mother is coming to pick me up, then I'll be there." She started crying again, hysterically, that scared little girl who always appeared with Kim's tears. Her face turned as red as the roses around that dead Derby winner's neck.

"I knew you couldn't handle this," said Justin Thomas. He lay in bed with her. "We'll just go to sleep."

LeBlanc sighed and took a Valium. It was a long time 'til 6:30.

The Thomas house was quiet with the passed-out sleep of drugs.

Anita Morales sat in her apartment and wrote neat, detailed notes, recalling everything that Regina Hartwell had told her just before she died, remembering everything that had happened since Regina had disappeared. She knew that, one day, she would have to remember, perhaps testify.

The detectives decided that Kim LeBlanc just might not show up in response to Morales's page and phone call, so they decided to send officers after her. Detective John Hunt,

Deputy Nelson, and two Travis County deputies left for the James Thomas house in Garfield, a tiny community in Bastrop County, near the Colorado River.

Drowsy on Benadryl, J. R. Kelly, James Thomas's nephew, was sacked out on the couch. Earlier, J. R. had climbed a tree to tie a rope around one of its big, thick limbs so that they could swing out over the Colorado River during the Fourth of July celebration. The tree was full of poison oak.

Now J. R. was covered in poison oak and crashed on Benadryl. Barking dogs woke him—the Rottweilers, he slowly realized as he moved from deep sleep to awareness and finally to alertness. He jumped up. He looked out the window. "Oh, my God!"

He counted five police cars parked in the yard, and a handful of cops were honking horns and spraying chemical Mace in the Rottweilers' faces. J. R. ran out the door.

"Is Kim LeBlanc here?" shouted Detective Hunt.

The dogs barked and yelped.

Hunt stayed in his car.

J. R. Thomas grabbed the dogs. "Yeah." He hemmed and hawed. "She was, but she left a while ago."

"When?"

"Noon, maybe."

The detective glanced at his watch. It read 5:45 p.m. He knew LeBlanc had been paged by the police at 4:45 p.m. "Who with?"

"Some friends."

"I know that not to be true." Hunt stared J. R. Thomas straight into his eyes—blue eyes like J. R.'s momma's. "I know she was here later than that." His voice was deep and gravelly.

"Uh." J. R. Thomas was scared, "Maybe she's inside."

"Well, let's go look." Detective Hunt took a step forward.

The dogs jerked on their collars. J. R. held them tightly.

"Why don't you go put up the dogs first."

J. R. Thomas put up the dogs. Then he said to Detective

Hunt, "I'll go get her." He started into the house. Detective Hunt followed. J. R. glared nervously at the officer. "I said I'd get her!" The cop followed J. R. into the house anyway. "Kim!" yelled J. R. He looked up the stairs. Detective Hunt stopped in the kitchen. Deputy Nelson of the Bastrop County Sheriff's Department and the two Travis County Sheriff's Department deputies started up the stairs.

They found Kim LeBlanc in bed with Justin Thomas. They woke up the couple. "Downstairs," they said to Kim.

The officers carefully watched Justin Thomas. He was hollow-cheeked and intimidating with a protruding brow that was made even more prominent by a Mohawk haircut. "Come downtown and answer some questions."

"I ain't going nowhere," said Justin. "I don't want to answer no questions." Even though he'd lain in bed, he hadn't slept for days. "If you ain't got a warrant, you can't do this."

Kim LeBlanc reached the bottom of the stairs just as Detective Hunt started up them. He stared at the young woman. She was gaunt and frail. She wore shorts and a dark-colored tank top. Her eyebrows were perfectly plucked, but she wore not a lick of makeup.

"Are you Kim LeBlanc?" asked Detective Hunt.

"Yes," she answered softly. She was dazed with the sleep of Valium.

"I need to talk to you about your friend Regina Hartwell, who's missing. Would you like to come voluntarily with me down to the police station? You don't have to. You aren't under arrest."

"Yes." Her voice was still quiet, but her dazed state was moving toward detachment.

* * *

She was still dazed and detached when Deputy Nelson came down the stairs with Justin. Detective Hunt couldn't help but stare—Thomas looked like Yul Brynner in *The King and I*, bald except for one black, top knot of hair.

"Justin Thomas," said Nelson to Hunt.

"Is he coming downtown?" said Hunt.

"He is," replied Nelson. "Let's place them in separate patrol cars until we talk to them."

CHAPTER 4

Amy Seymoure and her parents moved into their comfortable home in Pasadena, Texas when she was just three years old. Not long thereafter, Mark, Toni, and Regina Hartwell moved next door. It was a 1970s, middle-class neighborhood of sidewalk-lined streets, oak trees and yards big enough for touch football.

The Hartwells' was a modest, one-story, pink, brick home with three white columns on quiet San Jacinto Drive. But the quiet outside of the house was nothing like the inside. Inside, the home was volatile. Amy sensed the explosiveness, even as a child.

She and Regina played doctor at Regina's house. Amy, trying to be a good little play doctor, once took a Q-tip to Regina's ear to remove a pretend blockage from it. But the little girl with child hands probed too deeply and Regina yelled.

Regina's grandmother, who was watching the children, became furious. She ordered the two little girls onto opposite ends of the couch and then screamed at them. It was nothing like what Amy was used to. Regina's grandmother berated the two little girls so loudly and so strongly that twenty years later, Amy still vividly remembered the scolding. It seemed irrational to her. Regina's grandmother, Dorothy Rhoden, was harsh and stern.

Regina's mother, Toni Hartwell, was the same, and they were equally strict on Regina. In hot, humid Texas, in a community close to the Gulf coast, little Regina wasn't allowed to play outside in bare feet. If she did, she was disciplined. She wasn't allowed to wear pants or shorts. Toni wanted her beautiful daughter with daddy's cheekbones to be in a dress.

But the child Regina Hartwell was not one to be regulated. She screamed and yelled at her parents. She cursed at them, seeming to rarely ever hold anything back. She had a strong personality and fight-for-survival traits that would later be both her virtue and her death.

Regina Hartwell had had that wider-than-the-nearby-Pasadena-Freeway rebellious streak from the beginning. In kindergarten, once, she and Amy hadn't wanted to take their scheduled naps, so they hid under a school table. Of course, they got caught. It was a scene and memory that Amy never forgot.

A little girl can cope with only so much, and eventually Regina began to mutilate herself. It started out innocently enough—she would scratch mosquito bites until they bled and scabbed over, a tendency that seemed typically childlike at the time.

But Regina picked at the scabs until they formed scars all over her legs. This picking became an obsession with her, primarily because of her mother's overreaction to the situation. Toni Hartwell always grounded her daughter for two weeks for scratching mosquito bites. That harsh discipline for mosquito-bite scratching made little, hardheaded Regina that much more determined to scratch the bites.

When Regina Hartwell was seven years old, her mother was diagnosed with multiple sclerosis. Toni was only thirty-two years old then, and her life expectancy, because of the MS, was now only 43.4 years. Months later, Toni was discharged from her $4.25 an hour job at Channel Sheet Metal.

Life wasn't feeling so good.

Amy was back again at Regina's. This time, Amy infuriated Toni. Mrs. Hartwell was so irate that she walked next door to the Seymoures' and knocked on the door. Amy's mother opened the door.

"Amy and Regina are no longer allowed to play together," Toni Hartwell said. And she turned around and walked back into her own yard and house.

For the next six months to a year, the girls were not allowed to play together.

The two children had been playing together every day for five or more years. They had attended Children's University Pre-School and Kindergarten together. They attended the same elementary school. They saw each other at school everyday.

But when Regina and Amy came home from school, they saw each other only from their driveways. Little Amy stood in her driveway, little Regina stood in her driveway, and they talked to each other from their concrete drives. Because of Toni Hartwell, Amy was not allowed to step a toe into the green grass of Regina's yard. And Regina was certainly not allowed to step a toe onto the much greener grass of Amy's yard.

"Can I have a piece of watermelon?"

Toni Hartwell looked at her daughter and grimaced. She felt like hell. The pain from her MS was torture, creeping into her body, hardening her brain tissue, hardening her spinal tissue, causing tremors, nearing her toward paralysis, destroying her life. She hurt. Horribly.

"I just want a piece of watermelon," said Regina.

Toni didn't want to get up. She couldn't. It hurt.

"I want a piece of watermelon."

Toni got up, went into the kitchen, hefted the heavy melon

onto the table, ripped a knife into it as if it were a fish to be gutted, and slid the ripe fruit in front of Regina.

"Here."

Regina stared from the melon to her mother, and back again.

"You wanted watermelon, you got it. Eat it. Eat it all, and don't stop until it's all gone."

"But . . . ," stammered Regina, "I just wanted one piece."

"You don't get up from this table until it's all gone."

Regina ate the melon until she passed out in the sticky, sweet, red juice of one of Texas's best fruits.

Toni Hartwell wasn't ugly, but she wasn't beautiful either. Regina thought her mother was gorgeous. Toni often walked around in a housecoat, with a cigarette in her hand, and her brown hair in curlers. She covered the curlers with scarves or bonnets. The bonnets had feathers on them. If she didn't cover her hair with curlers and scarves and bonnets, she covered it with a wig. She needed glasses.

Antoinette E. Hartwell made a lasting impression.

The sweet aroma of mother mingled with the sickening scent of burning flesh. Toni Hartwell pressed her lit cigarette into her daughter's back. The hot, ashened tobacco made a perfect circle of black around red, blood red.

Toni did it time and again until Regina's fair-skinned back became dotted with scars, dotted like beautiful Swiss fabric.

Regina, Toni's sweet-eyed, twelve-year-old daughter, was proud of her mother. In fact, Regina hero-worshipped her. Toni had a couple of years of community college behind her, San Jacinto Junior College. She was an expert seamstress and marksman, and she'd won contests and medals for her sewing and shooting.

Regina couldn't get enough of her mom; they were a pair.

But her mother was busy. She had to work. It didn't matter that Toni Hartwell had multiple sclerosis. She was a working wife and mother with her own business, cleaning airplanes. Her cleaning service wasn't a big business, but it brought in a few extra thousand and nudged the family's annual income into the $30,000 range. Not bad for 1982.

So, despite her ever increasing physical pain, Toni still got up and made the minimum one-hour drive from Pasadena to Houston's giant, sea-of-concrete Intercontinental Airport.

There, Toni cleaned planes for Airesearch Aviation, a division of The Garrett Corporation, a sometime employer of her plane-mechanic husband, Mark L. Hartwell.

On April 22, 1982, while at work at Intercontinental, Toni walked out of an Airesearch personnel door that was built into a huge, sliding, metal hangar door. Just as she passed through it, another employee slid open a portion of the hangar with a tractor. He didn't see her. He didn't hear her. No one did. The hangar door slammed against the personnel door and snapped it shut. It snapped closed on Toni Hartwell. She was crushed to death.

She was thirty-seven years old.

At the time of her death, the whereabouts of Toni Hartwell's father was unknown. It had been unknown since the day Toni was born, November 22, 1944 in Kansas City, Missouri.

Toni's husband of almost fifteen years (they were married on May 20, 1967) sued Airesearch Aviation and his employer, The Garrett Corporation.

Mark Hartwell's lawsuit stated: "Antoinette E. Hartwell was a loving wife, parent and daughter, and her services to your

Plaintiffs have been lost forever. She was working and earning money to help support her family and was fully able to carry out her duties of employment and other activities and responsibilities of life provided by a wife and mother. But much more importantly, her life meant much more to her family than just her ability to help care and provide for her loved ones. The loss of inheritance of prospective accumulations is also gone."

The lawsuit also read, "The survivors' greatest damage and loss results from their deprivation of her comfort, care, advice, counsel, education, and loss of society. Moreover, they have suffered mental anguish."

After Regina's mother died, the tension and harsh discipline eased. But a new opposition arose—a tension between father and daughter. Before Toni's death, Mark didn't figure prominently in his daughter's life, but now he was her sole emotional support. Mark Hartwell didn't appear to know what to do with his only daughter or how to handle her.

Regina, lonely and yearning for a mom, recreated Toni in her mind. This Toni loved, adored, and cared for Regina with the soothing comfort of a listening friend. She was the perfect, fantasy mom. That ideal, as the years passed, became real to Regina.

Mark Hartwell, a short, heavyset man who drank and smoked like Toni, had a lot to live up to. As much as he may have wanted, as much as he may have tried, Mark Hartwell couldn't be the father his daughter wanted or needed.

So, young Regina Hartwell began looking for love in other places. She began clinging to other girls, idolizing older girls, in a constant search of female love, tenderness, and acceptance.

In the sixth grade, Regina hero-worshipped a girl who was two years older than she. Her freshman year in high school, she worshipped a girl who was a senior. It seemed to be one girl after another. She simply wanted a mother figure.

* * *

In 1986, nearly four years after Toni Hartwell's death, Mark Hartwell and his only natural child, Regina Stephanie Hartwell, were awarded a total of $2 million in damages. Mark received $1.6 million. Regina received $400,000.

Sixteen-year-old Regina's $400,000 was placed in trust. Prior to age eighteen, Regina's lawsuit money could be distributed to either Regina or her natural or legal guardian, Mark Hartwell. At age eighteen, if Regina wanted, she could receive $40,000 from her trust. If she wanted, from ages nineteen to twenty-five, she could receive varying amounts—from a low of $24,000 to a high of $42,517. The balance was to be distributed to her on her twenty-fifth birthday.

Regina Hartwell, a beautiful daughter with expressive eyes like her dad's, with smarts, with wit, with a smile that could light up all of Houston, with a sweet, innocent look of a young Reba McEntire, but with a sad wisdom that seemed beyond her years, tried to buy the friendship of these girls with her new money.

She bought them expensive gifts, pricey purses, even foreign cars. While still in high school, Regina bought a used Mercedes convertible and gave it to a friend—the same girl who was a senior when Regina was a freshman. Hartwell did this because she couldn't have the love of the two people she wanted most—her father and mother.

It became a pattern that she learned long, hard, and well— seek a woman you can't have and try like the devil to buy her.

Maybe that's what Mark Hartwell believed when Regina was sweet, sixteen years old and he bought her a beautiful, mint-condition, used Porsche 911. He drove up to Pasadena

High, a giant red bow atop the silver-blue convertible, and in a community where Regina's friends drove Buick LeSabres, Ford Thunderbirds, and Amy a Saab, Mark Hartwell presented his daughter with a $30,000 car.

"It's yours," he said, "under one condition—that when you start getting the money from your trust, you pay me for half of the car. $15,000."

"Deal," said Regina.

Maybe Mark Hartwell was just trying to buy his daughter's love. Maybe he was trying to alleviate his guilt because of what he was about to do.

Mark Hartwell bought a new house, got married, obtained a new stepson, and took off. He gave Regina the Porsche and the modest Pasadena house, then sped to Seabrook, Texas.

Another Houston suburb, Seabrook is close to NASA, its astronauts and engineers, and the Gulf of Mexico. Seabrook is prestigious.

December 29, 1987, Mark Hartwell married Dian Frances Cantrell Swate Corley, a thrice-divorced mother of four children.

Regina was not happy. She considered the marriage a betrayal of her own mother. To others, Mark Hartwell was just trying to move on with life after a devastating loss. But Regina never forgave her father.

Dian's youngest son, Brandon Swate, moved in with the Hartwells. He grew up in the 2,500-square-foot, four bedroom, two-and-a-half-bath, two-story, brick home in Seabrook with a hot tub in the back. He grew up playing football in Clear Lake, Texas, with Mark Hartwell attending most all of the games, cheering his stepson.

Regina was left in Pasadena to live by herself. This so concerned the Seymoures that they phoned Child Protective Services about Regina. CPS didn't do a thing. Regina had food in the house, a warm place to sleep, and a Porsche to say, "I love you" at night.

At sixteen, still a high-school student, playing saxophone and marching in the Pasadena High band, Regina Hartwell was on her own.

"Anytime you need us, we'll be here for you," the Seymoures told Regina.

The Seymoure family was tight-knit, supportive, and always there. Amy could not fathom the sorrow and hurt Regina went through.

Regina loved her dad, but she hated him. Mark Hartwell was a man who liked to brag about his stocks and bonds, who dabbled with race cars, who was red-faced, staggering, and slurring as his stepson's father arrived.

Mark and Regina both seemed to know that they couldn't live together. They both seemed to know that not living together made life more peaceful in the short run. But that living apart was also why Regina hated her father—he wasn't there for her, and she needed him.

On the outside, though, Regina's response to her father's move was, "All right! Freedom! No rules to follow!" After all, she was independent, strong-willed, stubborn, even hardheaded. Nothing was going to get to her or hurt her, not even the abandonment by her father on the heels of the abandonment by her mother, even if those abandonments were by marriage and by death.

Regina's devastation, although rarely spoken, came out in other ways.

She didn't know how to take care of her Porsche. She didn't even know how to drive it. In an attempt to gain friendship and adoration, Regina let other, older teenagers drive it.

But they abused her car, and they abused her generosity. So, Mark Hartwell took the Porsche away, then he gave it back, then he took it away, then . . . .

Regina became close to her band director—she was a good saxophone player—and a band director is better than no parent at all. And Regina desperately needed someone to look out for her.

After Mark Hartwell moved out and moved on, his relationship with his daughter didn't improve. When he came back to Pasadena for his occasional visits with his daughter, he and Regina stood in the driveway and screamed at each other. The yells rushed across the yards and filtered into the next-door windows, harshly nipping at the Seymoures' ears.

Few of Regina Hartwell's friends came from homes broken by death or divorce. Indeed, in Regina's childhood crowd, her family situation was considered the most tragic, and not simply because of her mother's death. Her whole upbringing was tragic from beginning to end.

But Regina was a survivor. She was charming. She was vulnerable, and yet she would stand up to anybody. Amy admired that. Regina was fun to be around, too. She had a great laugh and could make anybody smile, giggle, and feel good.

By Regina's senior year in high school, weekends were party time at her house. Music ricocheted off the walls of the modest house and shot out onto the sidewalks. Thirty, forty, fifty teenagers ran in and out of the front door. Regina provided the house, the food, the liquor, and the bedrooms. Lots of liquor. There were drinking games, which eased into sex. Lots of sex.

Regina was being used financially and physically. She never had any one boyfriend, but she did have intercourse with boys, despite the fact that males weren't particularly attracted to Regina. To Texas boys who like their belles soft and quiet,

Regina came off as abrupt. She had a loud mouth. She could be rough at times. Still, several of them slept with her in high school. Her sex life started young. She simply didn't know the difference between sex and love, tenderness and affection.

After each party, after the booze, after the sex, Regina was left to clean up the mess. But that was okay with Regina; she liked providing the wild parties for the Pasadena High teenagers. It made her the center of attention, and she thought it made the kids like her and be her friend.

Once again, though, what Regina felt on the inside and what she showed to the world were two different things. Her insides knew that her "friends" were just looking for a place to party.

That same senior year, Regina began hanging out with a woman who was five or six years older. Patricia was the sister of one of Regina's classmates. Amy Seymoure never understood why someone in her twenties would want to hang out with a sixteen-year-old. To her, it didn't seem right. It didn't seem reasonable.

"Patricia's bisexual," Regina explained to Amy. And Patricia introduced Regina into the world of homosexuality.

That didn't matter to Amy. Whether Patricia was or wasn't, did or didn't, was irrelevant. Amy just wanted to know why Patricia wanted to hang out with Regina. Again, it didn't seem right. It didn't seem reasonable.

But Amy tried never to question Regina or make fun of her, despite the fact that one never knew how much truth was coming out of Regina. Amy just listened and let Regina talk. Even then, she had some kind of understanding that things weren't like they should be for Regina, that her life wasn't stable and that Regina needed someone to listen to her.

"You don't have to lie to me. I'm your friend no matter what. You don't have to buy me anything."

Regina Hartwell grew numb to physical pain, but she was never able to numb out the emotional pain. To her, love always equalled pain. That was how it was supposed to be— that's what she had been taught by the mother who loved her so. They were buddies. They were best friends. Toni Hartwell was wonderful, beautiful, perfect.

And if Toni Hartwell was a wonderful, beautiful, perfectly loving mother, then Regina Hartwell must have deserved the hurt. That's how a child rationalizes abuse. That's the way an unhelped abused child thinks, even in adulthood.

Regina graduated from Pasadena High School in 1988. She bought a Ford Mustang convertible with her trust money and turned her Porsche over to her father, who put it up on blocks. "If you ever want to pay this off, it's here," he said. Regina moved to Austin, Texas.

CHAPTER 5

Young gay women in Wrangler jeans, cowboy boots, and blazers pounded their feet against the wooden floor and shouted, "bullshit" as they danced the cotton-eyed Joe. Country music bounced from the blackjack tables to the patio and back indoors. Sadie's was packed as usual. Near the Four Seasons Hotel in downtown Austin, Sadie's was where trendy, drinking, drugging, college-age lesbians went to shoot pool, dance, and find romance in 1989.

Ynema Mangum was a University of Texas coed working as a blackjack dealer at Sadie's when she spotted Regina Hartwell. There was no missing Regina. When Hartwell walked into a bar, everyone—friends and strangers alike—turned around and watched.

She looked enviously sure. A young woman who lifted weights, Hartwell was very physically fit. She wore immaculate dresses and long, dark tresses in a roomful of jeans and butch, short haircuts. She was confident, cocky, and charismatic. Everyone wanted to know Regina Hartwell.

Ynema Mangum was no different, and Regina and Ynema got along great. They were both twenty years old, they both loved to dance, and they both had a crush on Ynema's girlfriend.

But this was a world where girls bounced off girls like balls in a pinball machine, sometimes scoring, sometimes tilting. One night, in front of the blackjack table, Regina and Ynema kissed. Tilt.

Laughing, they backed away from each other, and not because of Ynema's girlfriend. For Ynema and Regina, kissing each other was like kissing a sister or a dog . . . or an alligator. "Izod," said Regina to Ynema. "From now on, I'm calling you Izod because you kiss like an alligator." Score, friendship.

Regina Hartwell was funny, and she was fun. She was powerful and intense. She had that strong, attractive build on the outside, but on the inside, Regina Hartwell was a little girl who was silly, immature and wrestled with personal demons of emotion, acceptance, and love.

Ynema Mangum was a young, slim, sweet, soft-spoken, Native American woman bent on destroying herself. She sipped wine coolers for breakfast, and she often threw up.

Hartwell loved to drink, too, but she never, ever seemed to throw up. It was just one more sign that on the outside, at least, Regina Hartwell was always in control.

Hartwell arrived each night at Sadie's looking drop-dead gorgeous with perfect hair, perfect makeup, and perfect clothes that all looked suave and sophisticated. She even danced perfectly.

She had her own place, which she paid for. She had a great car, a great stereo, a fridge full of food—chips and salsa— and she constantly hosted great slumber parties, just as if she were still in high school.

But Regina was a great chameleon. After she went home from Sadie's, she always broke out the chips and salsa for the slumber parties, jumped into a pair of cutoffs and a T-shirt, wiped off her makeup, and spilled hot sauce and queso on her clothes. She then stayed in those dirty clothes for days.

Hartwell's home replicated her turmoil within. There were

Cheetos under the couch, cigarette butts everywhere, and dog hair in the bed. She let her dogs sleep with her and lick her in the face. She was a lonely girl who continually took in strays of all sorts—dogs, cats, humans. She just wanted to love and to be loved, and she'd do anything to that end.

Samantha Reynolds had short brown hair, was a bit butch, and was chubby. She didn't stand out in a crowd, and she certainly wasn't the type to attract the lust of Regina Hartwell. Regina loved brunettes—toned, athletic brunettes—who presented themselves well and looked nice.

But Samantha Reynolds noticed Hartwell at Sadie's many times and wondered who was that young woman who was always dressed to the nines. Regina wore a black skirt, tight blouse, pantyhose and heels while everyone else wore their cowboy honky-tonk garb. Everyone else but Regina and two of her friends.

Still, Sam Reynolds never asked about Hartwell. It was Sam's first year in college, and she was shy and involved. She just didn't know she was involved with someone who was cheating on her. Everyone else in Sadie's knew, including Regina. Finally, Reynolds found out. With tears streaming down her face, she ran out of Sadie's.

Hartwell ran after her. She stopped Sam in the parking lot.

"Hi, I'm Regina," she said, sticking out her hand. "Look, I'm really sorry about what happened, but this always happens." Like an understanding and consoling mother, Regina shook her head. "Obviously, it wasn't meant to be. You deserve better than that."

She comforted Reynolds for an hour and half. Then Sam went home, and Regina went back into the bar. But they were friends from that day on. Regina Hartwell made friends fast.

* * *

Anita Morales noticed a Nissan 300 ZX parked outside of Sadie's. She couldn't help but notice it. Bright red and expensive, it was parked in the most prime spot. Morales and her college roommate, Sara, were out for a night of partying. They walked in and perused the bar.

"Oh, I know that girl," said Sara. "She's from Houston." She pointed to Regina Hartwell.

Anita Morales watched Hartwell, who was wearing a bold-colored, cheesy *Dallas* TV-show-style suit with big, gold buttons. She had Texas big hair. Regina was never without her hairspray.

"Who is she?" said Anita.

"Some really wealthy girl from Houston. She used to have the biggest crush on me."

Hartwell tended to get crushes fast and went directly for the woman. She spotted Sara and walked over.

But half the time, the woman wasn't receptive. But she was fully aware she could take Regina for what she wanted and not have to be very nice in return to the rich girl from Pasadena.

That was okay with Hartwell. She was often drawn to people who didn't care for her. They were a challenge, and Regina liked a challenge, thought many of her friends.

Believing Anita and Sara were a couple, Regina slashed Morales with a dirty look. *Oh, my God,* thought Anita, *this little girl is intimidating.* Both close to five feet tall, Anita and Regina stared eye to eye.

Regina shocked Anita, though, when she immediately began to buddy up to her. "Want to go with me in my limousine on New Year's Eve?" she said. She intended to buddy up to Morales to get to Sara. Still, it started a lifelong friendship. From that New Year's on, with the exception of one—Regina's last—Anita went with Regina in her limo every New Year's Eve.

* * *

"Don't forget, I'm buying you your first drink," Hartwell said to Ynema Mangum. She meant Ynema's first legal, alcoholic drink. "Don't forget. . . ." Regina said it over and over again as though she were obsessed with the idea.

On June 28, 1990, Mangum's twenty-first birthday, Regina took her barhopping. Hartwell disappeared for a few moments, and Ynema thought she was alone. She sidled up to the bar, ordered her drink, and, zoom, Regina was there beside her, slicked up next to her like a magnet picking up stray steel dust. "I'm gonna buy this," said Regina.

But Regina didn't buy Ynema just one drink. All at once, she ordered Ynema several drinks—mind erasers and amaretto sours.

Like a typical alcoholic, Regina Hartwell lied at every opportunity she got. Regina, the girl from down-home, hard-working Pasadena would hold out an apple and say it was an orange. At least that's what Ynema Mangum saw. Hartwell would tell Ynema all the virtues of the alleged orange. By the time she finished, Ynema would believe the apple was an orange.

Regina Hartwell was smart, and she was a smooth talker. More than once, she told her trust officer she needed money to go to college, and he gave her the money. Then she dropped out of school and used the tuition refund to party.

Hartwell just wasn't trustworthy. Ynema Mangum thought that was the reason Regina didn't trust many people herself.

But unanswered issues in her life, many unanswered issues, caused Regina Hartwell to appear self-confident when she was really still searching . . . soul-searching.

Ynema Mangum began to realize that.

Ynema noticed that Regina often didn't look her in the eyes when she spoke—lying. Or, Regina looked Ynema in the eyes, but Regina's eyes clouded over as if they were trying to hide something—lying. Ynema caught Regina in her lies and challenged those lies.

Hartwell stopped telling stories to Mangum, but she also stopped confessing to her.

None of that, though, was enough to stop Ynema from loving young Regina Hartwell. There was something inside of Regina that was sensitive and vulnerable, that made Ynema feel she needed to take care of Regina.

There were times when Regina got into trouble and someone wanted to beat her up; Ynema stepped in and protected Regina. Ynema Mangum, with a bit of a young Kate Jackson look, was Regina's Angel, and she knew Regina was afraid of being hurt physically.

Most of Hartwell's friends wouldn't believe that—they hadn't seen that side of her. Ynema had, and she loved Regina for that vulnerability. She knew the fear and vulnerability came from the loss of Regina's mother at such a needful age and from being abused at such an early age. But most of Regina's friends didn't know about that either. They didn't notice the scars on her pale arms.

They *did* notice how often she professed to hate her father. Her friends believed that Mark Hartwell didn't spend much time encouraging Regina, but they also knew that she didn't spend much time pleasing him. She wanted to separate from him, and to do that she had rebelled by moving to Austin and practicing a lesbian lifestyle.

Yet Regina Hartwell was much like her father. They shared the same hazel eyes, the same penchant for *braggadocio*, the same bigotries. She was uncomfortable that Mangum's skin was dark. She worried that Mark Hartwell would treat Ynema differently because of her skin color. And he did.

On one of Regina's rare trips back to Pasadena, she took Mangum with her. Mark Hartwell behaved just as everyone feared. He seemed surly to Ynema and made mention of her

American Indian heritage, so Ynema spent her time avoiding
Mark Hartwell. To her, he was wrapped up in himself.

In fact, as a salute to her father and his racist views, Regina
named her white husky dog Spook. When Spook got hit by a
car and had to be put to sleep, she held him in her arms and
wept until he died. Ynema was with her.

Ynema Mangum was one of the very few friends Regina
ever introduced to her father.

On February 6, 1991, Regina Hartwell turned twenty-one,
and Ynema Mangum bought Regina her first legal drink. February was always a good month for Regina Hartwell. It was
the month she received her annual disbursement from her trust
fund. Come February, she'd be rich and living high on the hog.
She'd often buy a new car, always with a souped-up stereo.
She'd pay cash for the car. By Christmas time, the money
would have disappeared, partied away into the smoke of some
lesbian bar in the fantasy of finding love, and Mangum would
be cooking to feed Hartwell and her girlfriends.

In those days, Regina never expressed her insecurities. If
she felt embarrassed by a weight gain, which came often, she
didn't show it. She just pumped herself up by bragging about
herself and how great she looked, and laughing. One thing
that caused such greats laughs for Regina was that her look
was so incongruent with her behavior—sophisticated look,
moronic behavior.

In fact, Regina was like Sybil; she had several sides. She had
a silly, immature side. If she wanted to get a laugh out of someone, that became her goal, and she wouldn't stop until she heard
the laughter. She had a serious side that manipulated others into
doing what she wanted. And she had that ever present scared
side in need of protection, the little girl still grieving.

She did tell a few friends that her mother had had a psychological problem and emotionally abused her. But she only let

them know just so much, never the whole story. She didn't want anyone to see the whole picture. It was a matter of control. Besides, it was easier to laugh and pretend that her mother tenderly adored her. It was always easier to pretend.

At first, Hartwell tried to hide her Austin life from her Pasadena friends and family. "I want to be a lawyer," she said to Amy Seymoure. "I'm going to the University of Texas," she lied. She also told her father she attended U.T. and that she had become a born-again Christian.

However, one day, a Pasadena friend saw Hartwell as she marched in a gay pride parade. He told someone, who told someone, who told Amy Seymoure. It was no surprise to Amy. She loved Regina no matter who or what she was.

On Regina's next trip to Pasadena, Amy made sure they got together. That was easy—every time Regina came home from Austin, she made a point to sit down and visit with Amy's parents.

She confronted Regina about Regina's homosexuality. "I support you completely. I love you very much. I don't care what you are, you're still my friend," Amy Seymoure said.

Hartwell sighed, embarrassed but relieved.

"You look like you're in the wrong place. You look like a bar hopper," Regina's friends said to her. They stood in Sadie's and pointed to her feminine clothes. These were friends who were close to her, who knew her for a few days, or for weeks.

"You don't have to dress like that. You don't have to draw attention to yourself because we like you anyway." Hartwell's appearance began to change. Gone were the dresses and the long hair. In their stead came fashionable Calvin Klein and Donna Karan.

But Sam Reynolds felt she and Ynema were the only ones

who really liked Regina for herself. Sam, Ynema, Regina: they made a great trio. Sam and Regina would dance together while Ynema dealt blackjack. After Sadie's closed for the night, they would go to Regina's house for more fun at a slumber party.

There they would talk. Regina knew that others were using her—using her for the drinks she bought them, the gifts she gave them, the limos she ordered to chauffeur them around each New Year's Eve when she was close to dead broke.

It hurt her that they were using her, but she accepted it. It was worth the love and attention—anything to be center of attention. Fake friends were better than being alone.

The only funny thing, though, was that some of those fake friends didn't believe Regina Hartwell when she told them she had money. Another one of her lies, they thought. But Sam Reynolds saw papers from Hartwell's trust officer, and she was there when Hartwell talked to her attorneys. She just never knew an actual amount. Two million, Regina told her.

Two million. Three million. Zero million. It didn't matter to Sam. She didn't need Regina to escort her around town in a limo or anything else. Her family had their own money. She certainly didn't need Regina's dough.

Hartwell found herself falling in love with Sam. It scared her, and she fought it. She didn't want anyone who was beautiful on the inside. She just wanted someone who was beautiful on the outside. Sam was beautiful on the inside, and she was reserved. Regina was everything that Sam wasn't—confident, outgoing, spontaneous—and Sam was drawn to that.

She was drawn to Regina's beauty and childlike heart. Regina brought out the best in Sam, and Sam loved her for that—for bringing her out of her shy shell.

Hartwell appreciated that Sam Reynolds loved her for simply being Regina, and she loved Sam back for that. Besides, Hartwell liked women who were pleasers, and Reynolds was a kind, sweet pleaser.

* * *

Everyone in Sadie's knew what was about to happen. Everyone but Sam Reynolds.

Regina Hartwell rushed up to the deejay, shouted in her ear, then tipped her well. She walked back to Sam with a huge smile on her painted on lips. She waited. The music started. She reached out for Sam. "This is for you," she said. The song in the air was Basia's "Time and Tide."

Everyone watched as Regina led Sam into the center of the dance floor, into the center of attention, and slipped an engagement ring on Sam's hand. It was a gold nugget ring in the shape of Texas, with a diamond placed strategically where Austin should be. Regina proposed.

Reynold's friends shuddered. They'd all known her since high school. They knew how she hated to be in control. They watched Regina in Sadie's and saw, in action, her need to control.

Some thought Hartwell wanted to be a man because of that need. Externally, she was often very feminine, but she could also be as butch as any dyke on the street. Lipstick and butch—she was an oxymoron. And she struggled with those two sides of herself.

To Sam, Regina talked about her father—how she didn't have a relationship with him, how she wanted a relationship with him, how she only saw him at Christmas. But the entire time Sam knew Regina, Regina rarely went to Pasadena for Christmas.

One night, Sam Reynolds overheard a conversation between Regina and her father, who was on a speakerphone. His voice was deep and Texan. He sounded loving, caring, like he longed for his daughter. But as soon as his voice grew sentimental, Regina picked up the phone, and Sam heard no more. Their conversation ended soon after.

"I've been with men before," said Hartwell.

Reynold's face squinched with pain, but she tried not to show it.

"I'm seeing a guy who's a dancer in a bar, like a Chippendale's dancer."

Sam relaxed and giggled to herself. *Regina's lying just to get my goat,* she thought. After all, Regina was known to frequent stripper nights in gay men's bars.

The control side ruled. It ruled everything, including Regina's sex life. Regina had to be the dominant partner, and she was a rough dominant partner. After Sam had been with Regina, she would find bruises on herself—on her arms, wrists, shoulders. But Regina Hartwell never had any bruises. Hartwell was a doer; she didn't allow herself to be done much.

Reynolds's friends just didn't know what Sam knew—the sweet scent of Regina's hair, her expensive aroma of Drakkar, her skin as soft as a baby's, or that Regina had a big heart under a big bosom, and that with Sam, Regina had orgasms.

In 1991, Regina Hartwell's stepbrother, Brandon Swate, petitioned the 309th District Court of Harris County, Texas to allow him to move out of Mark Hartwell's house. Court records state, ". . . that Dian Frances Swate Corley Hartwelle [sic] has participated, along with stepfather Mark Hartwelle [sic], in psychological and physical abuse of the child."

On March 11, 1991, in the same month the Hartwells began selling their Seabrook home, Brandon Swate signed an affidavit that stated, "I do not wish to continue to live with my mother, Dian Hartwell, as I no longer wish to be subjected

to the emotional abuse inflicted upon me by her husband,
Mark Hartwell."

"I hate having to live under my parents' rules. It's ridiculous. I can't come and go as I please. They ask me what time
I came in, who I was with, what did we do—everything. I
can't do anything," Sam Reynolds griped.

"Stop," said Regina Hartwell. "Just stop. Quit your whining. At least you have parents. At least you have your mom
and your father, and they love you. So just quit your whining.
I don't want to hear about it."

It was a common conversation between Sam and Regina.
If Sam complained about parents, school, whatever, Regina's
response was always the same. "Quit your complaining. Just
pee or get off the pot." She was a tough parent.

She was also a tender parent.

Reynolds was about to go over to Hartwell's when Reynolds learned that her aunt had died. Devastated, she ran to
Regina, breaking down and weeping, "My aunt died."

Hartwell wrapped her arms around her. She hugged Sam
and held her, letting her cry.

In shock, Sam whispered, "Why are you doing this?"

"Because I know what it's like to lose somebody, and that's
an okay situation to cry in," said Regina.

Regina Hartwell worshipped Madonna, the star-studded,
flashy celeb whose mother died when she was young. In her
own life, Regina recreated Madonna's persona from the movie
Truth or Dare—daring, funny, wild, sometimes crude, sometimes cruel. She even tried to walk and talk like Madonna.

Because of that, Hartwell loved "the scene," and she
couldn't give it up. But Sam Reynolds wasn't fast-paced,
glamorous, or able to fit into the scene. Sam couldn't be what

Regina wanted her to be. She could only be herself, just like Regina could only be herself, not what Sam wanted her to be.

"I do cocaine," confessed Regina.

"I don't approve," said Sam.

"I know," Regina answered, staring down at her toes, her hands deep in her pockets. "I promise I won't ever do it in front of you."

Both knew it was an empty promise. But in those days, it was a simple promise. Sam and Regina saw each other in the bright hours of daylight, rarely in the darkness of night. Sam never saw Regina do drugs.

Regina Hartwell and Sam Reynolds took jobs at Sadie's. Hartwell dealt blackjack while Reynolds shined boots. It was work that Sam loved.

One night, a group of male University of Texas psychology students walked into Sadie's. "We're here doing research for a psych paper—research on lesbians."

Regina Hartwell flirted with them and teased them.

They flirted and teased back. "Are you sure you're gay?"

"Yes," she answered, laughing.

"You can't be. You're too pretty."

Regina ate up the attention. "Oh, yes, I am."

Visions of sugarplum lesbians danced in the boys' heads. Visions of love and attention danced in Regina's hazel eyes. Suddenly, Sam started to believe that Regina had dated men.

Sex was a strange thing for Regina Hartwell. She showed signs of sexual abuse. "I've had sex with men and with women," Regina said to Ynema Mangum, "but I don't have any feeling inside." There was no hard evidence that she had been sexually abused.

In fact, many people didn't see Regina as a sexual creature.

They didn't think she'd let go of her feelings enough to be a sexual person.

Hartwell's body was too numb to feel. To feel sex, she had to have a fist rammed up her anus. To feel sex, she had to bleed.

Hartwell and Reynolds stayed together for four or five months before breaking up. Like many couples, they were growing in separate directions. They went to the Magic Time Machine restaurant to make their breakup official. They both grinned from ear to ear, especially Sam. She'd never experienced an amicable breakup.

Their waiter noticed their smiles. "What are y'all celebrating?"

"A divorce," said Regina.

He turned to Sam. "And what are you celebrating?"

"A divorce," she answered.

"Y'all are both getting divorced from different guys?"

"No," said Regina.

"Then who are you getting divorced from?"

Regina's big grin grew into a smirk. "From each other."

The waiter nearly fell to the floor, and Regina and Sam laughed and laughed.

But it was never a solid breakup. Regina Hartwell and Sam Reynolds came and went and bounced between others and each other. They got back together after a couple of Erasure concerts. They went to two last movies together—*Ghosts,* about a man who dies and comes back to see his lover, and *Flatliners,* the story of medical students toying with death and the afterlife.

After *Flatliners,* Sam and Regina talked long and hard about their afterlives. Then, Reynolds moved away from Austin. Today, she knows she'll see Regina again in their afterlives.

For Hartwell, things started going downhill after Sam. More and more people started using her. More and more, she needed people to use her. More and more, she wanted to feel love, to be accepted, to be a leader, the star, worshipped.

She told friends that, in high school, she'd had plastic surgery to make her nose look more like Marilyn Monroe's, another sweet, motherless child who just wanted to be loved and adored.

Mark and Dian Hartwell eventually returned to the home that Mark once shared with Regina's mother. He told the Seymoures, "Seabrook's just too uppity for Dian and me." Regina considered her father to be a gun-toting redneck, an opinion some other people shared.

But if there was one thing her airplane-mechanic father knew, it was airplanes. Mark Hartwell, the man who had left his nearby NASA neighborhood for Pasadena, owned a vintage '68, fixed-wing, single-engine Piper.

CHAPTER 6

"You don't scare me. You don't intimidate me. There's nothing that you have that I want," said Anita Morales to Regina Hartwell. Anita and Regina were temporarily roommates, and they were in the midst of a fight.

The fact that Anita stood up to Regina, that she didn't need anything from her, created respect and loyalty for Anita in Regina—so much so that if someone got mad at Anita, Regina would take a beer bottle to the person.

"You're not going to get to her without getting this bottle over your head," she'd yell. Regina was loud.

She burped loud, laughed loud, and farted loud. She was tough on the outside, scared and lonely on the inside. She loved to laugh at others and loved it when others laughed at her. She loved drama. And if Regina Hartwell thought a friend had wronged her, watch out.

Mike White was a 6'5", handsome, young man with a high IQ. He loved the fast life of the Austin gay scene, and he loved the fast drugs of the Austin gay scene, especially cocaine.

In the early nineties, he met Regina Hartwell, in a bar. She was a little overweight and complained about it at length. She had long, burgundy hair, and wore baggy jeans, Doc Martens, T-shirts, and baseball caps. Although she dressed like a little boy, she was very proud of being a woman.

They were introduced through Hartwell's best friend at the time, a young man named R. A. They partied and did drugs. The drugs helped them cope with "coming out," with disapproving families, and fogged their memories.

The drugs also helped them fight. R. A. ticked Regina off, they fought, they split, and Mike and Regina eventually became roommates.

In 1992, White and his friend Trey Lyons went through a string of bad roommates, and they needed a place to live. Regina Hartwell offered to help them out. After all, she was very good friends with Trey, and Trey was the kind of person Regina liked to be seen with. He was cute, he was a user, he would clean her house, he would take care of her dogs, he had a lot of friends, and he was good with the social scene. Mike and Trey could stay with Regina for a while.

They moved into her house on Lambs Lane in deep south Austin, east of Interstate 35, just past a trailer park. It was a small, stone-and-frame house in a neighborhood of overgrown weeds and rusted-out cars on jacks. Old pickup trucks and older boats were parked in driveways of homes with windows shaded by falling-down curtains and bent miniblinds. Year-round Christmas lights trimmed a few rain gutters.

But Lambs Lane was also just a fifteen-minute freeway drive from Sadie's and Austin's downtown gay bars. It was also indicative of Hartwell's increasingly oxymoronic life— good car, crummy home, friends who used her for her money, friends who loved her for being Regina.

Mike White and Regina Hartwell became close friends. They were a lot alike. They both had a heart of gold, and always wanted to make sure that everyone was happy, having a good time, taken good care of. They became good friends despite the fact that Hartwell, at that time, was very against men.

From White's point of view, it was a time of a lot of dyke drama—constant girlfriend switching, swapping, jealousy, anger, Regina seeing someone she thought was lofty or she couldn't have and setting that person as a goal.

From Ynema Mangum's point of view, Hartwell chose women for maternal reasons. She picked women who would discipline her and make her feel bad about herself. In Regina's mind, they gave her what she deserved.

New Year's Eve Regina gathered her children, as she often called them, for their annual year-end party rite—limo, champagne, and bar-hopping. Ynema was invited, but she didn't want to go. Regina begged, pleaded, and Ynema went. It was nice to be wanted that badly.

The limo pulled up, with a fully stocked bar and Dom Perignon champagne. Regina always had to drink Dom when she traveled in a limo. The driver treated Regina like a queen. She knew what she was doing; she drove Regina every New Year's Eve.

They stopped and picked up two more girls. Hartwell was giddy—friends, a limo, and two beautiful girls whom Regina lusted after. Regina couldn't decide which girl she wanted. Then, one of them turned cool to Regina, and Regina's ego hurt. The party ended as a night of drama.

Mangum didn't have one bit of fun. To her, it was all immature. Besides, Ynema had more important things on her mind—school, career. Life and self-images were changing, at least for Ynema.

Regina Hartwell walked into Sadie's. In the smoky, dim bar light, she spotted Joyce Cody. Regina called it love. Others called it obsession. Regina wanted Joyce Cody. So did Hope Rockwell. It was early April of 1992, and Cody was drinking with Rockwell. She was also flirting with Rockwell, who was flirting back. Hartwell tromped up to them and jerked Rockwell around. "If you don't stop sleeping with Joyce, I'm gonna rip your head off and piss down your throat."

At four a.m., April 7, Joyce Cody was at home, asleep alone, when Regina Hartwell came calling. But Cody didn't know Hartwell was there because Hartwell came calling through Cody's unlocked bathroom window.

Regina was detected only because a man named Calvin Pope caught her crawling out of Cody's window as he circled the house, pounding on the doors and windows. Pope was trying to wake someone as he needed a place to sleep. When he spotted Hartwell, she spotted him and crawled back into the house.

"Open the door," he yelled at her. "Open the door."

She finally did.

"Joyce's roommate is here," he lied to her.

Regina left.

Around noon that same day, Joyce Cody reported Hartwell for burglary. "She's threatened me with bodily harm," Joyce told the police officer. He searched the premises. Regina's muddy footprints were found in Cody's bathroom. "She didn't have my permission to enter my house or take my property," Cody continued. "I want to press charges."

On April 10, 1992, a criminal-trespass complaint was filed against Regina Stephanie Hartwell in Municipal Court of Austin, Texas. Six days later, at 7:10 p.m., Regina Hartwell was arrested and placed in jail. She listed her nearest relative and permanent contacts as Mark Hartwell, Amy Seymore

[sic], her high-school friend from Pasadena, and Tammy Weeks and Amy Teykl, both from Austin. Teykl was a neighbor of Hartwell's on Lambs Lane.

Today, Teykl claims to have barely known Regina.

Two hours later on April 16, 1992, Regina Hartwell was brought before Municipal Judge Celia Castro. Hartwell stated that she was an Austin Community College student and had lived in Travis County for three years. The judge ordered her to appear in Travis County Court of Law #1 on May 20, 1992, then released her on a $3,000 personal bond.

On May 20, Hartwell's case was continued to September because Calvin Pope could not be located. Court records speculate that he might have been in the Austin State Hospital.

That fall, Hartwell's attorney told her he didn't think she needed to worry about anything—the police couldn't find the witnesses.

Regina grinned. "I know Joyce won't testify. I tracked her down in Dallas, went there last weekend, and made up with her. She won't testify."

The charge against Regina Stephanie Hartwell was dropped.

On occasion, Amy Seymoure tried to talk Regina out of her gay lifestyle, not because she was concerned that Regina was gay, but because she was concerned about Regina's nightlife— the bars, the partying, the friends who used her. Seymoure was worried that Hartwell was in danger and that harm would come to her—that big mouth on such a small person.

"I just want you to be careful," said Amy.

Mike White, even though he was Hartwell's roommate at the time, never knew a thing about her arrest. Neither did Anita Morales. Not many did. Regina knew what she wanted to talk about and what she didn't want to talk about.

On many occasions White tried to get her to talk about her mother. Regina flat refused.

She did tell him, though, that she had received $6.5 million for her mother's death and that her father had received three times as much. He knew from her reluctance to explain to people how she got rich quick, the way she referred to her cash as "blood money," the way she called herself "rich, white trailer trash from Pasadena," that Regina's mother's death still pained her horribly.

She didn't hesitate, though, to talk to Mike White about her sex life.

Anita Morales's girlfriend Rosie Rulle roomed with Hartwell, White, and Lyons at a time when Rosie and Anita fought often; Anita and Rosie were in the middle of a breakup. Regina Hartwell had no qualms about calling the police to settle those arguments, and she had no qualms about sleeping with Rulle.

Rulle believed Anita was cheating on her with a girl with whom Regina was obsessed. Rulle told Regina, and Regina believed her.

"How could you do this to me?" Hartwell yelled at Morales.

"But I didn't. I'm not. Regina it's not true. Rosie's lying."

But Hartwell refused to buy Morales's constant protestations. She threatened Anita with a baseball bat.

"Regina, I swear. I wouldn't do that to you."

Regina backed off. Instead, she took Rosie to a nightclub, bought cocaine, and fed it to Rosie. They drank, snorted, got stoned out of their minds, and had sex together.

The next day, Rulle was bruised up. Hartwell was scratched up, fingernails dug into her back. White didn't want to know anymore. Morales had no choice.

"I slept with Rosie," Regina told Anita, her voice cold and hard, her eyes hot with anger.

The blow to Anita was as strong as a baseball bat. Rosie Rulle and Anita broke up for good.

Regina was finished with Rulle. She apologized to Anita.

Regina Hartwell was drugged and didn't know what she was doing. She wouldn't have done that if she hadn't been coked up, Anita rationalized. Her rationalizations flowed like her protestations had earlier. Although Morales forgave Hartwell, she never forgot the betrayal.

Regina knew she never forgot, even though Anita had forgiven her. It bonded them even tighter.

Regina, however, still didn't feel bonded to her father and still hadn't forgiven his betrayal to her and her mother, the betrayal of marrying another woman. Regina still didn't feel like she belonged with Mark Hartwell's current family, so she continued creating her own family in Austin, Texas. She and Ynema Mangum spent Thanksgiving and Christmas together.

Christmas was just the two of them at Regina's house. It was a Christmas that Mangum would always remember. Unlike Hartwell, she was used to huge family gatherings, so that Christmas seemed special and sweet with just the two of them placing presents under the tree for each other. They gave each other clothes and laughed when they found that one of their presents to each other was the same—huge, Odie slippers.

But not all times were so joyous. Ynema Mangum got a new girlfriend named Kathy Steng, who didn't like Regina. Regina didn't like Steng either, however she wasn't going to let that get her down. Instead, Hartwell fed off of Steng's disdain for her and tried to aggravate her. "Hey, let's do girls' night out. Sorry, Kathy. Just girls. Just us girls."

Kathy jumped at the bait. She and Regina fought, with

Ynema caught in the middle. "I don't want to choose. Hey, it's not fair. I don't want to choose between my best friend and my girlfriend," Ynema said.

Mangum decided she wanted to break it off with Steng, but each time she tried, Steng threatened her—she threatened to commit suicide and she threatened to "out" Ynema at work.

Then Mangum began to have an affair, hoping that that would cause Kathy to let her go. Kathy just complained to Regina about Ynema's cheating ways. She struck Regina in that vulnerable spot, that place in her heart that so desperately wanted and needed to be wanted and needed. Kathy Steng needed her.

Kathy and Regina began to bond, and Regina let Ynema know that she didn't think Ynema was doing the right thing by Kathy.

With that, Ynema Mangum began to feel that Regina Hartwell wasn't on her side anymore, and they started sliding their separate ways.

Besides, Hartwell was doing a lot of Ecstasy. She talked about it a lot and didn't feel X was really a drug. "Shit, X was legal for a while," she said. "Come on, try it, Y. It's not gonna hurt."

"No." Ynema Mangum was adamant. She was tiring of the drinking and partying. "No, Regina. No."

"You're not a very good party girl."

Mangum had spent a lot of years wasting her time because she wasn't in control of her life. She made a conscious decision to get rid of excess baggage in her life. That baggage included friends who she felt made choices that weren't healthy for her.

Ynema and Kathy parted ways. Regina and Kathy parted ways. And Regina and Ynema began to get together only on rare occasions.

* * *

Regina, however, had girlfriends for eighty miles up and down Interstate 35, from Austin to San Antonio. Some of the girls were just friends. Others were just one-night stands, like Rosie Rulle. Others were for love.

Pam Carson was for love. Pam was gorgeous, young, and worshipped Regina. Regina loved young girls to worship her.

Carson had heard a lot about Regina Hartwell. Regina was rich, she was generous, and she was interested in Pam's friend Fran Morgan. One January day in 1993, Pam was sitting alone in Fran's apartment in San Antonio when Regina called long-distance.

That didn't stop Regina from grilling Pam for an hour about Fran. "Well," said the young Pam, "I'm not going to tell you much, but I'm just going to say, be careful, and just don't get hurt."

Carson knew that Morgan was a bit of a "money sucker," and that she was more interested in what Hartwell bought her than in Hartwell herself. "Be careful," said Pam.

"I've heard that you're very cute," Regina replied, "and I'd like to meet you." Pam was a 5'7" tall, black-haired, blue eyed, fair-skinned beauty.

Regina later phoned Pam and invited her to Austin, and Pam accepted. But Pam and Fran got into an argument because Regina had told Fran that Pam had warned her to be careful. No longer trusting Regina, Pam didn't talk to her after that. In fact, they just plain didn't like each other, but, they didn't really know each other either.

Regina Hartwell and some of her friends drove down to San Antonio to party in the Alamo city's gay clubs. Carson was in one of the clubs with some of her friends, and her friends knew Hartwell's friends. They all drank and danced together until closing.

Afterwards, everyone, including Regina, went over to

Carson's, and Regina and Pam talked long into the night. They got to know one another and learned they had a lot in common: loss. Pam's sister had recently been murdered; Pam was grieving and drinking.

"My mother died when I was twelve," said Hartwell. "I've never really talked to anyone about that. She was crushed to death by a hangar door. It wrecked me. I loved my mother more than anything. The only thing that was broken was her little finger. That was the only bone that was broken. My mother was so beautiful. I'll never forget seeing her in the casket. I didn't know how to react."

Regina looked up at Pam. "It's weird how we've both suffered losses so young," Regina said. "A lot of our friends just don't comprehend that."

Regina was being real. Other times, she mouthed off or cut people down to hide her emotions. But Pam liked this Regina. They took each other by the hand and walked into a spare bedroom. They spent the night together. They didn't have sex, but they did everything else. Pam found it to be a very good night.

The next day, Hartwell showed up at Carson's workplace. "I've bought tickets to Europe," she said. "I've gone to talk to a travel agent, and I'm going to take you and Brandy to Europe." Brandy Wynne was an up-and-coming Austin singer and a good friend of Carson's.

"No, I can't afford it," said Pam.

"Don't worry, I'm going to buy it."

"No, no, no," said Pam.

Hartwell and Wynne went behind Carson's back and bought the tickets.

Regina Hartwell began commuting to San Antonio to see Pam. Hartwell made the trek so often, she had to quit her job at a North Austin clothing consignment store just to have enough time to woo Pam.

And to woo her, Regina bought Pam everything Pam even glimpsed. They'd go to the mall, Pam would fleetingly admire a T-shirt, and Regina would buy it. She wouldn't tell Pam about the purchase, however, until they got into the car.

Hartwell would step into her Nissan Pathfinder, shut the door, reach into a bag, pull out the gift and grin from ear to ear. "Look," she'd say, pulling out another gift.

Carson would shake her head. "Regina, you didn't have to do that."

"I wanted to."

Less than a month after they had begun dating, Regina's birthday arrived, and Pam went to Austin for Regina's usual birthday celebration, a party in a hotel suite. She gave Regina a lava lamp.

The following week it was Pam's birthday. The day before her birthday, Regina picked Pam up at work and said, "Close your eyes."

She took Pam to a hotel suite. "I've invited all your friends to come over tonight, and we're gonna go out."

But that night, before they went out, as they were dressing for the evening, there was a knock at the door. It was a delivery man with six dozen roses for Pam. An hour later, there was another knock at the door and there was another delivery, that time bunches and bunches of stuffed animals. Another hour later, champagne was delivered.

Then they sat down to dinner, and Regina said, "I have your birthday present."

"You're kidding me. What now?"

"Close your eyes." Regina handed Pam a box. Inside was a gold and diamond tennis bracelet. The two girls had known each other less than a month.

God, thought Pam, *I bought her a lava lamp for her birthday, and she buys me a thousand-dollar tennis bracelet. I'm a loser. Here's this girl who's coming down here, spending all this money, taking me out all the time, taking me shopping; I feel trapped.*

She especially felt trapped to go to Europe with Hartwell. But Carson also liked Regina a lot; they got along. Regina made her laugh (at a vulnerable time), and they didn't argue, not at all.

After a little over a month of dating, they finally consummated their relationship. It was then that Pam first noticed the dotted Swiss fabric of scars across Regina's back.

"I wanta bring home a guy," said Regina Hartwell.

"I don't know about that, Regina. I'm kind of boring," Carson answered.

"I just want to bring home a guy. You don't have to do anything. I just think that would be cool. And you can watch."

"Well, I'm not really into that."

They settled for trips to Forbidden Fruit, an Austin sex-toy shop, and talked about moving in together.

"But you can't bring your cats," said Hartwell. "I'm allergic to them." Her allergies bothered her contact lenses, and she was meticulous about her lenses.

"Well, if I move to Austin, you know I'm going to be very homesick without my cats," said Carson.

"I'll get you a little pet of some kind."

"I want to name it Emmitt."

They planned on moving in together upon their return from Europe.

Spring of 1993 came and the trip to Europe neared. Regina and Pam went to Houston to get Pam's passport. They shopped at the Galleria, a high-scale shopping mall. Pam leaned across a railing and stared at the ice skaters a floor below, and Regina disappeared.

"Hey," said Regina, excited, on her return. "I've found a whole roomful of Emmitts."

They ran to Petland.

"Wouldn't it be cute if we had a little puppy?" said Hartwell. She showed Carson all kinds of puppies. They narrowed their choices to two dogs in the same case—a pug, and a dachshund that looked like a Three Musketeers bar.

"Well, I don't know," said Hartwell. "I don't know." She was backing off from buying a dog after building up a puppy to Carson.

By then, Carson wanted that dachshund more than anything. That dog was Emmitt. "I'm not leaving this mall until you buy that dog for me," she said.

So Regina bought Emmitt for Pam. It was a thousand-dollar dog.

But Regina Hartwell didn't have the money to pay for a dog or a trip to Europe for four. Continuing her pattern of wooing the friends to "get the girl," she had paid for tickets for herself, Pam, Brandy, and Brandy's friend Carla Reid. She did so by requesting the cash from her trust officer, who gave it to her.

Hartwell then took Ynema Mangum, whom she still trusted, to the bank and placed Ynema's name on Regina's bank account so that she could pay Regina's bills while Regina was in Europe. After Ynema's name was placed on the account, Regina turned to her and said, "If I die, well, whee, here you go."

In May, Regina, Brandy, and Carla left for Europe. The plan was for Pam to join them later because she had to stay home for a while longer. She had to finish school and her father was ill.

But every day, Regina said the same thing. "I miss Pam. I'm miserable. I want to go back. I'm miserable." After three weeks, Regina returned home.

In June, Hartwell flew back to Europe with Carson. Separated from Brandy Wynne and Carla Reid, they were together every day for five weeks, sharing an apartment in Milan without anyone else around. Every day, twenty-four hours a day, Regina and Pam were stuck together. Pam was ready to kill Regina.

Pam suddenly had doubts about moving in with Regina upon their return to Austin, but she kept hearing in her mind Fran Morgan's words: *Oh, you're just using Regina to go to Europe.*

I'm not like that, thought Pam.

But, it made her angry, and she refused to fulfill Morgan's expectations. There was also another factor.

Regina Hartwell was dead broke and needed help. While they were gone, the rent money and bill money she had left her roommates had disappeared, but the bills remained there and unpaid. Her stereo had been pawned. Her house on Lambs Lane had been broken into.

Everything of value was stolen, including all of Mike White's clothes. Trey Lyons's clothes were left in a pile in the center of the bed—as if someone had interrupted the thieves in mid-burglarly. Bank statements were tossed about.

When White and Lyons cleaned up the house after the burglary, they looked at the statements. There were three accounts. One account had more than a million dollars in it. The other two had lesser amounts. When White added them together, the total came to more than $3 million.

But all of the cash Regina Hartwell was allotted for 1993 was gone—blown in Europe and on limos and on suites and roses and dogs and bracelets. She was behind three months in rent and bills.

Since Mike White's clothes had been stolen, and Lyons's

had been left on the bed, everyone believed Lyons had been the burglar. Many considered Lyons to be not just a druggie and user of people, but also a fast-talking, very skilled, pathological liar. Some thought he stole often. Hartwell kicked Trey Lyons out, but he talked fast and hard and convinced her that Mike White had committed the theft.

White moved out, Lyons moved back in, and so did Pam Carson, to help her lover.

Mike White was arrested on a drug charge.

To this day, White doesn't know if Regina Hartwell turned him in to the police. He does know that someone informed on him and that Hartwell liked to brag about things she may or may not have done. Regina bragged about turning him in to the police.

CHAPTER 7

Regina Hartwell and Pam Carson moved to a house in the Travis Heights section of Austin. It was a two-bedroom, one-bath home with a big, wood-and-glass door that was covered with decorative wrought iron. It had hardwood floors, a small kitchen, a sitting room/sunporch with crank-glass blinds that opened to a beautiful, hilly backyard full of trees.

The women had two dogs, Spirit and Emmitt, a house full of Marilyn Monroe memorabilia, roommate Trey Lyons, and even closer access to the downtown club scene than they'd had before. Yet, Regina had less time in those days for bar-hopping. She had enrolled in Austin Community College and begun to work at the Bookstop bookstore.

But Hartwell was a woman of habit. She had four or five pairs of shoes that she wore over and over again. The same was true for blazers, and she only bought Gap or Gibraud jeans.

Her extravagances were T-shirts, cars, and perfume. She had a closet full of V-neck T-shirts. She went through almost one vehicle a year—the red 300 ZX, a Nissan Maxima rental, a Nissan Pathfinder, a pink Suzuki Samurai, a big Dodge Ram truck, and, later, a return to the Porsche 911 she had driven in high school.

She regularly went to Dillard's department store at the local mall and bought three bottles of her favorite cologne—Bijan—at a time. She used a bottle a month, and her scent would fill a room long after she was gone.

That's what Regina Hartwell wanted—for everyone to remember her long after she had gone. Perhaps that's why the few clothes she had just disappeared so often—she gave them away to admirers so that they wouldn't forget her kindness, generosity, loveability. Perhaps she didn't think she'd need them. Regina Hartwell never thought she'd live past the age of thirty. That'd be too unlike her heros—her mother, Madonna's mother, Marilyn Monroe. It'd be too unmemorable.

Living a quiet life in a quiet home with the woman she loved and a dachshund wasn't memorable either. Constantly, rhythmically tapping out white lines on a bright, shiny mirror, in a disco with orgasmically pounding music and flashing lights, wiping the white dust from a Donna Karan blazer, clearing clogged nostrils with a slammer of Dom Perignon—that was more memorable.

The generous, tough, liquor-swilling, coke addict is what Regina Hartwell wanted everyone to see, to believe, because she thought it was cool and happening. Hanging with the so-called elite, the hip-hop crowd, the vampire people who came out only at night in black clothes and white makeup is what Regina Hartwell believed made her a better person, a more superior person.

Contorted truths of loveability are contrived in the mind of a child who rears herself. So Regina Hartwell and Pam Carson fought.

Often they fought about money.

"I'm sorry," said Carson, "I don't have the money. I give you all the money I have."

"Why don't you have the money?" yelled Hartwell.

"I give you my paychecks." Carson didn't have her own account; she and Hartwell just split their money.

"Well, if you hadn't gone out drinking the other night, you'd have the money."

"You gave me the money to go out. I'm sorry, but I don't get a $1,000 a month free."

"Well, I had to pay a price for that."

"Well, I didn't get any money when I lost my sister."

What money Pam Carson had she worked hard for managing a video store. But with the managerial responsibility, she didn't have as much time for Hartwell, and with the stress of work, she suffered migraines. Pam Carson just didn't have the time or energy to party with Regina Hartwell.

So Regina found new party mates, Rose and Timothy Vreeland, a swinging married couple. The Vreelands were Pam's and Regina's friends. Then suddenly, Regina began referring to them as *her* friends. Just as suddenly, Regina was back into drugs, back out of work, back out of school, and back into ambidextrous sex. She had an affair with the Vreelands.

Ticked at Regina's drugging and cheating, Pam went out with another woman. She also went home with that other woman, but nothing sexual happened between them. That didn't stop Regina, though, from a jealous fury. Pam and Regina fought again.

"I'm leaving," said Carson. She packed her things and went over to her friend's house.

The next morning, Hartwell showed up at the friend's. "I need to talk. I think I'm pregnant. I need you to stay," she wept. "I'm pregnant. It's Tim's."

"Are you sure?" said Pam.

"Oh, I know my body, and I'm pregnant." Tears flooded down Regina's face. "I need you. I'm really depressed right now."

Carson felt bad for Hartwell.

"I need you to stay." She wiped her cocaine nose.

Carson took Hartwell to get a pregnancy test, but deep down inside, she knew that Regina wasn't pregnant. She knew that Regina lied to get her to stay. As many times as Carson had threatened to leave Hartwell, this time she was serious. And this time Hartwell knew that—that's why Carson knew Hartwell had lied.

Pam Carson stayed.

Pam gave in to Regina's desire to have a threesome with a man. "Why don't we do it?" she said, and she and Regina brought home a guy. Pam thought they had all kinds of fun.

In February of 1994, birthday time and money time neared, and Regina Hartwell decided she wanted to buy her Porsche from her daddy. She and Pam Carson flew to Houston to get it.

"Please don't tell him anything about me," Pam pleaded the whole flight. Regina had told her about Mark Hartwell, and Pam was afraid he would verbally attack her. "Please, please don't tell him anything about me."

With a big smile on her face, Regina said to her father, "Well, Pam, she's the youngest of twelve kids."

"Oh, you're a good Catholic girl, huh," said Mark Hartwell, "a bee bumbler."

Pam didn't know what to say. She thought Mark Hartwell was a crude, arrogant bigot and sexist. He made her uncomfortable, and she couldn't stand to be around him. She was so uncomfortable that she and Regina stayed that night in a hotel rather than be around Regina's father.

For their actual birthday celebrations that year, Regina Hartwell played it low-key. She and Pam simply took some friends out to dinner. No hotel suite. No limos.

Regina was in a shockingly frugal phase. That phase lasted throughout the winter, the spring, and into mid-summer.

But in that spring, Pam Carson started seeing an old friend, Marion Casey.

"Look, Regina, you've got your friends, and I've got mine. I'm gonna see someone else," said Pam. She and Regina still lived together, but Carson vowed to herself not to rub her affair in Regina's face. After about a month, Carson and Casey had a falling out.

Hartwell took on her loved role as the good, comforting, consoling mother and was there for Pam. That tenderness created a bit of a reconciliation for the couple.

But Pam made it clear. "I'm still moving home, Regina. I want to go back to school. You and I are having so many problems, maybe distance would help."

At the end of April of 1994, Pam helped Regina move into the Château apartment complex on South Lamar.

"Pam, I need to tell you something," said Hartwell, as they toted boxes up the two flights of stairs to the apartment, a one-bedroom with gray carpet, pink tile, and a pink refrigerator.

"This is really going to freak you out, but I don't have nearly as much money as everyone thinks I do. I've never really told anybody this, but I only have $285,000. That's why I've been more frugal. I want to have children, and I really want to provide for my children. Don't tell anyone. Please don't tell anyone."

Carson thought Hartwell was being honest for the first time in God knows when because she believed Hartwell wanted to put all games aside and get back together.

It didn't work. Pam Carson moved back to San Antonio. She really did want to go back to school. She wanted to write, direct, produce; she wanted to make films. It was hard having dreams with Regina Hartwell by one's side, controlling every move, even if she did control out of love and need.

But Regina Hartwell and Pam Carson continued to dance in and out of each other's lives. They went down to the Gulf Coast together and took two male friends with them. On their return, Pam and Marion Casey, who both had moved to San Antonio by then, started to talk again.

"Are you seeing someone? Are you seeing someone? I know you're seeing someone," Regina panicked.

"No, I'm not," said Pam. But on the weekdays, Pam saw Marion. On the weekends, she saw Regina.

Then Pam and Marion got serious again, and Pam confessed her returned affair.

Pam Carson and Regina Hartwell broke up one week before July 4th, 1994.

Regina Hartwell had a faint yearning for normality, so she enrolled again at Austin Community College, and she worked for two weeks as a receptionist in a mall hair salon.

She also slept a couple of times with a body-builder she'd met at one of the gyms she frequented. She had one or two other one-night stands with men. She was lonely; they showed her attention.

"Look at him," said Jeremy Barnes to Regina Hartwell as they worked out at Big Steve's Gym. "Boy, he's cute. I could take him home."

Barnes was a young, gay man whom Hartwell had befriended at the Château. He was a kindhearted, gentleman who had survived his own battles with drugs and the law. Just a few years older than she, he was working to get his life together. Hartwell respected him, and she loved him like a big brother. They made good laughs together.

Regina giggled at Barnes's comment. "Well, that's okay because I've already had him."

Jeremy laughed back. He had never believed Regina Hartwell was completely gay. He thought she wondered if life would be easier if she were straight. Maybe it would be a normal life. If Regina were straight, then, maybe, she could have gotten along with her family.

Hartwell only told Barnes good stories about her mother—the contorted truths of kindness she had contrived in her mind. "We were very close. We were really good friends. But . . ." Regina's voice trailed off, "I really wanted and needed a mother's influence. Things would have been so much different if I had."

She took another gulp of Shiner Bock beer. A bit dribbled down her T-shirt. Regina ignored it and stared out at the pool at the Château, a place where they had many of their talks.

They talked there and in his bedroom, friends chatting on the floor, or sipping coffee. That was their thing together. To sip coffee. To talk of dreams. Hartwell wanted to have a coffee bar. She would own it and Barnes would run it. That way, they could share coffee and talks everyday.

But Regina and Jeremy didn't talk that much about her mother. He didn't feel they needed to go to that tender place of pain because of how Regina felt about her mother. To him, there were a lot of childhood memories and feelings that just shouldn't be spoken out loud. To talk about them, relived them, and, well, it's best not to relive them sometimes. That's what he believed.

Barnes wondered if that was why he and Regina bonded so well—they didn't have to talk about those kinds of things.

They just knew and understood what the other believed . . . about loneliness, love, acceptance.

One day Barnes was playing some Christian music on his stereo when Hartwell walked in. He quickly punched it off, knowing her lifestyle, her partying to three, four, five a.m.

"Oh, no, no, don't turn that off," she said.

"But it's Christian music."

"It doesn't bother me."

From that point on, their bond grew stronger. Regina knew how he felt and from where he got his strength—Jesus Christ. And he knew who she really was—the little country girl who wanted to be noticed, but who couldn't be if she were just a little country girl.

Regina and Jeremy argued only once, down by a railing at the Château. "You know what? I never can tell you anything without you arguing," yelled Jeremy.

"Fine. You just don't have to ever tell me anything again."

Regina went up to her apartment and shut the door. Jeremy went to his apartment and shut the door. They didn't speak for two days. On the third day, Jeremy was outside walking a neighbor's dog. Regina looked out her window and saw him. She went outside.

"This is stupid. I love you, and we don't need to be arguing like this. I'm really sorry."

Jeremy started crying, Regina cried, and they hugged and made up.

Regina Hartwell didn't have to think about her words. She knew what she wanted to say and got it out quickly. She also liked to have everything her way. And whatever she had to do to get her way, even if it meant paying for everyone, she would do it.

But if Hartwell didn't like someone, she had enough friends that she could make everybody in the whole gay community hate that person. In spirit, at minimum, she ran the downtown Austin gay club scene. Money did that. Strong will did that. Hurt, rejection, abandonment did that. It made one tough.

If someone whom Regina didn't like passed by her, she scrunched her face in a mask of disdain. But she could also love to the deepest pit of her lonely heart.

On July 4, 1994, Regina Hartwell jumped from bar to table to bar to table in Club 404 in downtown Austin. Nothing could keep her still. Madonna's "Justify My Love" pulsated from a giant video screen. Strobe lights flashed and undulated in rhythm as if tripping on acid. Drag queens strutted in and out of the restrooms, their noses tipped with white powder. The room was pitch black.

Finally, Regina lighted at a table of partiers—young, trendy, beautiful partiers. Erasure flashed onto the video screen, then the Pet Shop Boys. Regina spotted Diva, the giant drag queen drug dealer. She jumped up to talk to him. He was more than six feet tall, stocky and looked—depending on the night—like a man dressed as a woman, or a gargantuan, ugly woman. Diva, despite numerous arrests for drugs, was a much better dealer than drag queen.

Regina Hartwell bounced down to the basement, where music meant solely for tripping played, retro music from the 1970s.

When she returned to the upstairs room, Hartwell sat down with Sean Murphy, a University of Texas student and a Club 404 regular. Murphy smiled and waved at a handsome couple, Tim Gray and his best friend Kim LeBlanc. Murphy, an orientation leader, had just met the two in-coming students at freshman orientation. They had been hard to miss.

Tim was tall and slim, with flawless skin, sparkling blue eyes, perfect teeth, and a smile to die for. He was also gay. Kim was out-going, obviously popular, tiny, pretty, well-toned, and brunette, just Regina Hartwell's type. Only Kim LeBlanc was reputed to be straight.

"Hey," Kim said to Sean. God, she was excited. Life was about to change. College. A new start.

Sean pointed at the table. "Come join us. This is Regina."

CHAPTER 8

"On Earth as it is in Austin." For the hippies and high techies, that bumper sticker's not sacrilege, it's truth. Austinites passionately believe they live in God's chosen land.

Thirty minutes outside of town, on the shores of Lake Travis, the hippies and high techies believe it even more passionately. Rugged cliffs of limestone, dotted with the musky green of juniper and gnarled oaks, drop into the deep, blue waters of Lake Travis. Hawks soar over the tight sails of thirty-foot sloughs. There's almost always a good, solid breeze.

The wind can make rough waters for boaters. Still, they're there on wakeboards, kneeboards, inner tubes, and water skis every summer weekend. They toss their beer cans from cigarette boats and jet skis. The cans sink into the murky, dangerous waters below.

Lake Travis has one of the highest drowning rates in the state—booze, pills, pot mixed with too much speed and too little wisdom.

Kim LeBlanc was much like the Lake Travis region she grew up in—beautiful on the surface, stone-hard just below, dangerous waters down deep. Like the region, she seemed to have it all. She was smart—a National Honor Society scholar. She drove a cool car—a green Jeep Sahara. She was PPC— a pretty, popular cheerleader.

But it wasn't enough to escape the reality of life, at home and at school.

Kim was born Kimberley Alex Derrick on May 17, 1976 in Houston, Texas. She was a tow-headed baby with big, brown eyes and a smile that could light up the skies, especially when she was tugging on her stuffed rabbit's ears.

Less than a year and a half later, on August 20, 1977, Kim's mother, Mary Catherine (Cathy), married Kenneth Dwain LeBlanc, a man ten years her senior. As it did for Regina Hartwell, her parent's marriage altered Kim's life forever. Like Regina Hartwell, Kim kept smiling no matter what.

With a move to Dripping Springs, a cowboy community just outside of Austin, Ken LeBlanc became Kim's only father figure. She loved him, and she trusted him for almost thirteen years.

Her mother, Cathy LeBlanc, believed they had the perfect life. She spent her days working as a secretary for a prestigious Austin law firm. She spent her nights with Ken waiting on her hand and foot. She believed he was expressing his boundless love for her.

Kim believed his chivalry was proof that Cathy was incapable of taking care of herself, that she was naive, and couldn't make a good judgment by herself. Kim remembers Ken telling her these things, time and time again. So many times, that she came to believe them. Her mother did, too.

According to Kim, when the man she and her mother trusted made his move, she was only fourteen years old.

"My friend had sex," Kim told him. "She didn't like it. She said it was horrible. It hurt."

He smiled. "Don't worry. I won't let that happen to you. I'll teach you," she heard him reply. Kim alleges he then had sex with her.

Please God, make him stop, Kim prayed, her brown eyes wide and watering. *Please, God, please.* She begged and she pleaded with God. This is what she was being taught sex was like. *Please make him stop. Please, God.*

Kim's soul soared out of her body and up to the ceiling. There it stopped. Detached, it sat and watched. Numb. Unfeeling. Like a bad home movie projected on a clean, white sheet.

She remembers hearing him say, "Your mother can't survive without me. You tell her about this, and she'll divorce me. She can't survive without me."

Kim Derrick maintains she was molested repeatedly.

She didn't tell. Her heart raced with fear. She didn't want to hurt her mother. She wanted to protect Cathy LeBlanc.

Kim had no one to turn to. Not a natural father in Houston whom she didn't really know. Not a mother in Dripping Springs who worked days and was waited on hand and foot at night. Not anyone. Kim believed there was only Ken LeBlanc to turn to.

Kim decided she must be guilty. She must have done something wrong. It must have been her fault to lure his sex away from an adult and onto a child. Those are the thoughts of sexually abused children.

There was no adult for her to tell. He would leave Cathy if Kim told, she believed. Cathy and Kim would be out on the street if she told, Kim believed.

Ken LeBlanc was retired due to disability. He had taken a tumble from some scaffolding while working. On the surface, Ken provided a comfortable enough life for Kim and her mother. He had retirement funds and owned a bit of Wal-Mart stock. They owned the Dripping Springs home and a lot in the Highland Creek Lakes subdivision.

Sex, as Kim had now come to believe she'd been instructed, was the way to reap rewards. Sex, she'd been taught, was power. Sex, she believed, was one's only worth.

Kim believed her stepfather peeped on her as she showered. She believed he listened to her as she masturbated.

Ken LeBlanc bought Kim a bright, shiny Jeep Sahara, which she was so very proud of. She didn't dare let anyone else drive it.

"Don't tell your mother. She can't take care of herself." The words rang in Kim's brain.

Kim's young mind was too full of rape to remember that her mother worked and had worked for years for a prestigious, downtown law firm, that her mother made money, decent money.

But Kim Derrick was still a "sorta-have" in a Lake Travis region of haves and have-nots. In Lake Travis, there's no comfortable place for sorta-haves. Kim "sorta" had a nice house, but it wasn't in the Lakeway subdivision—home of pro football coaches, movie producers, retired generals, school teachers.

She "sorta" had a father. But he wasn't her real father. She "sorta" had a mother. But the haves have mothers who don't work. Everyone else has a mother who works to pay the grocery bill or to keep up with the haves.

Yet Kim Derrick was way too well-off to be a have-not—the world of scruffy-faced men who stand on the side of the roads in thirty-degree weather selling firewood out of the back ends of thirty-year-old rusted pickup trucks, who live in trailer homes parked next to the haves' subdivision, who own mongrel dogs, drink beer, smoke pot, and have no desire or aspirations to go to college.

On the surface, they are nothing like the haves. In reality, they are much like the haves who hide their woes in fine liquor, fine pot, and cocaine, in mystic crystals or Fundamentalist Bibles.

* * *

After Kim Derrick was raped, she cursed God. God, a real God, wouldn't let that happen to one of His children, she thought, her eyes glazed over. At fourteen, Kim also began having sex with boys closer to her own age. She began drinking alcohol and swallowing pain pills. Anything was better than reality.

Neither the haves nor the have-nots, though, want to think they are alike, so they draw a thick line of designer clothes between them. The only thing that pulls them into the same room is the school—Lake Travis Independent School District, 135 square miles. Half of the students are the haves from Lakeway, half are the have-nots from everywhere else.

This thick division affects the way one feels about oneself. The haves rule.

The haves like Chevy stepside trucks, Ford Mustangs, Dodge Stealths, country-music radio station KASE 101, Dr. Pepper, and Garth Brooks. They also think football is all-important.

Football was the number-one school sport in Lake Travis, although the Lake Travis Cavaliers rarely won a game. During Kim's sophomore year, she was a beautiful, blonde cheerleader. With her "megawatt personality," she always rode the top of the pyramids the cheerleaders built.

Their football team, however, won only two games that year.

Kim Derrick spent her time with her best friends, Meredith Swan, another cheerleader who was nicknamed the Princess of Darkness for her Addams Family-like makeup, and Tim Gray, a handsome blond, blue-eyed gay student. Both Meredith and Tim won fine arts awards that year.

The following year, Derrick was inducted into the National

Honor Society. She attended the prom, which featured a KASE 101 deejay. She made tamales for the school Spanish club. She built sets for the school's one-act play.

Kim and Meredith Swan were still cheerleading partners. Meredith was considered a nice kid who would look her teachers in the eyes when she talked to them. Both girls were fans of Nine Inch Nails.

Her fellow students considered Kim sweet; her teachers considered her brassy. She wore short skirts and tops that came down off her shoulders. They thought of her, in dress and personality, as outgoing, forward, and aggressive.

The football team only won two games that year, too. The players cried to their parents, the parents cried to their school board, and Lake Travis got a new coach.

Turnover in Lake Travis I.S.D. was high—often twenty-five percent annually. Coaches came and went. Band leaders came and went. Teachers came and went. School superintendents came and went.

Kim Derrick suffered instability at school and instability at home.

At first, Kim Derrick only abused drugs recreationally, meaning only Thursday, Friday, Saturday, and Sunday.

Her senior year, she asked not to be placed in honors classes. Derrick was always harried about deadlines and she didn't have time for study. She seemed to be separating from her high school crowd.

Kim took a job at the World Gym in Oak Hill, a ten- to fifteen-minute drive from her high school. Teachers thought she was working to pay for college. They thought she had the "want to" to succeed, to make something of herself. In reality, she was working to stay away from home.

Kim's boss at World Gym was a man named Robbye Cellota, a man who months later would hire a handsome, young trainer from California.

Kim chopped off her long, blonde hair. Her friends razzed her about it. She attended sporting events with a baseball cap slapped backwards over her locks, and a tank top for a blouse.

She made a poster containing photographs of brightly colored, fully inflated condoms for a school project about the book *Brave New World*. Teachers thought Kim had a curious ambiguity to her—sexually precocious while wanting to be a good little girl.

This is often the behavior of a sexually abused child, but, apparently, not one teacher in the Lake Travis School District noticed that. Instead, they sat in the teachers' lounge and gossiped about her homelife—rumors that her mother nagged her about her weight, that there were problems at home. No one asked Kim for the truth.

She only confessed the truth to a few close teen-aged friends, including Tim Gray.

She also changed her name from Derrick to LeBlanc.

Around Christmas time, Kim LeBlanc had sexual intercourse, for the very last time in a very long time. She also popped a tab of the drug Ecstasy that year. For the first fifteen minutes on X, there was a tornado of sensations—drunk, stoned, on speed, all at once. Then, elation. It settled like a gentle caress of fog.

For the next six to eight hours, there was a comforting feeling of love, euphoric love, love for everything and everyone. God, it was good. And for the first time in her life, Kim experimented with sex with a girl. It was with a close friend. And it felt good.

But to Kim, anything felt good under the influence of Ecstasy.

* * *

Graduation day was a big day at Lake Travis High School. In 1994, graduation was held in the school gym. With class valedictorian Amanda Dexter leading the way, each senior marched in holding a rose connected to the other roses and seniors by a single, long ribbon. A statuesque beauty and daughter of a Lake Travis High teacher, Amanda gave the valedictorian speech. U.S. Congressman Greg Laughlin also spoke.

There was a half-hour slide show of photos of the senior class. There were baby shots, graduation shots, and glamour shots from the local mall for the wealthier girls. There were photos of the losing football team, pictures of the Cavalette drill team, and pictures of the cheerleaders.

Meredith Swan sang a song. The class of '94 was introduced. Dr. Gloria Berry, the school district superintendent, spoke, then handed out the diplomas. The seniors talked among themselves while she was on stage. Then they threw their caps into the air and headed for Project Graduation, a non-alcoholic night of partying.

Kim LeBlanc graduated fourth in her class.

She cut her hair off shorter, dyed it black, and headed for the University of Texas and a life she'd never dreamed.

In the pulsating darkness of Club 404 on July 4, 1994, Regina Hartwell smiled at Kim LeBlanc. But Regina wasn't all that friendly to Kim. In fact, Kim wasn't even sure Regina liked her.

Kim was dead wrong.

Regina was immediately, intensely in love and lust.

Four days later, Regina introduced Anita Morales and Kim LeBlanc. Regina thought the world of Kim because Kim seemed to have it all together—she was in school, she came from a good family, she had a nice mom who loved her, and she was pretty. Regina liked to have pretty people around her.

* * *

Pam Carson and Regina Hartwell still communicated.

"I met this girl, Kim. I don't really like her, but . . . she flirted with me so much."

For two weeks, Hartwell told Carson how much she didn't like Kim LeBlanc. Pam wondered if Regina was trying to make her jealous, so she encouraged her to see LeBlanc, to see somebody.

"Why don't you see her? Why don't you go out with her?"

"Well, she's straight, and she's just a flirt. She's just playing with my emotions because she knows I'm going through a break-up right now."

At the end of that two weeks, however, Regina Hartwell was giving Kim LeBlanc money to buy drinks in 404. Soon after, Regina pulled Anita Morales aside.

"I swear to God," said Hartwell, "I would kill for Kim. I'd do anything for her. I love her so much. She is so beautiful. I swear to God, I'd kill anyone who tries to touch her. I'd kill anyone who tries to steal her away from me. She is so beautiful. God, I love her so much. She is so beautiful."

That was one of the few times Regina Hartwell saw Anita Morales during the rest of 1994. Morales was busy with school, only a few semesters from graduating with a degree in criminal justice. More than anything in the world, she wanted to be a cop, maybe even an FBI agent.

After she met LeBlanc, Hartwell abandoned her own friends so she could woo Kim's friends, in order to get to Kim, just as years earlier, she had wooed Anita Morales in order to get to Morales's roommate.

Hartwell gave LeBlanc an ATM card so she could access Hartwell's bank account. Then, she took Kim, Tim Gray, and Kim's friend Amanda Dexter, the Lake Travis High valedictorian, on a cruise to the Bahamas.

The need to waste her blood money clawed at Regina

Hartwell like a junkie's desperate need to waste herself on heroin—it killed the pain and alleviated the guilt of knowing that she had gotten the money through her mother's death.

"I have ten million dollars," said Hartwell, her scarred skin hidden behind a T-shirt.

Kim LeBlanc sunned in her bikini. "Uh-huh," she answered, not quite believing her.

Sure, Regina seemed to have money for anything she wanted—a cruise to the Bahamas for four, but $10 million? That seemed ludicrous. Regina lived in a not-too-spiffy apartment complex, and her place was sparsely furnished.

But there was that Porsche 911. The good clothes. The ATM card with access to $300 a day.

It was almost enough to turn a young girl gay, especially a young girl who was a "sorta-have" in a world of haves.

LeBlanc swallowed a tab of X. Soon, she tingled with euphoria, then that sense of affection floated over her body as if she could love anyone and everyone in the world. She reached out and hugged Regina.

CHAPTER 9

Regina Hartwell was infatuated with Kim LeBlanc. Kim knew that, and she was using that infatuation to milk Regina of her money, or at least that's what Pam Carson thought. Hartwell tried to make it seem to Carson that Kim and she were together sexually, but Carson knew they weren't. She heard the truth in Regina's voice; she knew Regina too well.

But that didn't stop Regina Hartwell from throwing the subject of Kim in Pam's face every chance she got, and it didn't stop Pam from retaliating by throwing the subject of Marion Casey in Hartwell's face. Such bitterness developed between the two former lovers that they fought often, mainly over LeBlanc. Still, they made a point to see each other regularly.

Pam Carson drove the eighty-five miles to Austin to spend the day with Regina Hartwell. They went to Manuel's, Regina's favorite, neon-lighted, trendy Mexican restaurant on Congress Avenue—a bird's-eye view from the Capitol and just steps from Club 404.

Kelli Grand, Hartwell's favorite tall, dark-haired waitperson served them. Whenever Kelli Grand entered the restaurant, she greeted everyone with a giant smile, an even bigger hug, and a kiss on the mouth. Hartwell hero-worshipped Grand, so much so that she often tipped Grand as much as the bill. Kelli Grand was the type who could put anyone at ease.

But on that day, Pam Carson was nervous about hanging out with Hartwell, just the two of them. They tried to agree not to talk about Kim or Marion. Carson started drinking, and she kept drinking—beer after beer after beer.

They left Manuel's and went to Oil Can Harry's, a gay bar within walking distance of Manuel's. There, they sat outside and drank more.

With Tecate beer moistening her lips, Hartwell put her hands out. Palms up, she wriggled her fingers. "I can still feel the X running through my veins from last night," she said and leaned her head back and rolled her eyes into her head.

To Carson, Hartwell looked like a frigging idiot. "I'm glad for you," she said, sarcastically. Pam made a few negative comments indicating right then, she thought Regina was a loser.

That didn't stop Regina Hartwell. "Oh, me and Kim last night, we couldn't keep our hands off each other."

The anger escalated until, finally, the two got up and left and went back to Hartwell's. Yet Regina was still calling Pam the sweet, private names she used to call her.

At the Château, they decided to take a nap. Hartwell went into her bedroom and climbed into the bed that she had once shared with Carson. Carson initially lay down on the couch, but eventually got up and walked into Regina's bedroom.

"You don't miss me at all, do you?" she said.

"Oh, don't even try it," said Regina. "I'm not going to sleep with you."

"That's not what I was trying to say."

Another fight erupted, and Carson left.

* * *

The next night, Pam Carson ran into Hartwell and Kim LeBlanc at Club 404. She immediately recognized Kim because she'd seen photos of her. "Hello," she said to Regina.

Hartwell put her Marilyn Monroe nose in the air and walked by without saying a word.

But the five-foot-tall Kim froze as though stuck in fear. Apparently, she had seen photos of Pam, too. LeBlanc's brown eyes were wide and big as though she was scared the 5'7" Pam was going to hit her.

Finally, Kim moved on.

My God, thought Pam, *what did Regina tell her about me?*

Lights flashed in the blackness of Club 404. Music pounded and ricocheted off the walls. It was perfect for thinking and drugging, perfect for tripping. Mike White, just barely out of prison, was by then a clean and sober, gay survivor of incarceration, who knew he could handle almost any situation with his smarts. He glanced across the room. "Shit." He spotted Regina Hartwell in the back of the club.

She'd cut off her hair, dyed it black, and lost weight. Her makeup was white, her lips were dark red. He thought she looked incredible, but she was the last person he wanted to see.

Hartwell spotted White. Not one bit intimidated by his 6'5" height, she lunged for him. "How the fuck dare you show your fucking face here after all you've done to me? I'm happy as hell that I'm the one who turned you in, you motherfucking ass."

White lunged forward. A friend held him back. His sobriety helped; he hadn't had so much as a beer.

A friend held Hartwell back, but she screamed. She yelled and she ranted, like a rabid dog tearing into meat.

White screamed and yelled, too. He felt his sobriety creep up his throat. It overrode his anger and placed terror in his heart of what would happen if he or she turned violent. He hated altercation. He hated confrontation. He put up his protective walls and walked away.

Later Regina Hartwell cornered Carla Reid, who'd traveled to Europe with Regina, Pam, and Brandy. "While Kim was on X," Regina's eyes were bright with excitement, "she hugged me. And she kissed me."

Love is a drug in a class all its own. Regina Hartwell started referring to Kim, Tim, and Amanda as her "kids." She bought them pagers so that they could all stay in touch. She bought Kim thousands of dollars worth of clothes. She took the "kids" to eat at Manuel's and introduced them to Kelli Grand. But it was Kim whom Regina wanted. It was Kim whom Regina provided with margaritas, X, and access to the clubs that Kim was too young to enter.

"Kim," said Hartwell, "I want more from our relationship. You know. . . . But I can wait until you're ready. I don't want to push you."

Everyone around could see that Kim LeBlanc was really straight, that her touches to Regina only got more sexual after she had done a tab of Ecstasy. But Regina couldn't see that. Her love was blind. Plus, Kim's mother liked Regina, and she was nice to Regina. Cathy LeBlanc even let Regina call her "Mom."

Cathy acted like a mom to Regina. She cried "ridiculous" when Regina talked about how she frittered away her money. "Regina, you shouldn't do that."

Regina Hartwell loved the attention. But even with Cathy LeBlanc, Regina got the attention by lying about her wealth. "After my mother died," she told Cathy, "I got most of the money. My father got less." The opposite was true. "I want Kim to use my ATM card. I've got all this money. It's just falling out of my pants."

"Regina has more money than God," Cathy LeBlanc told people.

"I hate my father," Regina said to Cathy, time and time again. "I hate him. I hate him so much. He used to beat me. He hit me all the time."

At first, Cathy believed Regina. Then Kim told her that Regina lied often, and Cathy didn't know what to believe.

Regina just knew it felt like an Ecstasy trip to have a family.

"I'm dating this girl," said Regina Hartwell to Samantha Reynolds.

Reynolds was always the one to do the calling after she left Austin. Hartwell never phoned her.

"Her name's Kim. She's really pretty."

Reynolds felt it was important to call Regina. It made her feel good to talk with Regina, who still had that much power over her.

"Kim's smart," said Regina. "She has a good family."

Sam wanted Regina to know that someone cared about her, that if Regina ever needed a place to detox, she had a place to go to. So, in late 1994, she called Regina.

"I really love Kim," Hartwell said. "But she's young. Real young."

"How young?" said Sam Reynolds.

"Eighteen. She really likes drugs."

"Don't do it," said Reynolds. "Just quit the drugs. Just quit doing this with her. Just quit it. She's using you. She's just flat-out using you. For your money. For what you can get her."

Regina Hartwell agreed to rent Kim LeBlanc an apartment starting January in 1995 and to take her, Tim Gray, Amanda Dexter, Kelli Grand, Carla Reid, Brandy Wynne, and several other friends to New York City for New Year's Eve. Hartwell loved New York. She fantasized about living there some day. This would be a celebration. The Plaza Hotel, limousines, Dom Perignon—it would be a trip worthy of Marilyn or Madonna.

There was just one problem: Regina Hartwell didn't have the money to foot the bill to New York City for ten friends and herself. It was her usual year-end poverty.

She also didn't have the money for cocaine, and she was going through withdrawal—badly. She shook, and she sweated. Her heart raced. She panicked and ran to Jeremy Barnes. Barnes sat up all night long and half of the next day, just holding her while she suffered.

But if nothing else, Regina Hartwell was a woman of her word. If she made a promise to a friend, she kept that promise— whether it was "you sorry son of a bitch, I'll send you to prison for doing that to me" or "I promise I'll take care of you." She had promised Kim LeBlanc and her friends a trip to New York, so, by God, they would get a trip, to New York.

Two or three weeks before the scheduled departure date, Hartwell went to her trust officer for traveling money. She begged and pleaded, but the officer wouldn't advance her the money. There was only one thing to do: sell her Porsche.

Regina Hartwell sold her beloved 1983 Porsche 911 and bought plane tickets and hotel rooms for ten people. So that she could drive around Austin, she rented a car from a cheap, no-name, day-rental agency.

"Will you go to New York with us?" she asked Barnes. "I have an extra ticket."

"No," he answered. Jeremy didn't want to be around her other friends, and he couldn't afford to pay his own way. He wished he could convince her that she was so wonderful that she would have friends even if she didn't buy their attention with drinks, drugs, and trips—she just didn't realize how big her heart was.

Regina Hartwell took the friends to New York. Some of those friends hadn't spoken to her in a month, but they were there in the snap of the fingers on the day they were to meet at the airport for departure. They were there because she had paid for the tickets.

The trip wouldn't be the fantasy she had dreamed.

In New York City, Regina Hartwell plied her friends with drugs, champagne, limousines, and parties. She did anything to make them laugh and be happy—answering her Plaza Hotel room door with her shirt stuffed in her cotton panties, making faces, making fun of others, mimicking Homer Simpson, doing the Beavis and Butt-Head marijuana "Huh, huh." It wasn't enough. Not for Kim LeBlanc. Not for Regina Hartwell.

They shared a bed on the trip, hugs in their hotel room, and kisses in their limousine. Regina gave Kim some expensive leather goods as gifts.

LeBlanc tossed them off as if they were nothing. This had gone too far. She knew she wasn't a lesbian. If she could only convince Regina of that.

It was time to say it plainly to Hartwell. "Regina, I'm not a lesbian." There, she had done it.

Furthermore, she confessed the real truth, but not to Regina. She was in love with Tim Gray.

Kim LeBlanc was in love with a gay man. Hartwell was losing LeBlanc to a gay man. Regina would die, if she only knew.

There was more. Around that time, Kim revealed her molestation. She told Regina. And if there was something that tugged at Regina's need to protect, it was a story of abuse, especially a story of abuse told by a girl who, like Regina, had been abandoned by her natural father.

LeBlanc left New York early. Regina Hartwell was left in her dream city with a bunch of coked-out and drunk-out-of-their-brains revelers whom she didn't particularly want to be with. She had to make the best of it. She decided she'd love and support Kim no matter what, even if she had to settle for just being like sisters. After all, they were bonded. They both knew abuse.

Friends noticed a change in Regina Hartwell after New York. She treated Kim LeBlanc differently, and not so sexually. She still paid LeBlanc's rent, bought her food, drink, drugs, and clothes, but there was a difference.

As before, however, the image Hartwell presented to her Austin friends was different from the image she presented to Pam Carson.

Pam Carson ran into Kim LeBlanc, Tim Gray and Amanda Dexter at a cocktail party.

"Hi, how are you?" said LeBlanc, leaning over and kissing Pam on the cheek.

Carson and Gray talked for hours. He told her, "Oh, my God, you're nothing like Regina described."

The next day, Regina Hartwell stormed over to Carla Reid's and Brandy Wynne's, where Pam Carson was staying. "How dare you hang out with my friends," she screamed. "How dare you talk to my friends." She threw things across the room. "Those are *my* friends."

"Regina," said Pam, "they're not your possessions. You don't own them. Just because you buy them everything, doesn't mean—"

Sam Reynolds phoned Regina Hartwell.

"I'm doing well," said Regina. "You'd be proud of me. I've

gotten Kim out of my life. I've been clean for a month. Everything is going great."

Hartwell even decided to get a job again. After all, Kim had taken one. LeBlanc then worked at Westbank Dry Cleaners in the community of Westlake, a so-called elite suburb of Austin that was home to successful writers, musicians, attorneys, and high-techies and where drugs, sex, and alcohol flowed freely among cheerleaders and football players. If Kim could work, so could Regina.

Ynema Mangum tried to help Regina get a job. As Regina's twenty-fifth birthday drew near, Mangum set up an interview for Hartwell with Xerox, Ynema's own employer, for a job as office assistant in the accounting department.

This is just the right thing to put Regina on the right track, to get her motivated, to get her working toward a career, thought Mangum. The two had been friends for about six years, and this was Ynema's last try at their friendship.

Hartwell went to the interview and aced it. Xerox thought she was smart, funny, outgoing, attractive, and a great dresser.

"They're going to do a drug test," Regina told Ynema.

"No problem," answered Ynema. "You told me you haven't been doing anything, that you're clean."

"Well, uh, I smoked some pot last week."

Just as in years past, Mangum knew Hartwell was lying. She knew that Hartwell had done drugs harder than marijuana.

"Rather than embarrass you," Regina said, "I'd rather just not go back and accept the job."

That hurt Ynema. It hurt because she believed it showed that she, Ynema, had become hardened. She was interested in huge corporations with health-insurance plans, with chances for advancement, with 401(k)s.

Regina was interested in making her friend not look bad for hanging with a druggie. That's the way Ynema Mangum looked at it. That's the way Hartwell's real friends always looked at her actions—as protecting them, not as protecting Regina.

Ynema knew something else about her friend. She knew Regina tried hard to be normal. She knew Regina wanted to have an education, to have a job, to be a professional woman, but that Regina didn't have the discipline or the roots in her spirit to do that.

Regina Hartwell wanted the whole panoramic view so badly that she couldn't focus on just one thing. She was a random person. Her most organized routine was to get up, go to Diva's, do drugs, and obsess about a woman she couldn't have.

On her upcoming twenty-fifth birthday she would gain access to all of her money—every single dollar of it. She could do whatever she wanted. No answering to trust officers. No begging, pleading or lying. Just cold hard cash.

The weekend of February 10, 1995, Regina Hartwell threw herself one hell of a birthday party.

She rented the Presidential Suite at the Embassy Suites hotel, then ordered three limousines and filled them with Dom Perignon. She took about a hundred friends to Manuel's, her favorite restaurant, with her favorite waitress. She ate chicken enchiladas verdes, her favorite. She wolfed them down in her usual fifteen seconds.

Eventually, everyone made their way to the hotel for drugs and drinks.

But on that twenty-fifth birthday, on that very special occasion for Regina Hartwell, few people gave her a birthday present.

Jeremy Barnes went to the Warner Bros. store and bought Regina a Wile E. Coyote pen, knowing her love for the *Road Runner* cartoon character, because she had said she was going to return to school.

Anita Morales gave Regina a very special ring, one exactly like her own.

Regina always gave away things that were important to her.

When R. A., her former best friend who had introduced her to Mike White, and with whom she had since reconciled, died soon after of AIDS, Regina placed the ring on his finger. It was buried with him.

Too familiar with death too young, Regina Hartwell was devastated by his death.

Regina Hartwell and Anita Morales sat down across from Regina's financial officer. Regina chattered, picked up a pen, signed the papers, and they left. They drove over to Kim LeBlanc's workplace, the dry cleaners. They got out, walked in, Kim signed the papers, and they left.

Hartwell had just created a $5,000 mutual fund account to help LeBlanc pay for college.

"Why are you doing this?" asked Morales.

"Because I love Kim." Regina beamed for joy. There was no more to be said. Incredibly hardheaded, once Hartwell had her mind set, there was no changing it. That's the way she was. Stubborn, and tough. Very tough.

She'd talked to Kim's mom about the fund, and Cathy LeBlanc had approved. As far as Kim and Regina understood, Cathy LeBlanc knew of and approved of every aspect of Kim's relationship with Regina.

That was good. Regina Hartwell liked getting the approval of a mother.

But there was a problem. Tim Gray was sharing LeBlanc's apartment. He slept in the living room while Kim slept in the bedroom. There seemed to be no hope of Hartwell getting physical attention from Kim.

"I'd do absolutely anything for Kim," said Regina. "Anything."

Anita Morales had heard that enough times to make her sick of hearing Kim's name.

* * *

"Regina, you've just gotta buy something for yourself. Look at this apartment." Jeremy Barnes glared at Hartwell's tacky coffee table. It was covered in plastic, black-and-white checkered shelf paper. "Girl, it's time you fix this place up. Do something for yourself for once. You deserve it."

Barnes had tried for months to get Hartwell to buy herself a couch. He knew she had the money. He cleaned her apartment on a regular basis, and had seen her financial statements. But trying to get Regina to spend money on herself was like trying to pull money out of Scrooge. Barnes took Hartwell by the hand and led her down to the furniture store to buy a sofa.

Regina couldn't find anything she wanted to buy, but she could find a million things she didn't want to buy, and a million reasons not to buy them. They walked down the aisles, Regina pointing her finger at this and that. "I don't like that. I don't like that. I don't like that."

"Reg, girl," said Barnes, "if you don't hurry up and buy something, I'm going to pick out something, and they're going to deliver it this afternoon. And I'm going to pick out the biggest, floweredest-looking thing that you can ever imagine."

She picked out a black, faux-leather couch.

She gave her old furniture to Kim LeBlanc to help furnish the apartment Kim shared with Gray, and for which Regina paid the rent.

"Is it silly that I bought a Jeep that matches Kim's?"

"Oh, no, no, no, it's not silly." Jeremy Barnes stared at the green Jeep Sahara with the huge tires and perfect sound system. "It's great, Reg. It's just great."

Regina Hartwell socked her hands into her pockets and grinned.

But Barnes really thought it was the stupidest thing he'd ever seen in his life. He wasn't about to say that to Regina, though. She was too happy, and it was getting rarer and rarer to see Regina happy.

"You deserve it, Reg. You deserve whatever you want because you have the biggest, bestest heart of anybody I know."

On Valentine's Day, Regina Hartwell gave Kim LeBlanc a diamond ring. It looked like an engagement ring. It was just one of many gifts Regina bestowed on her over the year. She gave the beautiful Kim a Gucci watch, her mother Toni's ring, a phone, and a CD player for Kim's Jeep.

"I want to sell it," Kim would later say to Regina of the CD player.

"No. Why?"

"I want to buy an eight ball of coke," Kim answered.

"I'll pay for it," said Regina.

But that would be months away, when Hartwell wasn't so flush with money. She was rolling at this time. She could buy LeBlanc anything she wanted.

Regina felt she could face anything, so she went home to Pasadena to visit her father and stepmother. Her visit with Mark and Dian Hartwell went well. They talked, listened, and bonded. They loved each other. Regina actually had hopes of building a wonderful relationship with her father, the kind of relationship Kim LeBlanc had with her mother.

Then, the words she'd spoken for so many years didn't seem so hollow. "If anyone tries to hurt me, I'll call my daddy, and he'll take care of them. I'll call my daddy, and he'll . . ."

Regina told Anita Morales about her great trip home. She told Jeremy Barnes about her great trip home. She really was on a roll. Life couldn't get much better than that.

* * *

"Jeremy, you know I really need my apartment cleaned, and the Jeep is looking really bad. You want to make some extra money?"

That was just like Regina—to know when Jeremy needed her. Jeremy's roommate had moved out, Jeremy had to pay all of the $700 rent himself, and he was short $200. He hadn't told Regina, but she just knew it anyway. That's the way Hartwell was; she cared so much about certain people that she instinctively knew when they were in need. At least that's what Jeremy believed—Regina loved certain people to the fullest.

On March 5, Jeremy's birthday, Regina went to The Gap to look for a present for him. But just like with shopping for a couch, she couldn't find a thing.

"Jeremy, I went to The Gap. Nothing looked like you. So, here, I'm over this." And she handed him a $100 bill.

She went out and bought a Honda scooter and registered it in the names of Regina Hartwell and Kim LeBlanc.

She bought an eight-foot-long Bombardier jet ski and registered it in the names of Regina Hartwell, Kim LeBlanc, and Tim Gray. She also gave Tim a ruby ring. She made plans to take Tim and Kim to Cancun near Kim's birthday. She planned on buying Kim huge, new tires for her Jeep.

Money went fast. Regina needed cash.

She also needed a friend, a real friend. Regina phoned Sam Reynolds.

"It's going okay with Kim," Hartwell told her.

Sam dropped to the floor, shocked that Regina had actually called her. She listened carefully.

"But it's not perfect," said Regina, her voice sounding sad.

Still, Reynolds was happy that Hartwell had phoned her. It made her feel that her love wasn't a one-way street . . . that Regina cared for her . . . that Regina didn't think Sam's calls were a pain in the butt. Reynolds was so happy that she remembered exactly where she had sat on the floor when Regina Hartwell had reached out to the past and groped for help.

By May, Regina had taken a job working beside her old roommate Trey Lyons, whose social connections Regina thought impressive—people who were good for the scene, who were good for the image. They worked at Kim's Dry Cleaners in Westlake.

Kim LeBlanc went back to work at World Gym in Oak Hill, her old high-school place of employment.

But work plays hell with partying. One has to make time for drugging.

CHAPTER 10

Kim LeBlanc was lonely, very lonely. It had been five months since she had broken up with Regina Hartwell, at least broken up in LeBlanc's mind. She guessed they were broken up in Hartwell's mind, too. Regina did, after all, talk to Kim about girls Regina was interested in.

LeBlanc didn't do the same back—she didn't talk to Hartwell about the guys she was interested in. That still didn't feel safe. LeBlanc was lonely for male companionship. Her year-long life as a pseudo-lesbian was making her feel incredibly uncomfortable.

She hadn't been with a young man, sexually, since the middle of her senior year in high school. That seemed like several lifetimes ago. Cheerleading. Partying. Making tamales for the Spanish club. Painting sets for school plays. Being feminine, frilly, with long, blonde hair.

She reached for a brush to comb her brown, cropped hair and glanced around World Gym. She glanced at the women on stairsteppers. She stared at the men clanking weights. At least she was this close to her old life, working out and working. *Here*, LeBlanc thought, *finding a guy should be easy.*

"The next guy who walks around that corner," she whispered to herself, "I'm going to ask out." LeBlanc ignored the phones she was supposed to answer in her job as a receptionist and watched the corner.

She couldn't believe her luck. There he was. Six feet, four inches tall, hazel-green eyes, light brown hair, built like a pro football player—a lean, mean, fighting machine. His hands had the faintest whispers of blond hair. They looked safe, loving. Kim smiled at Justin Heith Thomas.

He smiled back. He had a very sweet smile.

Justin Heith Thomas was three years old when he and his parents, Judy and James Thomas, went fishing with his father's brother, wife, and son Michael. Times seemed okay in the Thomas household. There were big gallon jugs of wine around, and cold, cheap wine was always good on hot, sunny fishing days down at the creek. They lived just outside of Riverside, California, on land good for growing crops and raising chickens.

Justin and Michael sneaked in and out of the trees. They spotted the jug wine and giggled. They'd seen how it made their parents laugh, joke, love. Justin and Michael squatted like little Indians and tippy-toed over to the wine. Together they juggled the bottle until they each got a few little nips.

"Justin! Michael!"

The boys froze.

"Jim," yelled Judy, "Justin and Michael have been sneaking the wine."

"Oh, leave 'em alone," said Jim. "Just leave 'em alone."

Justin continued to sneak his little nips. By the time the family walked the road toward home, Justin was wobbly. In fact, he was downright drunk, and he fell over and passed out in the road. His daddy picked the toddler up and carried him to the car.

* * *

Before little Justin reached puberty, his mother attempted suicide twice. He remembers his mother and father arguing, while he stared at his daddy's truck, which was loaded to the hilt with his father's worldly possessions.

"Please don't go," his mother cried as she begged Jim Thomas to stay.

Jim Thomas got in his truck and drove off.

Judy Thomas walked back in the house and wept more tears.

Justin didn't know for sure what happened next. It was the same year he had drunk the wine, so he was still only three years old. He thought Judy had gotten lots of pills and taken them. He didn't see her do that, but he came across her, lying on the floor, looking dead.

"What's wrong, Mom? What's wrong?"

Judy didn't answer.

Justin paced by her, time and time again. "What's wrong, Mom? What's wrong?"

Judy couldn't answer.

Terrified, Justin called his grandma, Judy's mother. How he knew her number, he wasn't sure. But children, even three-year-old children, can often dial the number of the one they know will come no matter what.

The scream of an ambulance broke his mother's silence. Then Justin's uncle Andy, Judy's brother, arrived and he took Justin home.

Justin's daddy kept driving—clear across the states of California, Arizona, New Mexico, and halfway across Texas. Jim Thomas drove to where his mother lived, in Gonzales, Texas, a small town just east of San Antonio, just south of Austin.

That was when Justin Heith Thomas started staying with his mother's parents.

Both Judy and Jim Thomas had grown up in the farming region of Sunnyhead, California, a city in the desert foothills not far from Los Angeles. Judy's family managed a local chicken ranch. Jim's family migrated throughout the U.S., from farming community to farming community, before finally settling in the Riverside County town.

Jim's uprooting and rerooting and uprooting again were just one foreshadowing of the history of chaos in the Thomas family. There were six children in Justin's father's family. One child died quickly after a premature birth. Another died at age twenty-one after being hit by a car.

Justin's grandfather Thomas was an alcoholic. His grandmother Thomas drank only occasionally. But when she did pull her wine out from underneath the sink, behind the washing powders, she drank until she was drunk, which led to argument between man and wife.

"You son of a bitch," she yelled at her husband.

"You're not calling my mother a bitch," he yelled back and slapped her across the face. The hand belted across the face by the six-foot-tall man and the sudden black eyes on the four-foot, eleven-inch tall wife put an end to the argument, always.

Justin Thomas was said to bear a physical resemblance to his grandfather Thomas.

To escape the tyranny of Justin's grandfather, Bonnie Thomas, Justin's aunt, ran away from home when she was sixteen years old. She was considered her father's "baby girl," and her father hated all of her boyfriends. He particularly hated the one she was in love with at that young teen age and who, over the decades they were together, provided her with four children to mother.

Bonnie eventually did return to the Thomas fold. She and her brother Jim became as close as entwined fingers, and she became more of a mother to Justin than his own mother.

Jim, in contrast to Bonnie, was considered his mother's

"baby boy." His escape from the family dysfunction came in the form of a stint in the Army and a trip overseas to Vietnam. He was eighteen years old. There, like many soldiers, the teenager managed to smoke a little dope in the jungles.

Upon his return from 'Nam in the early 1970s, Jim met Judy. Jim was a handsome, six-foot-tall war vet who was particular about his appearance. He liked his jeans perfectly creased by the dry cleaner's and his shirts perfectly ironed. Judy was a pretty, eighteen-year-old Hispanic just out of high school who worked as a teller in a local bank.

Judy and Jim dated. They fell in love, and after Judy got pregnant, they married. Justin Heith Thomas was born to Jim and Judy on November 3, 1971. Jim's and Judy's marriage lasted about four years. Jim agreed to pay child support, agreed to visitation rights, and remained in Gonzales, Texas. Every month, he sent Judy child support. And every summer, Judy sent Jim Justin.

Judy maintained a stable work history and landed a managerial position in the bank, but her personal life and work life were diametrically opposed. There were the suicide attempts, multiple relationships, and multiple divorces. There was little time for Justin, and her son ended up being raised by her parents.

Justin was six or seven years old when he first found his daddy's marijuana.

"What's this?" he asked.

"Marijuana," said Jim Thomas. "It makes you high."

Justin didn't quite understand. "Can I light it?"

"Yeah."

The young boy touched a flame to his daddy's joint and watched Jim Thomas as he inhaled on the reefer with a loud, sucking wheeze. His daddy's often sad face washed into a silly, little, satisfied grin, and Justin leaned back with contentment.

For Justin, it was a thrill and an honor, a bonding moment, just like all those many times before when he had been allowed to light his daddy's tobacco cigarettes for him. Justin had been doing that since he was three years old.

Justin's memory is more vague regarding his mother's second suicide attempt.

He was at his uncle's when he was told, "Something's wrong with your mom. We're going to the hospital to see her."

But no one told Justin what had happened to his mother. He just peered his eyes over her body, as she lay quietly in her hospital bed, and he desperately searched for something visibly wrong with Judy. He couldn't find a thing.

Later, he learned she had once again tried to commit suicide.

After the two suicide attempts, Jim requested full custody of Justin. Judy turned him down.

Justin lived with his mother two or three years at a time, when she was involved with a man in a good relationship and when it was time to try the "family thing" again. Mom was good then; Mom was stable then.

But when the relationship fell apart, as it always did, Justin remembers Judy blaming the wreckage on him.

"I hate you!" she yelled at Justin. "It's all your fault! I hate you!"

She repeated the words to her son, over and over, until her anger echoed in his brain without his mother even voicing the words. And Justin was angry back.

He was angry, then he was lifeless, so very lifeless. All he wanted was for his mother and his father to love him, to physically love him—for his mother to tuck him in bed and to hug him and kiss him goodnight, for his father to wrestle with him on the floor like little boys and daddies do.

It wasn't to be. Justin was returned to his grandparents and his uncle Andy. They provided him with his values and life lessons. But they weren't his mother and father.

Justin was twelve or thirteen years old and with his uncle Andy when Judy's third husband threatened to leave her. Judy and her husband had been out drinking, they'd done some fighting, Judy phoned Andy, and Andy and Justin rushed over to Judy's.

They found Justin's mother with a bandaged hand, in a cast or a splint. She'd cut herself with a piece of glass. There weren't a lot of cuts, just one deep, telling slash.

That was about the time Justin began to understand the high of marijuana his daddy had explained, the euphoria of drugs. In junior high, Justin Thomas's daily routine was simple. His mother woke him for school. His buddies came by the house for him. They left together, then stopped and picked up a couple of more friends. On their way to school, just after the stores and just before the schoolyard, they stopped in a field and smoked a joint.

At lunchtime, they went behind the handball court and smoked a cigarette, sometimes a joint. After school, they smoked another joint. Justin was cool and having fun; no square or preppie friends for him.

But one day, behind the handball court, the boys got caught.

"You have a choice," Justin was told at school. "Join this drug-rehab group, or we tell your parents."

To save my hide, thought Justin, *I'll join the group.* He was thirteen years old.

It was better than facing his stepfather.

Justin maintains there were no ifs, ands, or buts about it; whenever he screwed up, his stepfather belted him.

According to Justin, one time when he smart-mouthed off to his stepfather, he was smacked. Justin argued back, his face painted over with rage. The stepfather took a wooden paddle and broke it across the thirteen-year-old boy.

I wanta kill you! Justin yelled in his mind. But Justin Thomas was a child. He was helpless against a full-grown man, and he was smart enough to know that. He was smart enough to know he needed an equalizer. *I wish my dad was here to beat you up!* thought Justin.

Judy worked during the day, and at night she went to cosmetology school—with a goal of earning extra money. She was materialistic and a gold digger in Justin's eyes, traits he had picked up from her, and her attempts at gaining wealth from men weren't working.

Justin's mother hired a young girl, who lived up the street, to stay with Justin until Judy got home. Sometimes the sitter came to Justin's home. Sometimes Justin went to the sitter's home. He was thirteen. She was eighteen. She had a pool.

Sometimes, they went swimming.

Justin stared at the young girl's breasts, full and tanned in the hot desert sun. He kept his eyes on them as he slowly, quietly swam up to her side. She lay there serenely, floating on a raft, looking like an Egyptian goddess, dark hair, blue eyes, legs firm, curved, sensual. They made a young boy's body beat. Justin Thomas was in lust.

He reached one hand out to her raft, barely touching the plastic as he thought about what he'd do to her. The kisses, the touches, the caresses, the being loved, the passion. He could stroke his hand up and down her thighs, between her legs.

Justin popped up out of the water and pushed his sitter from her raft. She fell on top of him, her dark, oiled skin rubbing against his chest. He wrapped his arms around her and kissed her.

They had sex by the side of the pool. He wasn't even sure if he did it right, but the experience made him go softly quiet, like his father after a joint.

Except for lust, Justin Thomas didn't have any other sexual contact until he was fifteen. After that day at the pool, he knew what masturbation was.

At fourteen, Justin fell in love. Every inch of his being felt it. When Justin Thomas was in love, he was in love. He'd do anything and everything for the woman, fly to the moon and back.

However, at the same time, his mother's third marriage fell apart. Per the usual pattern, when his mother's marriage fell apart, Justin's and his mother's relationship also fell apart. She went off on a Pentecostal Christian kick and got tough on Justin, forcing religion down his throat. He didn't like it or the extremeness of it.

He got a cross tattooed on his left arm. He was fourteen years old, and his mother didn't like it.

"Either get rid of it or you go," she said.

So Justin got rid of it. He took a pair of pliers and a needle. He got the needle hot, and touched it to his cross time and time again until he had burned the tattoo off and it was no longer visible. More than a decade later, the burn scar is still visible, though, barely—hidden beneath new tattoos.

But back then, burning off the tattoo didn't stop the fights. Justin and Judy argued about his school work, about his school friends, about his pot-smoking.

"Leave, just leave," she yelled at him.

He started smoking pot in the house. They argued about his

behavior, about how he spent his time with his friends, about his performance at school.

He told her off. She had no control over him.

"Leave, just leave," she yelled at him.

They fought more than her child could handle, so Justin called Jim Thomas, who was then living in a small town in central Oregon.

"I want to come live with you," he said.

"Come on up here," said Jim Thomas.

CHAPTER 11

Justin and Jim Thomas lived in a trailer house parked on the butte of a volcano near Bend, Oregon. Justin's aunt Bonnie and her former teenaged sweetheart, now her husband, lived nearby with their children. It should have been a beautiful time in beautiful country.

But Justin hated it. His heart ached because he missed his girlfriend, but most of all, Justin was bored.

He was a spoiled, rowdy, wild, party boy who loved to boast tall tales and hated school. The only things he liked were football, fishing, and getting high. As far as football went, though, Justin couldn't play in the games—he didn't maintain the required B average.

Just like in California, Justin wouldn't handle the responsibility of school. Nor could he handle the fact that Jim insisted he do household chores—like making his own bed, mowing the lawn, washing the dishes, washing his own clothes, and doing a little cooking.

"You gotta carry your own weight around here," Jim told Justin in one of their many arguments. "Just 'cause you say 'gimme,' don't mean you always get what you want. You have to work for what you get."

Justin didn't buy it. He already had his mind set on his ways and what he wanted. His family in California had always given Justin everything he ever wanted, materially at least. He thought attempts at death and gifts like good cars and great stereos were a part of life, normal for any family. Justin Thomas just didn't know any differently.

His teachers constantly phoned Jim. "Justin's not here to learn," they complained. "Justin' s here to be the class clown."

With that, Jim demanded that Justin pull out his school work and do it in front of his dad. Justin didn't like that. He spent his time bragging about alleged drug, alcohol, and sexual victories back in Southern California.

"Me and my buddies, we used to go downtown cruisin', and we'd pick up these girls, eighteen-, nineteen-year-olds," said the fourteen-year-old, "and, you know what I'm saying, we'd party all night, drinkin', fuckin', fuckin' all night long, and smokin'. You know what I'm saying, we had us some high-grade pot. The highest-grade shit you can get."

Jim didn't buy it. Instead, he went out, bought some low-grade pot, and brought it home. "I tell you what, son," he said to Justin, "we're gonna smoke this, and we're gonna get high together, and we're just gonna see."

Justin puked his brains out all night long.

That wasn't the norm. The norm was Justin handling his drugs.

Each morning, on his way into town, Jim dropped Justin off at Aunt Bonnie's. Then Justin and his younger cousin J. R., his "number-one cuz," spent the day fishing. They got high and fished. Sometimes, they got drunk and fished. It didn't really matter as long as they were doing the two things they loved most—fishing and getting wrecked.

But Justin didn't like the taste of alcohol. To him, liquor was good for only one thing—to get blitzed. He much preferred pot . . . or something stronger.

And it was there, in Oregon, on the side of the volcano, where Justin Thomas's life began erupting out of control as drugs went from a recreation to a dependency.

Justin Thomas and his friends were going out, just hangin' with the homeboys. A few blocks from the trailer, he realized he'd forgotten something, so he turned around and went back home. He walked in the back door, which was closest to his bedroom, went into his room, got what he'd forgotten, and then heard his father in another part of the trailer. It sounded like Jim Thomas was in the kitchen.

Both Jim and Justin Thomas loved to cook. It was one of the few things they had in common. Justin was a growing, hungry fourteen-year-old, so he decided to go see what his dad was cooking. He walked into the kitchen, and there, on the table, was a scale and a pile of crystal methamphetamine—the poor man's cocaine, a drug that can turn a boy paranoid and violent in a matter of months, that can turn him into a murderer in no time.

"What's that?" Justin asked innocently, meandering over to his dad, staring down at the white powder. "What are you doing?"

Young Justin was just playing dumb so he could play his father. He knew exactly what his dad was doing.

Jim Thomas looked up at his son, sat there, and laughed.

"Is that meth?" Justin asked, his voice sweet.

"Yeah."

Justin Thomas knew meth from his friends in California, from the parties he frequented. "Can I do a line?" he said.

The fourteen-year-old Justin did, and from then on, it was on.

"Twice a week Jim Thomas drove to Eugene and Salem to

get crystal meth. He sold meth, his son sold pot . . . and, in between, anything else that came along . . . including cocaine and acid.

On occasion, Jim provided Justin with the pot. But "on occasion" wasn't enough. Justin needed it every day. Every day, like an old, western, coal train rounding the Oregon mountain, Justin smoked.

He smoked to kill emotional pain—to try to kill feelings, to try to fill an emptiness, a void.

Ever since Justin Thomas could remember, he knew there was another plane of consciousness or another reality right next to the one he was in at that very moment, one just over his shoulder, and that confused him. It confused him as a kid. It confused him as an adult—because he didn't know what that other plane of reality was.

He only knew that there was something more to him, his person, his being. There was just no book of directions that told him how to find out what that was. A toke of pot, a hit of meth, and that confusion and emptiness magically went away.

Justin became addicted to meth and pot. Jim was addicted to meth and booze.

Addiction was a Thomas family tradition.

Justin phoned his mother's parents in Riverside County. "If you'll come back," they said, "we'll buy you . . ."

And Justin was gone.

Jim later moved back to Texas and his mother.

But the one good thing that came of Oregon was football. Justin Thomas loved it, and he wanted to make it his career.

* * *

High school was the "funnest" time of Justin Thomas's life. He was sixteen years old, good-looking, popular, a blue-chip football player with a letterman's jacket and a car, and girls fawned over him. It was a time when his easy, sweet smile often slow-danced across his face and changed an angry, young man into a Prince Charming of a pussycat.

His future wife Dawn saw both sides of Justin Thomas.

The first time Thomas saw Dawn was at a post-football-game party, one given by mutual friends. Dawn was with another guy when Justin walked in wearing his letterman's jacket, sweats, and tennis shoes and carrying a case of beer under each arm, looking like a typical jock.

Dawn, a 5'2", petite, brunette beauty who often modeled and won beauty pageants, took one look at Thomas and turned away. "What a loser." Dawn didn't like guys who drank.

But Justin took one look at Dawn and instantly fell in love. "Wow," he said. Maybe it was lust. First lust, then head over heels in love so that he would try to do anything in the world for her. Love was becoming another drug.

At the party, they drank, they ate, people carried on, music blared. Justin tried to make sure he was always in the same room as Dawn. He wanted to watch her and look at her; she was so beautiful.

He drank some more, he smoked too much marijuana, he showed off and showed out, he got louder and louder and louder, and he started acting like an ass.

"You've gotta leave," he was told.

"Back off, you asshole," Justin responded, and he shoved the boy who had told him to leave.

The boy shoved back. He and Justin got into a fight.

"What a loser," said Dawn.

Justin's repertoire of emotions consisted of two: extreme love and extreme anger. That's the way it is with an addict.

* * *

Wipe away his sweet smile with a flash of anger, and the 6'4" star football player became an imposing, big-browed Frankenstein's monster of a character. It was a turn-off to Dawn, but it was a turn-on to drug dealers. And Justin Thomas was equally attracted to them.

He met a few people who introduced him to a few people who. . . . He remembered the cash that flashed through his father's hands in Oregon. He wanted to see that cash flash through his own hands. Justin Thomas, after all, had his mother's love for the material. Visions of riches danced in his sweet, hazel-green eyes.

Some of those people who were attracted to him made him an offer Justin Thomas couldn't refuse.

Justin Thomas became a drug dealer.

The next time Justin saw Dawn, he turned to a friend and said, "I'm gonna make her my wife—watch. I'm gonna marry that girl."

Justin Thomas started living a split life. For his family and everyone who was important to him, he tried to do good and be good—go to school, make good grades (mostly Bs, a few Cs, an occasional A), graduate, go to college, play ball, play pro football.

To his friends, he was making his first steps toward being an influential person in the drug world. He thought, *I'll make it big in playing football or I'll be the boss telling everyone else what to do. I'll be the boss of a part of something that's a money-making operation.*

Drugs and money became his lord.

He sold pot then graduated to selling coke, heroin, acid, and pharmaceuticals. When he found out he could get crystal meth, too, Justin Thomas got very, very happy. He knew what kind of money he could make from that. He knew he liked to snort crystal meth. So as quickly as he could tap out a fat rail, he chose that track.

Justin and Dawn continued to run into each other around town, and each time Thomas ran into her, he tried to talk to her.

"Wanta hook up with each other for a while?"

Dawn ignored him.

That drove Justin nuts. To him, the blue-chip football player, it seemed like hundreds of other girls fought to get close to him, to touch that hard body of his. But Dawn played hard-to-get. That intrigued Justin, and it made him fight harder to get her.

On a hot summer day, during football practice, one of Thomas's homeboys phoned. The sweet, high pitch of girls' voices drifted over the line and Justin smiled that sweet smile of his. "Whataya doing? What's going on?"

"There's a girl here who wants to talk to you," said the friend.

"What girl?"

"Dawn."

"Dawn?" There were too many girls chasing Thomas. "Who's Dawn?"

"You know, *the* Dawn. The girl from the party."

"What party?" Justin's brain just wouldn't snap into gear.

"The girl you've seen around town."

"Where around town?" Brains don't snap into gear after too many parties, too many beers, too many joints.

"The girl you say you're gonna marry."

It can wreak havoc on a young man's sex life.

Dawn got ticked when she realized Justin didn't remember

who she was . . . after following her around at the party, after pursuing her around town, after claiming he was going to marry her.

She yelled in the background.

Thomas heard her voice. "Oh, shit, yeah." His brain had finally kicked into gear at the sound of her voice. "Lemme talk to her. Stick her on the phone. Lemme talk to her."

"No, I don't wanna talk to him now," she said, still in the background.

In Justin's mind, Dawn was playing a little game with him. He could play back. He sweet-talked her into getting on the phone and smooth-talked her into getting together—that day. There was no winning against Justin Thomas. He could be a charmer.

On the way to meet Dawn, Thomas stopped at a liquor store. *Okay, we're gonna party,* he thought. *I'll get some party favors.* He bought two pints of vodka. He left his stash of pot behind—that split life.

With a big grin on his face, Justin walked in to meet Dawn. Like a little boy thrilled to be pulling two huge catfish out of his pockets, Justin Thomas pulled two pints of vodka out of his pants.

But Dawn wasn't thrilled.

"Oh, no. Oh, no," she said. Dawn remembered too well what Thomas had done at the party, the fight he had gotten into. "I'm not going out with you if you drink."

"All right," said Justin. After all, he lusted after her. He thought he loved her. He'd do anything in the world for her, fly to the moon and back. Justin handed Dawn the two pints.

She threw them away so hard that they both broke on the ground. The smell of vodka permeated the air. Dawn and

Justin and two of their friends then went to a movie and to Taco Bell, Dawn's favorite restaurant.

"Can you and me go out?" said Justin. He bit into his taco and seemed a bit shy.

"Yeah," said Dawn. She smiled.

In fact, Dawn wasn't ready to go home just then. She and Justin drove around town, just the two of them, to talk, to get to know each other. His curfew arrived, and he had to go home. They sat in the drive of his grandparents' house.

Justin was nervous, like a little boy. "Uh, is it cool that we can go out again, just me and you without the other two?"

"Yeah." Dawn leaned over and kissed Justin on the neck, the left side.

Justin Thomas was a goner, smitten. Nearly ten years later, at the memory of that tenderness, he still softly touched his neck where Dawn had first kissed him.

That kiss on the neck, however, eventually led to pregnancy. It seemed that Justin Thomas was more like his parents than he might have dreamed. Like his mother, he liked money. Like his father, he liked drugs. Like his mother and father had once been, Justin Thomas was young, unmarried, and had a child on the way.

"You can either have a wedding in Hawaii or a big wedding here," said Dawn's mother and stepfather. "What'll it be?"

Dawn's parents and Justin's grandparents had old-world values. So, like Justin's mother and father, there seemed nothing to be but married. Justin and Dawn chose the big wedding in California—a $30,000 wedding.

Like his mother and father, Justin had a little boy, Prestin. From the beginning, Prestin was a daredevil and a show-off who craved the attention and spotlight, like his father, Justin.

* * *

Like his mother, Jim Thomas, wasn't an everyday drinker. But when he did drink, he drank to get obliterated. He was depressed and had been so for decades. Jim was so distraught that his hair fell out. It didn't merely fall out of his head; it also fell out of his arms, his legs, everywhere.

Jim went to a general practitioner, who told him the hair loss was caused by nerves. But the doctor didn't give Jim anything to remedy the situation, so Jim went to a dermatologist. The dermatologist gave Jim a prescription, and the hair started growing back.

But Jim Thomas decided he didn't need a doctor—he could do his own prescribing. He ran down to Mexico and got pills on his own. He did that regularly and also began drinking, a lot, regularly, to the point of obliteration.

After Prestin arrived in November, the college football recruiters departed—USC, San Diego State, Cal Berkeley, UTEP, Texas A&M, Rice, Northwestern, Washington, Oregon State, and Hawaii. Justin Thomas was left with one fewer dream.

But Justin loved Dawn. It was either love or anger, the only two emotions he knew. At eighteen, he was in love—to the moon and back for Dawn.

A friend of Justin's uncle Andy got Justin Thomas a job in construction, and Justin played the good boy. But that split life was ever present. He dealt enough drugs to have a nice, little, extra amount of money, and he screwed around on Dawn. He thought it was normal for a man to cheat on his wife. He thought every man was allowed to do that.

To Dawn, he hid his lying, cheating ways. In Justin

Thomas's eyes, if he didn't flaunt his philandering, that meant he was being respectful to Dawn, that meant he was being loving to her.

That worked for the first year of their marriage. Then Justin got that first-year itch—he thought he was missing out on something in life. He was frustrated in his job. He felt he was doing the work of a foreman, but not getting the pay or the title. His boss refused to give the young man the pay or the title.

On top of that, his drug-dealing "family" was tugging and pulling on his emotional shirt sleeve. "Come go to work for us. Come go to work for us, and look what all you can have." It was as if the devil had Jesus by the sleeve, flying him over the universe, saying, "Just follow me and all of this too can be yours."

Justin Thomas had too many good avenues of distribution to turn down the devil. He accepted. He raked in maybe $200,000 in drug profits, and he spent maybe $200,000 in drug profits—on parties at beach condos, on limo trips to Vegas, on drugs, cars, jewelry for this girl and that. He and Dawn split, then got back together several times.

When they split, he got tighter with his drug family. Hard headed, he called it. But he also always had to have what he didn't have. If he had the drugs, but no Dawn, he decided he had to have Dawn. If he didn't have the drugs, but he had Dawn, he decided he had to have the drugs.

"Please, please, come back to me," he begged and pleaded with Dawn, like his mother had begged and pleaded with his father fifteen years earlier. "Please stay with me. I have nothing without you. If I have you, my life will be all right. All this other stuff won't be important no more."

And Justin was right. He did have nothing without Dawn, only the pull of the drugs, the attraction of the money, the power behind those things. They clutched at him like the gnarled fingers of Satan.

"I'll leave it alone. I won't do none of that if I'm with you."

But Dawn knew Justin didn't speak the truth. He was too far gone, too spun out on crystal meth. He'd dropped from 250 pounds to 195 pounds. And he paid for his drug abuse with his career as a drug dealer. He missed phone calls. He missed meetings. His drug-dealing family began to question Justin Thomas's loyalty. The money he turned in to them was short. He'd messed up with these people, and they went looking for him. It was time for Justin Thomas to pay his debt to them.

CHAPTER 12

There was a part of Justin Thomas that didn't consider Dorothy Brown good enough to be his girlfriend. She was ugly, she was fat, and she was too old. She was about eight or nine years older than twenty-year-old Justin, only a few years older than the sitter he claims had sex with him by the swimming pool when he was thirteen years old.

But age or no age, Dorothy Brown was a good meth dealer. She and Thomas met through mutual friends in the early summer of 1992. Justin had methamphetamine connections, and Dorothy needed a supplier for her own drug-dealing business.

Quickly, she became a "major distribution avenue" for him in one of the nine cities in which he did business. Justin Thomas thought he was on his way to being king of an empire, but he let his emotions and a woman tie him up and distract him from business.

Brown and Thomas saw each other every other day throughout the summer. On those visits to Brown's little Moreno Valley home, three or four times a week, Thomas used her phone to make his own drug connections. He spoke Spanish on the phone, like a native, like his Hispanic mother.

Then he and Brown exchanged drugs and money. Generally, he fronted her drugs, and she paid for the product after she'd sold it. He told others that Brown was his girlfriend. She thought he loved her, but she thought he loved her like a mother or a sister.

One day around dusk, Brown rode with Thomas a little ways outside of town to a working chicken ranch, in an area known as The Hills. Justin's uncle Andy ran the ranch, and Dorothy met the uncle there. She also met a thirteen- or fourteen-year-old named Josh. But that was at another time and another place.

That day, she went there to do a drug deal. The police had long suspected that that was what went on at the chicken ranch. Thomas kept his drugs there because it was quiet, and it was a great hiding place, camouflaged by the terrain and the chickens.

That was one of the few times Dorothy Brown went to the chicken ranch, but she never, ever went with Thomas to meet his suppliers . . . until the wee, dark hours of a September morning in 1992.

In Thomas's eyes, he was betrayed by love on that September morning. In his eyes, Dorothy Brown set him up to get jacked, to get rolled that September morning. Drugs that no longer existed without any cash behind them was something he couldn't explain away to his people. Considering the amount of meth he snorted, they wouldn't believe he hadn't done the drugs himself. His integrity was already being questioned by his drug family.

Whenever he got into trouble because of drugs, Justin Thomas always ran to the safety of his Thomas family. He couldn't go to his mother or maternal grandmother. They knew something was wrong—he was skinny, hollow-cheeked, and had smudged, black circles around his hazel-green eyes.

They knew he was doing weird things like staying up ten to fifteen days at a time. But his blood family in California didn't know why. They didn't know it was because of crystal methamphetamine. And he didn't want them to know.

Justin Thomas went to Texas to sober up. He thought he'd get to know his father, too. There was just one thing wrong with that plan. From Justin's point of view, like a lover's triangle, drugs were always involved with his father and him. Justin Thomas could think of nothing cooler than to sit down and party with his old man.

Justin Thomas had a good amount of pot and a good amount of methamphetamine on him when he crossed the Texas border sometime around the middle of September of 1992.

On September 14, 1992, the landlady for Rafael Noriega called the cops in Riverside County, California. Rafael Noriega was a supplier for Justin Thomas. Rafael Noriega was missing, she told the authorities, and she filed a missing person's report.

On September 18, 1992, Justin Thomas was handed a traffic citation in Texas.

About the time Thomas was receiving his traffic ticket in Texas, Noriega's abandoned pickup truck was found just east of Riverside, in the golden foothills of Southern California.

Justin's dad was no longer messing with drugs . . . until his son got into town. Then Justin and Jim partied until the drugs ran out.

* * *

On October 17, 1992 Noriega's decomposing body was discovered in a gully, half a mile from the working chicken ranch that was managed by Justin's uncle Andy, under some wooden pallets and a bit of dirt, his corpse partially burned, a few ounces of methamphetamines tucked into his clothes.

The story hit the Riverside papers. When Brown saw it she called Thomas. "They found him," she said.

"Don't say nothing on the phone, baby."

She didn't.

But with the drugs gone, Thomas had to start to think and cope with life again. He missed the hell out of Dawn and Prestin, but he knew he'd screwed up his chances for a normal life in California. He knew he couldn't go back to his drug family.

Dawn wasn't going to leave California, and Justin couldn't live without her. Justin Thomas returned to California.

He tried to get back his old construction job. It wasn't available. Even though friends were keeping an eye out for him, telling him where it was safe to go and not to go, it just wasn't smart for him to stay in California. It was just too dangerous.

Justin got an idea. Like his dad, he'd join the Army. The recruiter made it enticing—Thomas could learn, work, travel, tote a gun, play with guns, blow things up, play war—something that fascinated him, something that he loved. And, in the Army, he thought, he'd be protected from his drug family.

Justin Thomas joined the Army.

He got a deferred entry.

On November 15, 1992, twelve days after Thomas turned twenty-one, at approximately 8:16 in the morning, he drove north on Perris Boulevard in Moreno Valley, California, the same area where he had spent his years with his mother and grandparents.

As he approached Ironwood Avenue, two cars in front of him stopped for a red light. Thomas bent down to get a cassette tape off of the floorboard. He crashed the new red Toyota Paseo he was driving, into the new brown Ford Ranger truck in front of him. The Ranger then crashed into the new maroon Toyota Corolla in front of it.

"I was upset because I found a phone number in the vehicle I'm driving," he told the police officer on the scene. "The car's my wife's."

Justin then walked to his house, got Dawn, and the two of them walked back to the accident scene.

"The vehicle's not insured," he told the officer.

The cop cited Thomas for having no proof of financial responsibility and requested that the accident report be submitted to the district attorney's office for follow-up on violation of Section 22350CVC—unsafe speed for prevailing conditions.

The following spring, Dorothy Brown got a call from Justin. "Mail me some pot," he said.

She did. She mailed it to Gonzales, Texas.

"Dad, how come you weren't never around when I was a kid?" Justin Thomas looked up at Jim Thomas. "We never got to play cars and trucks or nothing."

Jim Thomas got up and left. He went to the store. A little while later, he walked back in the door, his arms full of cars and trucks.

He and Justin got down on the floor, lay on their bellies and played cars and trucks for hours and hours.

Dorothy Brown stared up at the clock on the wall. She had a legal problem, and it was more than a traffic citation. Just a month after Justin Thomas had phoned her about the pot, someone had phoned the Riverside County Sheriff's Department about Brown. They had tipped them off about her meth business. It was March 1993 and the Sheriff's department had raided her home.

Dorothy Brown sat in the Moreno Valley sheriff's station. She was scared, she was crying, and she was frantically trying to figure a way out of the mess.

"Do you know anything about the murder of Rafael Noriega?"

Brown sniffed and cried. Justin Thomas and Rafael Noriega might be her way out. The cops had found Justin's name and Texas address in her house.

"Yes," said Dorothy Lee Brown. "Justin Thomas did it." Detective Daniel Wilson moved in closer to listen. He had been on Noriega's unsolved murder since September, when Noriega's landlady had filed the missing-person's report.

Detective Wilson weighed Brown's words against her woes. She was a thirty-year-old woman with a drug problem. And she had legal problems.

She sniffed again.

"I'm listening," said Detective Wilson to Brown. But his eyes revealed neither belief or disbelief in her words. He flipped on his tape recorder.

Brown continued to cry. She was scared to death of Justin Heith Thomas. She swore to herself to tell the truth, but not the whole truth. She started talking.

On that cool September night, at a dark hour when only coyotes, drug dealers and users are hunting, Thomas had gone over to Brown's house. Everything had seemed to be as usual. Brown had given Thomas some money she had owed him for drugs. He had gotten on the phone and spoken in Spanish. He had argued, then he had gotten angry.

He had hung up and yelled, "That son of a bitch Rafa." Rafa was Rafael Noriega, Justin's supplier, and thus a member of Justin's beloved drug family. Justin Thomas owed Noriega money and Noriega had just demanded payment.

Thomas had turned to Dorothy. "Come with me. I wanta make sure I ain't ambushed out there in the middle of nowhere." He had picked up his car keys. "Take your own vehicle."

Brown had gotten into her Toyota truck, the one she had stolen earlier that night.

Thomas and a seventeen- or eighteen-year old, male friend had gotten into Thomas's truck, a light silver-blue Nissan. Brown had seen the young man around the neighborhood, but she hadn't paid him much mind. She wasn't interested in him. She had followed them alone in the Toyota.

Deep into the foothills she had followed until Justin had pulled off to the side of the road, stuck his arm out the window, and motioned for her to park on a trail.

"Wait here," he had ordered.

A ways down the road were a few houses and the chicken ranch.

"Signal, if anyone comes," Thomas had ordered.

He and his young, male friend had driven around a bend and deeper into the foothills. Brown had waited with her drugs and her radio in her stolen truck. She had been scared and nervous and high.

"You shouldn't be out here."

She had jumped. It was around 3 a.m.

"It's dangerous."

She had turned to find an old couple staring into her car window. "I'm . . . uh . . ." She hadn't signaled. "I'm . . . uh . . . I'm with my boyfriend. He went to use the bathroom. We'll be leaving soon."

* * *

As soon as the couple had gone, a shaking Brown had jumped out of her truck and high-tailed it down the trail. Two car lengths from Thomas, she had slammed to a halt. Thomas hadn't been able to see her, but she had been able to see him, clearly. He had been sitting in the light of his open truck door with its headlights beaming.

He had gotten out of his truck. "Rafa," he had yelled. *"Mi compadre."*

Rafael had hustled out of his small, silver-blue car, moved to the back of the vehicle, and opened the trunk. Brown had seen a weird green colored duffel bag in the trunk.

Thomas had stayed by his truck. He had reached into it and gotten a gun from the seat. He had opened fire—one, two, three, four, five, six, seven, eight shots—automatic gunfire.

Rafael had fallen to the ground.

The night air had fallen silent.

Brown had run back to her truck, jumped inside, and turned on the radio, loud. She had been so scared that she had been sure she was glowing white, like the moon.

Slap.

She had leapt.

Thomas had slapped his hands on her window. "You hear that?" he had said.

"What?" she had answered.

"The gunshots."

"Yeah, but hardly at all. I could hardly hear it at all."

"Get out and come with me."

Brown had walked with Thomas the block and a half or so, back around the bend. She had seen tail lights fading into the darkness—the tail lights of Rafael's car, driven by Thomas's teenaged cohort. She had seen Rafael lying dead in the dirt.

"Get in the truck," Justin had said, "and drive."

She had gotten into the truck.

Thomas had picked up the dead body and tossed it into the

truck bed. He had jumped into the back of the truck with the body and yelled, "Go."

Dorothy had gone. She had driven what seemed to her like forever down the trail, with Thomas barking directions to her the whole time. In reality, Brown had only driven in a circle. When she ended up right back where they had started, Thomas had said, "Your car's right down the trail, just over the hill."

She had gotten out. She had seen again the weird green-colored duffel bag in the back of the truck between Thomas and Noriega's corpse, and she had run. She had run back to the safety of her stolen truck.

With the sun rising over the California foothills, with the coyotes bedding down for the day, Dorothy Brown had driven back to her home in Moreno Valley. The last block or two, she had pushed the truck so as not to wake anyone.

But scared coyotes can't always sleep, even in the day.

Two hours later, Thomas had arrived on Brown's doorstep, showered and clean-shaven. He had shoved a broken shovel into Brown's face. "Here," he had said, "I borrowed it earlier."

She hadn't known that. "I don't want it," she had said, still shaking.

Thomas had thrown it in her backyard. "I've gotta leave town." He had handed her a large bag of crystal meth and Thomas was gone. To Texas. In a pickup truck with blood in the bed. "Deer hunting," he had explained to others. "I went deer hunting. That's what the blood is."

Dorothy Lee Brown and Detective Wilson stood in the same general foothill area where Noriega's body had been found. There was no doubt in Wilson's mind that Brown had witnessed the murder.

Over time, Dorothy Brown was convicted thrice—on the charges of the sale of methamphetamine, possession of firearms, and grand theft auto.

Justin Thomas was not pursued.

On April 18, 1993, Justin Heith Thomas' driver's license was suspended for six months. The suspension was a culmination of a string of many California vehicle violations and convictions dating back to 1991. It didn't matter, though; he was in Hawaii with Dawn and Prestin. The Army had stationed him there.

In the land of paradise, everything was good. For the first time in years, Justin didn't smoke dope every day. He focused instead on his war playing. He, after all, had a self-admitted fetish for guns.

He also spent time playing chicken with other soldiers, burning his arms with lit cigarettes. The sting of the ash, the sizzle of the flesh hurt, but it showed how tough he was.

Thomas got Dawn's name tattooed on his right forearm. The needle cut his skin so that his blood oozed. It hurt, but the hurt felt good. He got four more tattoos. The more tattoos Justin Thomas wore, the more he silently shouted to the world, "I have pain inside this heart." That's what he believed—the more tattoos one had, the more pain one felt inside one's soul.

Emotion, to Justin Thomas, as it was to his dad, Jim Thomas, was not something that was easy to deal with. Extreme love, extreme anger, those two he could deal with. But depression, sadness, he didn't know what to do with them.

When Thomas was in the field, on maneuvers, depression and sadness weren't factors. In the field, he was the best of the best.

He agreed to let Dawn go to work in a bar, and that created a whole new world of problems, particularly a problem of trust.

As an infantryman, Thomas was gone on deployment for days at a time. It meant that he often wasn't there for his wife, but that an island full of military men was. Justin returned from deployment to hear rumor after rumor—Dawn was with this person and Dawn was with that person. Dawn had allegedly succumbed to the shine of temptation, just as Justin always had back in California.

But he didn't think on that, not on his own past. Or maybe he did. Extreme love. Extreme anger.

"What the hell's going on here?" he yelled at Dawn. "What the fuck are you doing?"

"You don't trust me? You don't love me?" she answered.

Justin felt he had to believe her; she was, after all, his wife. The men telling him these stories were a bunch of drunk, stoned, horny, GIs.

Still, it got to Justin, and he started drinking. Whereas he was the best of the best in the field, when he was on base, he was the best of the best at screwing up. He drank a fifth of vodka and a twelve-pack of beer at a time. Just as Dawn had told him years earlier that she wouldn't go out with him if he drank, Dawn and Justin's relationship deteriorated even faster after he resumed drinking.

They were growing further apart, yet he loved her so much. Justin Thomas didn't know how to cope with the pain. So he coped through violence. The 6'4" infantryman grabbed his 5'2" bride by the throat. He threw her on the bed, and he belted her, forcing Dawn to listen to his tirades, his accusations, his pleas as to how much he loved her. Manhandling her, beating her, that was the only way, Justin Thomas believed, to get his wife to listen to him.

That wasn't the first time he'd struck Dawn. He'd done it in California too. He'd pushed her to the ground. He'd thrown her on the bed.

And Dawn had stayed with him.

Dawn Thomas, according to court records, had been molested as a child. Justin Thomas, according to court records, boasted that he had murdered Dawn's rapist. To the moon and back for the woman he loved.

On Valentine's Day, Dawn Thomas planned a special celebration. She planned it to please her husband, who constantly complained that she always went to work early and came home late, which led him to believe even more deeply that she cheated on him.

At the time, Justin had a broken leg. Carrying a 120-pound rucksack on his back, a machine gun, and more, he had tripped and fallen through the mountains and canyons and gulches of Hawaii on a training mission. He had survived all of his falls intact, until he crossed a man-made road. There, he fell in a crack, twisted his ankle, and broke his leg.

Thomas was left to work company quarter duty on the base while his unit was out on deployment. The day he was assigned to CQ duty was Valentine's Day.

"Can't you stay?" said Dawn. "I'm going to cook dinner."

"I've gotta go. You know, I've gotta go when they call."

Dawn got angry. She was really trying to work on her relationship with her husband. They had a son together. She loved her son and her husband. She thought about the good times they had together—the way Prestin had watched his daddy with awe as Justin had jumped off a sixteen-foot cliff on the North Shore. Three-year-old Prestin had grinned and clapped for his daddy and jumped up into his big arms as Justin had swum ashore.

Dawn really wanted her marriage to work.

"Are you sure you can't stay?"

"Fuck you, Dawn. I told you. I've gotta go. It's my job. Don't you understand anything?"

"Fine. Just fine," shouted Dawn.

Justin went on duty. He phoned Dawn to tell her he loved her—that "if I can't have her I want her" thing.

"I'm busy," she said. "I'm getting ready to go out."

"Whatdaya mean you're going to go out? Why are you going out? Are you pissed because I had to come to work?"

Dawn hung up on Justin.

He called back.

She hung up on him again.

The wife of Justin's sergeant-in-charge was the Thomases' babysitter. The sergeant said, "You know, your wife dropped your son off."

"Nah, I didn't know that," answered Justin.

Justin phoned Dawn again. She didn't answer. He phoned her throughout the night, but she never answered. He left messages on the machine. "What the fuck are you doing? I know what the fuck you're doing!"

At 7 a.m., he phoned her again, that time to tell her to come pick him up, he was off from work. Still no answer. At 9 a.m., 10 a.m., 11 a.m., still no Dawn, still no ride home. When she did finally arrive, Justin was livid. He screamed at her. He berated her. He belittled her.

She didn't want anything to do with him. "Let's just pick up Prestin and go home. I want to go to sleep." She refused to talk.

They picked up Prestin and went back to the house. Dawn took a bath and went to bed. Justin took his son and went to the liquor store—a fifth and a twelve-pack. He went back to the house and drank.

Two hours later, Dawn came downstairs and sat down on the couch, next to Justin. He looked at her. He spotted a hickey on her neck. The bottom dropped out of his gut; Justin Thomas felt destroyed, annihilated. They fought, violently. But it didn't matter. Justin didn't care anymore. Nothing mattered anymore. He was dead inside. Just like he had been when his mother shouted, "I hate you. I hate you."

* * *

Dawn's mother soon arrived for a visit. She watched her drunken son-in-law. She overheard his loud, profane verbal attacks on her petite, beauty-queen daughter. She took Prestin back to California with her.

Justin started snorting cocaine and smoking pot on a regular basis. He'd smoked a little pot and snorted a little coke in the Army before, but he'd never gotten caught. The drug NCO had warned the men when there would be urine tests, so Justin had always been clean for them.

But not anymore. He failed a urine test for cocaine.

"Since you're an exceptional soldier in the field, I'm giving you a chance," his captain said. "But you have to complete the program to stay in the Army."

Justin entered a six-week drug-and-alcohol-rehab program, his second introduction to rehab, including that quick stint in junior high.

Just like in junior high, the anti-drug program had not one iota of influence on Justin Thomas. Rehab, doing drugs while in rehab, it was all a joke to him. Justin tripped on acid and did cocaine. He told his drug counselors what he thought they wanted to hear. Inside, he laughed and sneaked more drugs into his body.

At the same time, Dawn said to him, "I'm sorry. I know I messed up."

Justin Thomas began to care about life again. It was near the fifth week of rehab, and just as he was beginning to care, he was told, "You're not working the program. You're not showing that you want to do this."

He was kicked out of rehab.

Justin was devastated. Getting kicked out of the program meant he was to be kicked out of the Army, and he loved the Army. Guns, grenades, fighting, killing, war, drugs, alcohol, and the U.S. government paid him to do all that; life couldn't get much better than that.

What am I gonna do now? How am I going to support my family? he worried. *I can always go back to getting my hands dirty, but I can't go back to the people.* He was already in deep trouble with his drug boss in California. Afraid, panicked, Justin's heart raced as though he were on bad coke.

He went home to Dawn, but she still worked in the bar, and nothing had changed. He got that don't-care attitude again, lit up a joint, and got another bad urine test.

"There's no way," he told his officers. "Can't be. There's no way."

They retested him.

That second test came back bad, too.

But Justin Thomas, the fast-talking, smooth-talking charmer, convinced the Army to let him try to be a good military man again. They let him stay in for another year.

Dawn started seeing someone else. Justin started seeing someone else. He failed a third urine test. Justin Thomas was booted out of the Army. It was September of 1994.

He moved his family back to California.

Dawn was pregnant.

I'm still young. I'm only twenty-three, he thought. *Maybe I can still give this football/college deal another shot.*

He called his dad in Austin.

"Can I come back there? I want to go to school." Justin knew he was telling his father what he wanted to hear, just like he had the rehab counselors.

On Halloween night, Harlie Thomas was born to Justin and Dawn Thomas. Harlie developed into a shy little girl who liked to get her way.

Her daddy, Justin Thomas, left for Texas, just like his own daddy had two decades before—Austin, Texas.

It wasn't long before Justin fell into another drug-dealing crowd of people. But most of all, he found out how much money meth was bringing in Austin. Good money.

Justin Thomas returned to living a split life, good-boy fitness trainer by day, bad-boy bouncer and drug dealer by night. He made $20,000, maybe $30,000 in Austin over six months time. It was easy to sell drugs when you were a tall, good-looking, well-built bouncer at some of the fastest bars in town—Shakespeare's, the Coppertank.

CHAPTER 13

The day Kim LeBlanc smiled at Justin Thomas in World Gym, Thomas had been working there as a trainer for about six months. He checked his clients' weights, took their measurements, set them up with their training programs. He was a popular guy; customers asked for him specifically.

He looked like he knew what he was doing—no more than ten percent body fat, a diet of protein drinks and egg whites, muscles that bulged.

Kim watched him as he walked up to the reception desk to check his appointment book.

"So, how do you use that machine?" she said as she pointed to an abductor, her thin arm just grazing Justin's taut belly.

He looked at her as though she were stupid, but inside he was smiling. Justin Thomas was a womanizer, and Kim LeBlanc was just his type. Short. Small. Brunette. Beautiful. Like his wife, Dawn, in California, the mother of his two children. In fact, she looked like Dawn. Shockingly like Dawn.

And Kim was pursuing him. That was pure pleasure to Justin Thomas, who'd spent his months in Austin doing the pursuing. He thought of the way Dawn had pursued him in California, played him, kissed him on the neck. He touched his hand to his neck. Dawn had later cheated on him.

Justin Thomas had drug deals to do.

Kim LeBlanc rubbed up against him.

He reminded himself that he had let a woman and his emotions distract him from his work before, and now he had to sneak back into California to see his children. He hadn't seen them since he'd last sneaked back in January, just after he'd been to Tennessee to meet someone, to assist in a . . . to help a friend, to make sure everything went the way it was supposed to go, without any funny business.

Justin Thomas went back to work. There were drug deals to do.

Another day Justin Thomas stood in the World Gym's manager's office. He and a few co-workers had just done a few lines of coke, and they were in the midst of their final sniffs to get the drug well into the sensitive membranes of their nostrils when Kim LeBlanc walked in.

She grinned, obviously savvy to the boys' quick sniffs and snorts, and she rubbed her body against Justin. "We ought to get together sometime," she said, and she rubbed her back against his front. "You know, call me sometime."

Kim walked out the door.

"She's hot for you, buddy," said one of his friends.

Justin dismissed it. Nope, no way, no way was he going to let another female distract him from succeeding, from being king of an empire.

Kim LeBlanc made sure she got Justin Thomas's pager number.

It was Wednesday, and Thomas was on his way back from a little drug deal in Marble Falls, a resort city on Lake Lyndon Baines Johnson, about forty-five minutes from Oak Hill and World Gym. Just before he reached Oak Hill, before turning north to head to the other side of Austin to meet a drug connection, Kim LeBlanc paged him.

Justin didn't recognize her number on his pager, but he dialed it on his cell phone anyway. "Who's this? What's up?" he said.

"It's me, Kim. What are you doing?"

"Why are you paging me so late?" It was about one in the morning.

"Well, you're up and around, aren't you?"

"Yeah."

"Well, what are you doing?"

"I'm on my way to North Austin."

"Wanta get together?"

"Okay, that's cool. I have a vehicle. Let me pick you up, and you can come with me."

They met at the Stop-N-Go convenience store near LeBlanc's South Austin apartment. They made Thomas's drug run, but Thomas didn't tell her why they were driving to North Austin. They returned to Kim's apartment.

"You party?" said Kim.

"Yeah, I party." Then Justin realized what he'd said. "But, well, what kind of party do you mean?" he backed off, wanting to play Mr. Innocent, Mr. Square.

Kim brought out a mirror that had a picture of Trent Reznor of Nine Inch Nails on its face. Trent was her favorite singer. Justin, who had a passion for music, liked Nine Inch Nails, too. On the face of Trent Reznor was a bit of cocaine.

Thomas laughed, again trying to play innocent, just like his dad had ten years before with the crystal meth in Oregon.

"Wanta do a line?" said LeBlanc.

He also laughed because he had a few tastes of drugs on him. "Yeah, sure," answered Justin. A couple of ounces on him.

So they did a line, sat on her bed, chit-chatted, and listened to music. Kim touched Justin, she glanced over at the mirror as if she wanted another bump of cocaine, she caressed Justin's thigh, played with his ears, then picked up the mirror as if she wanted another line. They talked and they got to know each other. Kim wiped her finger across the shiny surface to sweep up any excess grains of cocaine.

Damn, thought Justin. *Either this coke's no good, or she's addicted to this stuff.*

He looked at Kim. "You wanta try something?"

"If you wanta do something to me, that's okay," she said, her voice flippant.

He meant drugs.

She meant sex.

That caught him off guard.

"No," he replied, "I'm talking about this right here." He pulled some meth from his pocket. "You know what crystal meth is?"

"I've heard of it."

He spread out a hefty boulder on the mirror. "This stuff is better than that stuff you're doing there. All them little bumps you keep doing there, well, you do one little, good line of this, and you'll be all right until tomorrow, know what I'm saying?"

LeBlanc didn't quite seem to believe Thomas, so he did a little line to prove it. Then Kim did one. And the grin on her face proved to Justin Thomas that Kimberley Alex LeBlanc liked crystal meth, like sugar to a horse.

They talked a little more. He spoke with a sweet, soft slur. They got a little physical, kissing a bit, petting a bit. Then they got a lot physical. They had sex in the bedroom. They had sex in the bathroom. They had sex in the hallway. He stayed the night.

To Justin, they were making love. He was a young man with two emotions—extreme love, extreme anger. And for him, it was a firecracker number-ten evening on a scale of one to ten. Justin Heith Thomas was smitten.

So was Kimberley Alex LeBlanc. At least she seemed to be. Kim was a young woman who liked to have sex, a lot, all the time. She wanted Justin to go slowly with her and to be a gentle lover. She also wanted him to dominate her, tie her up, then make slow, soft love, and torture her with his tenderness. She phoned him the next day.

Thomas was carless. "I've gotta go see a friend," he said.

LeBlanc chauffeured him in her Jeep that had the tires and stereo Regina Hartwell had bought for her. Justin directed from the passenger seat. He directed her to a house in South Austin. They wound around so LeBlanc didn't really know where they were.

"You wait here," he said and disappeared into the house.

A few minutes later, he was back in the car, and they drove off.

"I've met somebody I really like," Kim whispered. She had that half-glazed-over, faraway look in her eyes. Most people couldn't tell if it was sleepiness, drugs, conceit, bitchiness, or what. It was disassociation, safety, protection. "A guy," she said.

Regina Hartwell shook inside. "Yeah," she said, calmly, refusing to betray her anger and fear. "Who is he?"

"I want you to meet him. I want your approval."

"What does he do for a living?"

"He's a trainer at World Gym."

Regina made a face of disapproval. "You can do better than that. You are better than that."

Stay detached. Stay out of your body. It's safer that way. "I'd like to bring him over for you to meet," said LeBlanc.

"Yeah, sure," said Hartwell. She could get through this, she told herself. She could win this, she told herself.

"You'll like her," said Kim to Justin. "Y'all are a lot alike." Kim didn't realize just how much alike. "But you gotta understand, she pays my rent, she buys my food, she buys my clothes."

Thomas nodded and thought back to how his dad always

told him you have to work for what you get. Justin was out to impress. Hartwell was out to impress and protect.

Out to control, thought Justin when he met her. *She has to be in control.*

Regina took one look at Justin and knew he was a dealer. To an obvious user, he was an obvious dealer—with his pager and cell phone.

But Regina Hartwell was nice to Justin Thomas, just like she had been to all of Kim's other friends, just like she had been with all her previous obsessions' friends. She played as though she thought he was the greatest thing since sliced bread.

A controller, yeah, thought Justin, *but a real cool person.*

Yep, they were a lot alike.

The phone rang at Kim LeBlanc's apartment, the apartment Regina Hartwell paid for and furnished. "Come over," said Regina.

"Uh," replied Kim. She stared at Justin with frightened, wide eyes. Her body tingled and shivered. "Now?"

"Of course." And Regina hung up.

"We can't go over there," said LeBlanc. She couldn't stop the tingling and the shivering. "She'll know."

"Not if you stay calm, you know what I'm saying," said Thomas. "She'll know if you keep acting like a cat on speed."

"Well, hell, I *am* on speed."

He tapped his straw clean of crystal meth and stuffed it in his pocket. "Let's go." Justin opened the door.

Kim LeBlanc couldn't sit down. She bounced from couch to floor to kitchen to bathroom to bedroom and back again.

Regina Hartwell stared at her.

LeBlanc tried to turn away. "Got a beer?" she said and lit a cigarette.

"What up?" said Hartwell. She looked from LeBlanc to Thomas and back again.

"I can't lie to you, Regina. I just did some crystal meth. Right before you called."

Regina looked again at Justin and back to Kim. "No big deal," she said. She reached underneath her couch and pulled out a mirror. Streaks of cocaine residue clouded the glass. A small, brown vial balanced atop it. "I've got this."

Kim gasped. She'd never seen Regina with cocaine.

The girl from Pasadena tapped out three fat lines.

There was just something bonding about doing drugs together.

Hartwell phoned Ynema Mangum. "Wanta get together for lunch?"

They met at Pappadeaux's, a loud, popular, expensive (for Austin), seafood restaurant off of Interstate 35. They had an appetizer of oysters *Pappadeaux*, and they ate the fish special of the day.

It was the last time Mangum saw Hartwell.

"I love Kim so much," said Regina. "But she's involved with this psycho named Justin. I love Kim so much. But things are really weird with Kim and Justin. He's crazy."

Bonnie Thomas put the key into the lock of the apartment door she shared with her brother Jim Thomas and his son Justin. Jim had asked her to move in with them if he bought a house. The only problem was that the hunt for his dream home was taking a hell of a lot longer than he had expected, and he was damned depressed about it. He and Justin and Bonnie and her two Rottweilers were living on top of each other in the one-bedroom, South Austin apartment. And Bonnie's son J. R., Justin's "number-one cuz," stayed with them on weekends.

On Friday, about 4:30 or five o'clock in the afternoon, they were dog-tired from work. They had cut fine, wood cabinets.

Bonnie, 5'2", tanned, gray-haired with sapphire blue eyes and tattoos, pushed open the apartment door when, whoosh, two almost identical-looking brunette girls jumped up off the couch and started wrapping blankets around themselves. The girls scooted and maneuvered their arms under the blankets as if they were shoveling on their clothes.

"Where's Justin?" said Bonnie, her drawl thick, her blue eyes wide.

"Oh, he went to the store," one of the girls answered.

There was awkward silence as Kim LeBlanc and Regina Hartwell gathered their clothes and purses and ran into the bedroom to finish dressing.

Bonnie swore she knew what the two girls were doing naked under the blankets.

Regina Hartwell wouldn't go for a threesome. "The thought of having a dick inside makes me sick," she told Justin. Then she bragged about the size of her dildo.

It drove Justin Thomas nuts. He could only watch the two girls together for so long, then he had to leave. Either he got so excited that he had to go to another room to masturbate or he got so jealous that Kim was with Regina, and not him, that he plain had to leave.

Hartwell stood at the bar in Oil Can Harry's. So did her former roommate Mike White. She turned around, and they saw each other. In fact, they stared at and studied each other. Mike had to because he didn't recognize her. *God, she looks so different,* he thought. Weight loss. Regina was so much skinnier than in the past.

So was White. Prison had done that. The 6'5" man was down to less than 200 pounds.

But Hartwell seemed proud of her new body. She wore jeans and a tight cropped top, and her navel was pierced. Regina didn't seem to Mike White to be the type to pierce her navel.

"This is stupid," he said to Hartwell, the woman who had sent him to prison for drugs. "Why should we fight anymore? I didn't do anything to you, even though I know you think I did."

Regina sighed inside. God, she needed a friend. This thing with Kim hurt too much. "You're right." She needed someone she could talk to, someone she could confess to, someone who cared.

And Mike White did care; he felt he owed Regina Hartwell his life. If it hadn't been for her, he'd still be messed up on drugs and screwing up his life. He'd needed to be told, he'd needed to be shown what he was doing to himself. Prison had told him, had shown him. Regina had done him a favor. Coke had damaged his heart. She'd saved him from himself. He had nothing to do but thank Regina Hartwell; that's what he thought.

They made up and shared the evening. She showed off her drug-thinned stomach. She shared her pain.

"I'm dating this girl. I really love her. I don't know what to do. She doesn't return my love. I don't understand why. I do everything for her."

"You have got to start getting it together and detaching from the situation," said Anita Morales. Though she had barely seen Regina for months on end, since the beginning of May, Anita and her new roommate, Carla Reid, had seen Regina almost every night.

And almost every night, trying to put some meat back on her bones, Anita and Carla fed Regina. Hartwell had been wasting away to nothing since she and Kim had been hanging with Justin Thomas.

But Morales and Reid didn't know that it was drugs, coke, crystal meth, and speed draining Regina's body, soul, and spirit. They thought she was bulimic. Hartwell vomited a lot; her stomach couldn't hold anything down because she was always upset.

They thought it was Kim LeBlanc. Kim this. Kim that. Kim does this. Kim does that. Anita and Carla were sick and tired of hearing Regina complain about Kim.

"This is hurting you more than it's making you feel good," said Morales. She stood outside in the darkness of the early May night, barbecuing steaks on her back patio, and struggling to find the words that would soak into her hardheaded friend's brain.

"You've gotta realize that it's only going to get worse."

Hartwell jammed her hands deep into her baggy blue jeans' pockets. She wore the jeans and plaid shirt that she often made fun of as the *de rigueur* lesbian uniform.

"It's not going to get better. Kim's not going to wake up some day and say, 'Okay, I'm gay,' or 'Okay, I'm gay and I want to be with you, Regina.'"

Regina Hartwell stared at the ground and studied her toes in her favorite Doc Martens sandals. There was no way she could look Anita in her brown eyes. Anita was just too intense, just too serious for Regina right then.

"I don't like the way you're still supporting Kim when Kim is off doing her own thing. You don't have to do that anymore."

Hartwell was serious, too. At least she looked like she was seriously listening, like a kid who was getting in trouble with her school teacher. But she wasn't listening. When Regina had her mind set, there was no changing it. And Regina had her mind set.

Anita Morales flipped the steak she was grilling for her thin friend. "Regina, it's time to do something about it. Get out of it. It's not working out. You've got to make some changes or something because this is really getting old."

Anita might as well have been talking to the wooden fence.

* * *

Regina Hartwell called Ynema Mangum at work. Regina was antsy. "Hey, I really need to get your name off of my bank account," she said. "Somebody's taking money out of my bank account."

"Regina, hey, no problem. I'll do whatever it takes. You just tell me."

"Okay, I'll go to the bank and check it out."

A few days later, Hartwell called again. "You have to sign something at the bank to get your name taken off my account."

"No problem, Regina. I'll do it."

Mangum had no qualms about getting off Hartwell's bank account, but she felt Regina was talking in front of Kim LeBlanc and saying those words for LeBlanc's benefit. She felt she was playing a role in their scenario of drama. She felt all of this because Regina Hartwell never took another step, other than those spoken words, to get Ynema out of her banking life. They were the last words Regina ever spoke to Ynema.

Jeremy Barnes and Regina Hartwell stood outside and talked in the breezeway. "Kim and I have never really slept together."

"What?" said Jeremy. "You're paying her bills and taking care of her and you're not even getting sex in return? Girl," he joked, "if you're gonna spend that kind of money on some body, get something for it."

"Well," she shuffled around some, "we've kissed and fooled around just a little bit, but we've never actually had sex."

"Well, um, okay," replied Jeremy.

A few days later, Barnes told a friend, "She really, really needs to go see somebody because she's not getting anything out of this. And it's beyond obsession. It's crazy."

* * *

Folks just didn't understand what it was like to feel you had another person's blood flowing through your veins, making your heart beat, your skin tingle, your mind want to work, your arms want to reach out and touch and hug and love and breathe and feel loved and fulfilled for the first time in your life, like you're not alone in the world, like there's a mother to care for you, a family who won't abandon you, someone who accepts you even when you feel all ugly inside. But Regina understood. And it was worth life.

CHAPTER 14

Regina Hartwell didn't want to get up and go to work. Working was a pain in the butt. It interfered with the partying and with the image she wanted to create. It wasn't fast-paced. It wasn't glamourous. At least the name of where she worked was good, Kim's Dry Cleaner's.

Hartwell got up, threw on her shorts, her cropped T-shirt, jumped in her Jeep that matched Kim LeBlanc's, and drove the ten to fifteen minutes to Westlake, the Austin suburb. She swerved into the parking lot and stared across the street at Westlake High School. It was really a rather ugly school, 1960s construction of bricks mortared into boxes—not even interesting boxes—just big, ugly, square boxes of bricks.

Anyone with half a sense of creativity could have done better. Hartwell knew that. If nothing else, she had style. Her pierced belly button danced between her cropped top and her baggy jean shorts. Her keys dangled from her belt loop. She loved to go butch in this Republican neighborhood.

But there was a part of Regina that was envious. The kids who went to Westlake were glamourous. They were the children of country singers and pro football players. They had money—born money, parents'-worked-for money, not blood money. And they had expensive, designer clothes, fast cars, cell phones, Junior League moms, and doctor dads, not redneck plane-mechanic dads.

Regina wouldn't let anyone know about her envy. She would cover it in humor that sacrificed her targets like clown-faced balloons in a carnival shooting gallery.

"Regina," said her boss. "No more midriffs. Wear something that covers your stomach."

Regina nodded. "Fucking pigs," she said to herself and laughed. A portrait of the boss's daughter embracing a pot-bellied pig hung in the dry cleaner's. Regina reached for a rice cake and gulped down some water.

"Seventy-five pounds," she told her fellow employees, "I've lost seventy-five pounds. My personal trainer helped." Hartwell picked up the phone to call Justin Thomas.

Her boss watched and shook her head. Regina Hartwell was thin and drawn. Her legs were so crepey that she looked like she'd been heavy for years and now had lost too much, too fast. Her conservative, straight employer just didn't know what to make of this closed, distant employee with the strange tattoo on her ankle, another tattoo on her shoulder, and the friend with the matching Jeep who came by to talk too often.

The other workers weren't like that, and Regina was far from the first gay employee at Kim's. In fact, Regina's old roommate Trey Lyons worked there, but he had done so many drugs that his parents had made him move home.

"My personal trainer," bragged Regina again.

"Regina, you've got flowers up here."

Regina walked up to the front counter, glanced at the dozen red roses, and grabbed the card. She read it, looked at the flowers with disgust, and said, "Anybody want these?"

Everyone stared at her like she was looney.

"I don't want them. They're from my boyfriend. He's trying to make up." She turned to her boss. "Don't forget that I need a few days off for my trip to Cancun." Regina glanced out the window to Westlake High School. "It's a present from my dad."

Regina Hartwell was released from her job at Kim's Dry Cleaner's.

The trip to Cancun wasn't really a gift from Regina's father. It was Regina's gift to Kim LeBlanc. Kim's nineteenth birthday was in just a few days on May 17. She'd already bought Kim new tires for her Jeep, bigger ones like her own 31 by 10.50s. The trip was seemingly a last-ditch effort to win LeBlanc away from Justin Thomas. No way could Justin Thomas give Kim LeBlanc what Regina Hartwell could—a vacation in Cancun, Mexico.

Justin held Kim in his arms. Sometimes, she just wanted to be kissed and cuddled. He never knew what mood she would be in, tie-me-up or hug-me. She was the strangest girl—she was like Dawn. In the middle of making love, sometimes, when Justin grabbed her or held her in a certain way, Dawn had totally freaked out.

But Justin had loved Dawn. And he loved Kim. Justin Thomas had cheated on Kim three times before. Remembering how his cheating had hurt Dawn, he stopped screwing around on Kim.

He leaned down and kissed Kim. "I want to have kids," he said. "I want two or three kids."

Kim closed her eyes. "Well, we're gonna leave that up in the air."

"Why?"

Kim was silent for a very long time, never looking Justin in the eyes. "My stepfather," she said, "he would try to watch me take a shower. Sometimes he listened to me masturbate."

Justin's gut tightened. He hated these discussions. He

thought about Dawn. "Well, why did you keep doing it? If you knew he was trying to listen or trying to watch, why did you keep doing it, you know what I'm saying?"

Kim couldn't believe that he could ask her such a question. "You just don't understand," she said.

"What does that mean?" said Justin, angrily. "Did he ever touch you? Did he ever try to have sex with you?"

"I hate God because there is no God. If there was a God, He wouldn't have let what happened happen. I don't believe in God. There is no God. If there is a God, I hate him."

Justin thought about how, whenever he and Regina got into a discussion about religion, Kim always detached herself from the conversation. "Why?" said Thomas. "Why don't you believe in God?"

"I prayed to God to please make him stop. I begged with Him. I pleaded with Him. He didn't stop."

"If he's physically touching you and doing things to you, why are you going to masturbate and let him listen to you?"

LeBlanc was so angry that she just shut up. Justin held her. It never occurred to him that she may not have had a choice.

A week before the Cancun trip, Regina Hartwell walked into Jeremy Barnes's apartment. She had her financial statements, checkbooks, jewelry, and a bag. She shoved them all toward Jeremy.

"Here. Keep them for me until we get back. Jay's staying at my place while we're gone, and I don't want any of this stuff in my house while he's there. I don't trust him." She opened up the bag and pulled out a gun. Hartwell called Justin Thomas, Jay.

Barnes freaked. "I want you to get that out of my house," he said. "I don't know what it is." It was a black gun with a screen of holes around the barrel. To Barnes, it looked like an Uzi. "I don't care to know what it is, but I want it out of my house."

"Jay brought it over, and I don't know what to do with it." Hartwell pulled out a second gun.

"Get rid of them. If there are guns in your house, I'm not going to take care of Spirit, and I'm not going to clean the house."

"They're just collateral for some money I'm loaning him."

"Get rid of the guns. We don't know if they're stolen. We don't know if they've been used in drug deals. Reg, I've lived in New York. I know about these things. We don't know what these guns have been used for."

"He got the guns because, if we're going to start dealing drugs out of the bars, he needs protection."

"What?"

"Jeremy, I'm scared for Kim. Jay always carries a gun because he's a drug dealer. He wants me to sell drugs, too . . . in the bars . . . and guns. He wants me to be his partner."

"Number one, if you need that kind of protection, you don't need to be doing that in the first place. Number two . . ."

Regina's heart sank and jumped with joy. She wanted Jeremy's approval, but she wanted Kim more. To keep Kim, she'd break the law, live with Kim's boyfriend, break the law for the boyfriend, anything. But she also liked having someone pay that much attention to her, showing her that he cared—a father, mother, a parent.

"I'll get the guns out of the house," she said.

Justin Thomas took a trip to Louisiana just to help out a friend, again, to make sure everything went according to plan.

Hartwell took Thomas over to Diva's so that Diva could get a little sweeter deal on his drugs. She provided Justin with front money to buy their meth. She got him into the gay clubs so that he could sell the crystal.

Justin Thomas, an admitted homophobic, was spending a lot of time with lesbians and drag queens. The money was too good not to.

However, his homophobia wouldn't let him move in with Kim LeBlanc, because she had Tim Gray, a gay man, for a roommate.

"But you're not his type," said Kim.

"But that's beside the point," said Justin.

Gray didn't like Thomas. He didn't like the fact that Justin always had drugs. He only spent time with Thomas because Kim liked Justin.

Anita Morales and Regina Hartwell spent almost every Mother's Day together. Mother's Day, May 14, 1995 was no different. They were going to Manuel's, where Kelli Grand worked. Fridays and Sundays were always the same for Regina—chicken enchiladas verdes with margaritas at Manuel's.

Morales drove over to Hartwell's to pick her up. She walked into the apartment. "Jesus Christ," Anita whispered to herself. "What's happening?" Regina was standing in her bra and panties. She was so skinny that Morales could see Hartwell's pelvic bones.

Anita Morales looked around the apartment. It was a wreck. Kim, Regina, and Justin had stayed up the entire night doing drugs. A gun was laying out.

"Jay," said Regina as an explanation. "He deals guns. I bought them all to keep them away from Kim." She motioned toward the bedroom. "There's more in there. Under the bed."

"You do not need to be messing around with this," Morales said, as she emptied out the chamber of the one gun she saw.

"But I've gotta protect Kim. It's this guy she's dating. He's a dealer. He deals drugs. He deals guns." Her speech was rat-ta-tat-tat rapid. "He hangs out with gangs in California.

He deals drugs. He deals guns. He's killed people, too. He's a hit man."

They drove to Manuel's. Regina Hartwell spent most of the time there on the pay phone, screaming and yelling at both LeBlanc and Thomas.

"If you really loved her, you wouldn't be doing this. You wouldn't be dealing drugs. You wouldn't be putting her in your world of danger. If you really loved her, you'd stop."

As much as Anita Morales loved Regina, it was hard for her to hang out with Regina. What Regina was doing with her life was the complete opposite of what Anita wanted to do with hers: law enforcement, FBI agent, investigator, the white-hatted, good guy.

She was soon to graduate from college with a major in criminal justice, and she was currently interning at the Austin Police Department. She was scared that if something bad happened she would be involved in some way.

Jeremy Barnes thumbed through Hartwell's checkbook and financial statements. Regina's bank statements rang up $143,000.

"We need more drugs."

Kim, Justin, and Regina sat in Regina's apartment. Justin reached for the phone and made a call. He knew some heavy hitters. He'd been to Laughlin, Nevada on a drug run. He'd taken Kim to Mexico to pick up a load, and she'd met some of his "family."

"Be back in a few," he said and grabbed the keys to Hartwell's motor scooter, the scooter that Regina had registered in her own name, LeBlanc's name and Gray's name.

* * *

A bit later, the phone rang in Hartwell's apartment. She listened, hung up, and turned to Kim. "Jay wrecked the scooter."

"I was going down Seventh Street," Thomas explained to Hartwell, "making a right on Lamar, when a fuckin' truck came up behind me and jumped in the lane like it was going to make a right turn, you know what I'm saying? I thought it was going to fuckin' cut me off. But it kept on straight, and the front brakes locked up on the scooter, and I had to dump it."

Hartwell looked at Thomas. She didn't quite believe him.

Justin stood in the doorway and studied his road rash. Droplets of blood slowly oozed from his arm, legs, and back. "It's not that bad, Regina. The scooter still runs, you know what I'm saying? Just the right side is a little scraped up." He still stared at his own scrapes, heat burns mainly, on his right side.

"You want a paper towel?" said Kim.

"Nah." Thomas grabbed the keys to Hartwell's Jeep and left.

The next day, Regina Hartwell dropped Thomas off at his dad's workplace.

"I was coming home from work," he said to his dad and his aunt Bonnie. "It was about 11 o'clock, and a truck cut me off."

He showed them his wounds. His legs weren't scraped badly, but both of his arms and his side from back to front were pretty well scabbed over.

"Why didn't you call us?"

"It was too late," said Justin, and he lit a Marlboro.

* * *

On May 20, 1995, Anita Morales was tired. She'd had to search around for luggage to use for the trip to Cancun. Regina had told her to go by her apartment and borrow her luggage. Morales didn't want to do that. Justin Thomas was there dropping off some of his things, and the last thing Anita wanted was to be alone with one of the two people whom she believed was destroying her best friend's life—Justin, the man she thought was a dealer and hit man.

Anita took a plane to beautiful, sunny Cancun, Mexico, a resort made for happy times and partying. Great discos, great food, great drinks—she should have been thrilled. She wasn't. At that time, Cancun was the last place in the world Anita Morales wanted to be. She was about to walk out of the concourse, into the sun, and see Regina . . . and Kim, the other person whom she believed was destroying her best friend's life.

Anita had gone because Regina had always been there for her when she had needed her, and Anita had always been there for Regina when she had needed Anita. Anita could tell Regina really needed her right then. Carla Reid had figured it out, too, and pointed it out to Anita.

"Go to Cancun. Regina really needs you. If she didn't, she wouldn't have begged you to go."

Anita Morales didn't know she was a last-minute replacement for Kim's roommate Tim Gray. She did know her ticket was nonrefundable. Hartwell had told her that much of the truth.

"You have to go, Anita. The ticket's already paid for. Are you going to make me flush $500 down the toilet? Because that's what I'll be doing. It's nonrefundable."

Regina smiled big and handed Anita a drink. Morales tried not to reveal her shock. Regina was emaciated, as though she'd been living in a concentration camp. She was probably losing a pound a day.

They rode to the plush Omni Hotel and went up to Hartwell's

room where she opened the mini-bar and handed Anita a tiny bottle of Bacardi, Anita's favorite liquor.

"Drink it," said Regina.

Morales did.

Regina handed her another bottle of Bacardi. "Drink it. Morales did.

"Do you have a buzz, yet?"

"Yeah, sorta. Regina, whatever you gotta tell me, I can take it without me having a drink."

"No, I don't think you can," said Hartwell.

"No, I can," Anita Morales insisted.

Regina handed Morales a third bottle with a third order to drink. "Drink it down."

She did. "What's wrong?" Anita's dark brown eyes demanded an answer.

"Well," said Hartwell, her head down, "I've been going to the doctor lately." She shoved her hands into her pockets. "And I came out HIV-positive. I won't be around much longer. You've gotta swear to me that you won't say anything."

"Regina," Anita begged.

"Swear. You've gotta swear."

Anita Morales didn't know what to say . . . how to act . . . whether or not to believe her friend. She didn't want to believe Regina was lying, but there were old rumors that Regina liked to pick up guys and have one-night stands. There were even recent rumors of sex with guys. But . . .

Regina Hartwell had lied to Jeremy Barnes. While she was in Cancun, he spotted the bag with the guns on the top shelf of her closet.

He went to Justin Thomas and fell once again into a protective parent mode. "Justin, I want these guns out of her house now. I don't care what you have to do with them. Just get them out."

Barnes didn't leave any room for argument. But Thomas didn't try to take any room; he didn't balk at Regina's homosexual friend. He didn't say one unkind word to Jeremy. In fact, Justin was so kind and polite that Jeremy thought Justin Thomas, Kim LeBlanc's homophobic boyfriend, was coming on to him.

"Regina told me that you're her friend," said Thomas, "and that if I'm rude to you or anything she's gonna kick my ass when she comes back."

Barnes laughed. That sweet, soft slur of Justin's could charm.

At seven p.m., when Justin Thomas knocked on Jeremy Barnes's door, Jeremy wasn't laughing.

"I have to to get rid of these guns and get them out of the house," said Thomas, nicely. "So can I borrow Regina's Jeep to take them over to a friend's house? I'll be back in an hour."

"No," said Barnes.

"C'mon. Just for an hour."

"No."

"That's all I need it for. Just for an hour."

"No," said Barnes, again.

"I just need it long enough to go get rid of the guns. You want them out of her house."

Barnes said no to Thomas five times before finally giving in. "Okay, if you take the guns and get rid of them and come right back."

Eight o'clock came, and there was no Justin. Barnes was ticked. Nine o'clock. Jeremy was dying with nervousness. Ten o'clock came, and there was a knock on his door. Justin Thomas . . . with a friend. As a rule, Barnes thought Thomas generally looked a bit worn from drugs, but he certainly didn't look like anyone to fear. His friend, however, was another matter. To Jeremy, the son of a military mom, Justin's friend was thuggish, white trash, scum of the earth.

"The alarm's going off on Regina's Jeep," said Thomas, again politely. "I can't get it to stop, and with the alarm on, the Jeep won't start."

Barnes knew how to turn it off.

"Come go with us, and you can just drive the Jeep back."

Jeremy reluctantly got into a pickup truck with Thomas and his thuggish friend. *God, just get me through this,* he prayed. The friend drove like a bat out of hell. *God, please, just hold my hand and get me through this,* Jeremy prayed more fervently.

They pulled up to an apartment complex. Barnes got out, turned off the alarm, and noticed that the face plate for Hartwell's compact disc player was missing. He searched around until he found it hidden underneath the tire of a nearby car.

"One of your friends was planning on stealing Reg's stereo," said Barnes to Thomas. "I'm taking the Jeep. I don't care how you get home, but if you don't come with me right now, then I'm out of here."

Justin and his friend both rode back with Jeremy.

Barnes pulled into the Château parking lot, turned off the Jeep, turned on the alarm, went to his apartment, and stayed up all night watching Regina's beloved car. He was terrified they were going to try to take it.

Anita Morales felt as though she were living in the middle of a horror movie about an American tourist on a nightmarish foreign vacation, and she didn't know why she was in it.

Days were miserable. Nights were rotten. Kim LeBlanc cried constantly. Regina Hartwell cried continually. They all fought constantly. And all anyone wanted was for everyone to be happy and have a good time because Regina was dying and they wanted their friend to go out happy.

"You're not having fun. You're not having fun," said Regina to Kim.

"Regina, what do you want me to do? What do you want me to say," Kim answered, frustrated.

Angry, Regina turned to Anita. "What do you want to do? What do you want to do?"

"Regina, what do you want to do? We're going to do whatever you want to do. We're here. You wanted us here. So anything you want to do, let's go do it. Let's go on the Seadoos. Let's go windsurfing. Let's go snorkeling. Let's do whatever. Let's go do whatever you want to do."

"Well, you're not having fun."

With that, Morales pulled Hartwell off to the side and yelled, "You're too busy taking care of other people to take care of yourself, and worrying about whether the other person is happy or having fun. You're not worried about yourself. You're not taking care of yourself. You never take care of yourself. You care more about other people than yourself. It's time you start taking care of yourself. We want you happy just as much as you want other people happy."

It was the biggest argument of their six-year friendship. It was also the only time that Anita was on Kim's side because Kim was saying the same thing to Regina as Anita was.

"Regina, we want you to be happy. We want you to do what you want to do."

Apparently what Regina Hartwell wanted to do was drugs. Hartwell and LeBlanc never did drugs in front of Morales on that trip, but she knew what was going on. Regina barely ate. In fact, all the morsels of food Regina swallowed in three days totaled perhaps one meal.

When the three petite, young, women frequented Cancun's marketplace, Hartwell disappeared down back alleys for an hour at a time, with people she didn't know, to buy drugs for another cocaine spree.

"Don't you ever do that. You're being stupid," said Anita Morales.

But that didn't stop Hartwell. At night, in the discos, she took off again with strangers to buy drugs.

And she bitched at LeBlanc. "Kim, you're not dancing. You're not having fun. Go dance."

Kim got up and danced.

"You're only dancing because I want you to dance," Regina groaned.

"Regina," Kim answered, "what do you want me to do?" There was just no winning with Regina. "How do you want me to be?"

Morales noticed that there was no winning. She also noticed how Hartwell expected certain things from LeBlanc, how Hartwell was too sensitive and took things too personally. And she noticed how hard LeBlanc tried to please Hartwell on that trip.

Regina looked down at Kim's hands. "Where's my mother's ring?"

"It's at home," said Kim.

"Why don't you have it on?"

"It really doesn't fit me."

"I told you to get it fixed."

"It's your mom's ring, Regina, I'm not gonna go get that fixed."

"I told you I wanted you to have it. It's yours. So you need to go get it fixed."

That started another argument, and Anita Morales left the room. The argument lasted throughout the long Cancun night.

"Anita," said Kim, as she cried, again, "I've got to get out, and I don't know how." The two sat alone.

"If you don't do it now," Anita answered, "which I think would be the best thing, not only for you, but also for Regina, and I really want to see Regina happy again, then I think you should do it, because Regina will never do it."

It was the first time Kim and Anita ever had a real conversation. It temporarily changed Morales's opinion of Kim LeBlanc a little bit.

When Anita finally walked toward that hotel door to escape to a plane that was headed for South Texas and the sanctity of her parents, she left wondering, believing that Kim actually did care for Regina, but not in a sexual way. Kim LeBlanc cared because Regina Hartwell took care of her. She cared for Regina as a friend she could count on, like a sister. In fact, for a while, Regina had referred to Kim as her "little sister." Kim, at one time, had sent Regina roses with a card signed, "Your little sis."

Morales wondered if Regina was the one making things hard on herself, instead of Kim.

"I'm leaving, too," said LeBlanc, as she threw her clothes into her bag.

"Why are you saying that?" pleaded Regina. "What do you mean?"

Kim turned to face Regina, red eyes to red eyes. "Regina, you expect me to be all okay about this, and you don't even give me time to deal with this on my own. I need some time to myself to deal with this. You tell me you're HIV-positive, and you expect me to be, 'Everything's fine, let's have a good time, we're in Cancun.'"

Kim LeBlanc left Cancun to go home to Austin.

Regina Hartwell stayed in Cancun for a couple more days. She brought three bottles of Jean Paul Gaultier back to Austin. One bottle was for Anita Morales and Carla Reid, one was for herself, and she planned to give one huge bottle to Kim's mother, Cathy LeBlanc.

But when Regina Hartwell died on June 29, 1995, there were two cannisters of Jean Paul Gaultier on her bathroom cabinet, one small, one large.

CHAPTER 15

Regina Hartwell was tired when she got back from Cancun. "Kim and I had a really good time," she said to Jeremy Barnes. "We fought once or twice the first few days, but I'm glad we got away. Kim and I really became friends."

Not only Kim and Regina, but Justin and Regina appeared to have become friends, too. Upon her return home, Thomas presented Regina with a black, leather recliner. However, he told his aunt Bonnie that Regina had given the recliner to him, proof that Regina and Justin really liked each other and that they weren't jealous of each other.

"Regina's the coke queen of Austin. She feeds Kim coke, and Kim feeds me coke," he also told Bonnie. "Regina used to be worth $9 million, but she only has $3 million left," Thomas told Bonnie and Jim.

"Those girls are gonna get you in trouble," said Jim. "I'm warning you, get away from them."

Justin gave Kim a titanium navel ring. He also gave her roses, tulips, candles, and balloons. They were her nineteenth-birthday present from him.

But what Thomas didn't tell his father was about the many times Justin had been the one to present the girls with an ounce of cocaine at ten or eleven in the morning, and how by six or seven in the evening the cocaine was gone, snorted up the noses of the two just-barely-five-feet-tall young women.

Memorial Day weekend, the Thomas family loaded up their pickup trucks and moved from their tiny apartment in South Austin into their new home in Garfield, on the banks of the Colorado River, near the community of Del Valle.

They left behind a place where they had been a family, where Justin and Jim Thomas had finally had some good father-and-son talks, where Justin had quietly come in late at night, fixed his pallet on the floor next to the couch where his aunt Bonnie had slept, and had risen the next day to say to Bonnie, "Momma B, did I disturb you last night?"

They left behind a place where Justin Thomas had been a pussycat.

"You're more of a mother to me than my own mother," he had told Bonnie. She loved him for that. She also loved the way he had wrestled with her son J. R., as though Justin and J. R. were brothers. She loved to laugh at the way she had had to take a broom after Justin to sweep him and J. R. outside as they had wrestled on the floor. J. R. had always put up a fight, but Justin had always been the victor. It was his size that had won out.

Justin Thomas could put up a tough front for people he wanted to impress.

But the Thomases were also thrilled to be getting out of that one-bedroom apartment. "Can you please be a little tidier?" Jim Thomas had asked of his family. He loved a clean, organized kitchen, bathroom, home.

The house in Garfield, with its stilts, three floors of rooms, and a view of the river, country, and sky was James Thomas's dream home. It was quiet. It was a place to drink, to relax, to fish, to listen to the wind in the trees, and to watch the fireflies at night. It was a place where the crickets chirped, the bullfrogs burped, and the dogs were free to run.

Life couldn't get much better than that.

For Tim Gray, Kim LeBlanc's roommate, life couldn't get much worse. First, he'd had it out with Regina Hartwell so that she'd cancelled his trip to Cancun. Then he'd had it up to his eyeballs with Justin Thomas, his drugs, and his guns. "I'm sorry, Kim," he said, "but I'm gonna move out. This is getting too crazy."

Tim Gray eventually moved back to the safety of his family.

But Justin Thomas didn't help his family move that Memorial Day weekend. As far as his family knew, he spent the weekend with Kim and Regina.

On Monday, Memorial Day, May 29, 1995, Regina was without Kim and Justin, at least for a while. As usual, when she was without Kim, she was upset.

Carla Reid was upset, too. She hadn't seen Anita Morales in weeks, not with Anita's travels to Mexico to see Regina and to South Texas to see her family. Now Anita was coming home, and Regina was already calling for Anita and already on her way over. *Can't she give us any time alone?* Reid wondered.

When Morales walked into her apartment, Hartwell was sitting there waiting for her. Regina reached into her pocket and threw Anita a baggie. "That's what they're into now."

"Who?" asked Morales.

"Jay. And that's what he's getting Kim into. You know what this is?"

"No."

"It's called crystal meth. This drug is, like, totally evil and it keeps you up for days and it's really bad."

Anita sat down, staring at the bag. "Well, you're not doing it are you?"

"No."

"Then let me have that then." She reached for it.

Hartwell's thin hands quivered. "Nah, I'll just take it with me. You don't need to have it in your house."

"Well, no," said Morales. "I was just gonna flush it."

Regina took it from Anita. She talked on and on about Kim. Then she left, crystal meth in jittering hands.

Morales looked at Carla Reid, sadness as dark as her brown eyes. "She's doing it." She shook her head. "This is just Regina's subtle way of saying, 'This is what I'm doing.'"

Anita reached for a cigarette as the Cancun nightmare replayed in her mind. "You know, Kim may be selfish, Kim may be a bitch, but in a way, I can see how she can't get out of this so easily, even if she wants to, because Regina has a strong hold on her."

Anita Morales jotted in her calendar, "Regina came over to talk, talk, talk about Kim."

Regina Hartwell phoned Pam Carson in San Antonio.

"I've been working out," she said, her body vibrating from crystal meth. "I want to get back into school. I realize I was obsessed with Kim, and it's over. I've stopped hanging out with Kim entirely. I've bought a jet ski, and I want you to come up for Splash." Splash was an annual gay celebration of sun and fun on Lake Travis, the same Lake Travis Kim LeBlanc's high school was named for. "I want us to play on the jet ski. I can't wait for you to come up."

Hartwell was different than she'd recently been with Carson. Gone were the anger, the insults, the cutting remarks. Present was Regina's wonderful heart. They talked and talked.

"Marion's coming home soon from Europe," said Pam.

"She's going to break your heart," said Regina.

"No, no, no, she's not."

"Pam, I tell you. Marion's going to break your heart. I know, and I don't want to see her do that. I don't want to see you hurt like that. But she's going to break up with you when she gets back from Europe."

"No, no, no," insisted Carson.

"Pam, I just want you to know I love you so much. You're just so special to me. I'm really sorry that for the last year we've argued."

An hour and a half later, they closed. "I can't wait for you to come up," said Regina. "I love you."

It was almost as if Regina knew something was going to happen to her.

Regina Hartwell traveled back to her old home in Pasadena, the little, pink, brick house with the three white columns on the quiet street in the alleged land of rednecks and hicks, the home of recreated fantasies of a perfect mom who loved her daughter more than life itself.

She stopped by to visit her neighbors, the Seymoures. "If I had found the right guy who really loved me," Regina said to Mrs. Seymoure, "I'd probably switch over."

Mrs. Seymoure didn't know if what Regina said was true or if the sweet, lonely, abandoned child was just telling her that to make the kind, Christian woman happy. After all, Regina had once told her father that she was a born-again Christian attending the University of Texas.

But that last conversation between Regina and Mrs. Seymoure was tender and loving, just as their conversations had always been. And as always, Mrs. Seymoure tried to be a bit of a mother to Regina.

Then Amy happened to stop by, and she and Regina talked

in the driveway, just as they had as little kids. *Regina looks better than she has,* thought Amy. Gone were the white, white makeup and the dark, dark lipstick. Regina's hair wasn't dyed as darkly black, and there was nothing dark or serious or heavy to the conversation. There was absolutely no mention of Kim LeBlanc or Justin Thomas.

"I love you. Take care of yourself," said Amy to Regina.

They were the last words she ever spoke to her friend.

Regina Hartwell became nearly impossible to reach. She cut off her friends, even her cocaine-using friends. She barely returned phone calls. The only person she saw each day was her drug dealer Diva. Her life became Kim, Justin, and crystal meth. Her philosophy became, "If you can't beat them, join them."

Hartwell was beginning to get what she thought she wanted: Kim and a lifetime connection to Kim. Regina just didn't comprehend the cost.

"Dad, the girls want to go swimming," said Justin to Jim Thomas. "Can I have them out?"

Jim Thomas looked hard at his son. He wanted his boy away from those girls. They were no good and up to no good. But at the same time, he liked Regina. They got along well, like peas and cornbread. Regina had Valium, and Jim liked Valium. Jim shook his sad eyes. "Just for a little while, a couple of hours maybe."

Soon, Kim LeBlanc and Regina Hartwell roared up to Jim Thomas's quiet retreat. They ran into the bathroom, changed into their swimsuits, and came out wrapped in Bonnie's best bath towels, recently purchased.

"Uh-uh, no, ma'am," said Bonnie to the girls.

"Huh?" they replied. Kim and Regina were used to having

what they wanted one way or the other. And they liked good things.

"You're not taking my good towels swimming." Bonnie took away the towels, went into the bathroom, got Kim and Regina a couple of different towels, and the girls went down to the river to swim and have a good time.

Regina left her $150 Doc Martens boots behind. They sat lined up for most of June, outside, under the carport, next to the door of Jim Thomas's dream home.

She later told Anita Morales that the Thomas family had charged her, cornered her and frightened her, wanting drugs.

"1 don't have any on me," she said.

"You're lying," they told her.

"No, I'm not. I don't."

Kim LeBlanc spent more and more time with the Thomas family. "Can I help?" she said.

Bonnie stood outside, hanging clothes on the line. "Sure, Miss Kim."

"What do I do?"

Bonnie looked at Kim. "You don't know how to hang clothes on the line?"

LeBlanc shook her head no, flicked her cigarette to the ground, and looked down.

Bonnie glanced at Kim's shiny, new Jeep parked next to her own Dodge Ram. Staring at the fancy Jeep, Bonnie thought Kim seemed to have it all. Looking back at Kim, Bonnie realized little Miss Kimmie was a young girl in a jungle, who had been cut loose and who didn't know what to do. Bonnie felt a bit sad for her nephew's girlfriend. *If Kim were just taken under the right apron strings, she might have a little horse sense,* thought Bonnie. She quickly showed LeBlanc how to hang the clothes on the line.

Kim LeBlanc began to open up to Bonnie. She told Bonnie about being molested. Bonnie was a good listener.

Just weeks earlier, Mike White had introduced Regina Hartwell to David Franks. Now it was David's birthday, and they gathered beneath the neon lights at Manuel's for the celebration on June 10. Regina made sure she was seated next to Mike. "I've rented a boat for David," she said brightly. David, she knew, wanted a boat for Splash. "Things aren't going well with Kim. She's dating a guy."

White thought about the Jeep Hartwell had bought to match LeBlanc's. He knew she was obsessive about her girlfriends, but now Regina seemed to be taking it to a whole new level. It seemed too weird to him. He felt that Kim was using Regina. *But who hasn't?* he thought. *Everyone has at some time or other.*

"I don't know what to do. She's not returning my feelings. I'm not getting what I need from her."

"Regina, just get away from her," said White. "If you're not getting what you need from her, get away from her. Go on a vacation. Do something. Just distance yourself from her. I've got a real bad feeling if she's dating a guy and she's trying to date you. There's something wrong here. I just don't like the situation. You've just got to let it go. There are plenty of girls out there. You'll be fine."

After dinner, they went to Oil Can Harry's.

It was the last time Mike White ever saw Regina Hartwell.

Anita Morales looked over at Kim LeBlanc. It seemed rare to see her with Regina Hartwell since Justin Thomas had arrived. "Why's Kim here?" she asked.

"She's all worried about Justin. He went to Florida . . . to do a hit."

The weekend of June 16, Regina Hartwell returned to Manuel's again, without Kim. That time, it was the birthday of Kelli Grand, Regina's favorite waitress with the big, friendly smile and lots of hugs and kisses for males and females.

Hartwell wore her favorite pearl-colored blouse tied at the midriff so that her pierced belly button showed above her loose jeans. She wore a ruby ring she had once given Tim Gray and now had back. Regina looked happy, even radiant. But she told Kelli, "I'll kill Justin because of what he's doing to Kim with the drugs and guns."

Kim and Regina lay on the bed in Hartwell's apartment, coked up and naked.

"Make sure you don't touch me," said Regina.

Neither one of them wanted LeBlanc to get AIDS.

On Friday, June 23, 1995, Anita Morales and Carla Reid decided to have a barbecue. "Wanta come?" they said to Hartwell over the phone.

Later in the day, Anita and Carla changed their minds about having the party. They called Regina. "Forget it. We're not going to have a barbecue." To them, it was no big deal, but to Regina, it was a big deal.

"Kim thinks it's because of her, because she was going to go and that y'all don't want her over there. Is that true?"

Cocaine makes a user paranoid.

"No, that's not true. No, we're really not going to have a barbecue."

"Okay, I'll tell Kim that."

A few minutes later, Regina phoned Anita and Carla again. "Can we come over anyway?"

"Sure, you can come over. We're just hanging out, and we're not doing anything."

Morales and Reid believed Hartwell was having to prove to LeBlanc that they truly weren't having anyone over for dinner.

Crystal meth makes a user paranoid, too.

When Kim and Regina arrived at Anita's and Carla's apartment, Kim and Regina looked like Auschwitz hell—mere skin and bones, as if they were both about to die from anorexia and hadn't slept in God-knows when. With black-circled eyes, they were nervous, paranoid, fidgety. So fidgety that they made Carla and Anita fidgety and nervous.

Hartwell wore a baseball cap to hide her usually perfect hair and heavy base of makeup to cover what appeared to be a bruise on her left cheek. But Regina had long since passed the point of always seeming to be hiding something . . . to protect someone.

Hartwell grabbed the phone, and she spent most of the time they stayed there on the phone, presumably trying to make a buy. Suddenly, she said, "I've gotta go take care of some business."

Anita Morales never saw Regina Hartwell again.

On Sunday night, June 25, 1995, Hope Rockwell and a friend went over to Regina Hartwell' s apartment, the same Hope Rockwell Regina had pursued to her own arrest in 1992. Hope and her friend had just gotten out of drug rehab and needed a few party tools to celebrate—cocaine.

While they were at Regina's, Kim LeBlanc phoned. "We're coming over."

"Not right now," said Regina.

LeBlanc paged Justin Thomas. He was downtown with

some friends, cruising Sixth Street, the straight, teenage
hangout for live music and beer. It soothed Justin's passion
for music—Nine Inch Nails, Pearl Jam, Smashing Pumpkins,
Jane's Addiction.

"Meet me at Regina's," said Kim.

Thirty minutes later, LeBlanc arrived with Thomas. Rockwell and her friend were still there. Kim looked at them, and
they looked at her. Kim looked coked up as hell. She looked
at Regina, furious, and dragged her into the bedroom. "What
the hell are you doing giving away our drugs!"

A few minutes later, LeBlanc stormed out of the bedroom,
turned to Thomas, and said loudly enough for everyone to
hear, "I'm so mad, I could just kill her."

Regina's neighbor Brad Wilson only saw Regina in passing that last week. Jeremy Barnes didn't see her at all, except
for the last night of Regina Hartwell's life.

A few days later, friends phoned Mike White. "Have you
seen Regina?" He just presumed she'd taken his advice and
gone out of town. He presumed she'd gotten away from Kim
LeBlanc.

CHAPTER 16

Wednesday, June 28, 1995 in Austin, Texas was hot, muggy, cloudy, and humid. In fact, it was downright steamy with thunderstorms threatening. Around noon, there was a change—a sudden drop in humidity. It didn't last until the summer sunset. This was Texas, and the phone was ringing in Kim LeBlanc's South Austin apartment.

Kim was high, she wasn't dressed, and Regina Hartwell was calling. "Meet me at my place," said Regina, from her drug dealer Diva's house. "We need to talk."

God, thought Kim, *Regina was always wanting to talk.* But Kim LeBlanc was tired of the long discussions, of rehashing the same ole same ole, of trying to convince Regina that Kim just plain wasn't interested . . . in women. Not at all.

But how could Regina Hartwell understand how Kim LeBlanc felt about men when Regina and Kim had hugged and kissed, when Kim had taken Regina's money, drugs, clothes, and jewelry, when Regina had given Kim all the material things that Justin Thomas never could—even an apartment?

LeBlanc sighed under her breath and glanced over at the futon. Justin Thomas was lying there watching TV. Kim thought he was so beautiful, that long, hard body.

Justin flipped channel after channel, talk show after talk show.

"Can Jay come?" asked Kim. She rubbed his belly with the soft palm of her hand.

"Fuck, no," said Regina. "He can't wait in the car either." Regina slammed down the phone so that Kim couldn't argue.

Justin Thomas's firm pecs rose and fell as if he were trying to contain jealousy, maybe rage. He detested the way Kim spent her days with Regina and only her nights with him.

Kim hated it too, but there would be drugs—fresh drugs. "Shit," she finally said.

Thomas held her arm. "Tell the cunt . . ."

LeBlanc snorted a line of cocaine and tossed on a pair of shorts and a T-shirt.

"We'll get the money, and we'll go to Mexico, you know what I'm saying? Just tell the fuckin' cunt . . ."

A man she wanted, a woman she needed, Kim's frustration heated. "You know, I have to go." She grabbed her car keys and walked out the door, 6'4" Justin following behind 5' Kim.

"Tell the cunt . . ."

He climbed into the passenger's seat of her Jeep Sahara. She climbed behind the wheel. LeBlanc threw her bright, shiny, green Jeep into gear, whizzed past the partially painted cars that lined her parking lot, and pulled onto the street.

It was getting hotter and more humid, and the sun kept moving in and out of the clouds.

"You know what I'm saying? Just tell the—"

"Fuck," said Kim. "Just goddamned fuck. I'm getting so damned sick and tired of this, you know. All I do is what Regina wants." She lit a Marlboro. "Do this. Do that. Go here. Go there. You know, dance. Don't dance."

And she was doing it again—dancing to Regina Hartwell's beck and call. Turn to the right. Turn to the left. Grab your partner and do-si-do.

"I don't even have my own life. God." She inhaled deeply

on her cigarette, "I might as well be back with my parents." She cursed to Thomas.

He smiled to himself.

Still, Kim LeBlanc knew the benefits of keeping quiet. She'd kept quiet for five years—anything to get along. Her hands shook on the steering wheel. She took another puff of her cigarette. She squeezed her toes so that the accelerator grazed the floorboard.

Her Jeep raced past the only two nice apartment buildings in the neighborhood, past the Ramada Inn, across Ben White Boulevard, and past the Assembly of God Church. Keep quiet, she told herself, anything for peace. She swerved down tree-lined Gillis Street, past home after home that had once been a dream but now was broken and bruised.

Keep quiet. Useless furniture was discarded on the porches. *Anything to get along.* Rusted equipment was abandoned in the yards. *Keep quiet.* It'd been her unspoken mantra for so many years. *Anything for peace.* She didn't know what else to do. Kim LeBlanc pulled into the drive of Josh Mollet's house. Josh was Justin's cousin. Thomas got out. "Tell the . . ."

Anything for peace. Kim drove the five minutes down Lamar Boulevard to Regina Hartwell's apartment. *Keep quiet.* By then, it was perhaps noon, maybe even one o'clock. Time was hazy in the hyperkinetic fog of cocaine and Valium. *Keep quiet.* Kim LeBlanc felt so trapped. Like a fly caught in honey. *Anything.*

LeBlanc found herself standing again in Hartwell's one-bedroom Château apartment, posters and cutouts of Marilyn Monroe watching over them, a photograph of herself entwined with Regina nearby. Kim's fragile hands trembled. Too much coke. Too much crystal meth.

Hartwell jammed her hands deep into her pockets and yelled, as she often did. LeBlanc bowed her head like a shamed child, as she often did. They were like two battling, injured fawns—too young to know their limitations, too scared and too thin—each had dropped thirty pounds from the drugs.

Regina's voice was firm. Too much hurt, too much loss, too many years to let anyone see the fear. "I want you to stop seeing that sonofabitch," she yelled. "He's no good. He's a drug dealer, a gun runner. You can do better than that."

Hartwell's meticulously applied red lipstick made a perfect bow across her soft, white face. Her freshly cut, dyed-black hair bounced when she spoke. She could look like a joy when she wasn't being so controlling.

LeBlanc lit a Marlboro. Her dark brown eyes and cropped brown hair did make her look like a fawn, a fawn that'd been struck by a killer truck.

"I don't know what you see in him. He's dumb, Kim. Just plain stupid." Regina flopped into the black, leather recliner that Justin had bought for her just a few weeks before, a gift between supposed friends.

Kim thought about Justin. He had such beautiful hands. Strong hands. Such beautiful, frightening hands. She closed her eyes and imagined a line of coke. Regina often kept a mirror and a few lines hidden under the faux-leather couch on which Kim sat. Those lines were just a few fingertips away.

"He's a big lulking, shithead retard." Hartwell made a face to mimic Thomas. "Duh." She slapped a limp hand against her breasts. "Couldn't even pull off a drug deal." She kept pounding her full breasts. "Has to make me put up the front money for him. And still can't make a living. I pay for him. I pay for you. Everything you own, everything you wear, I fucking bought for you!"

LeBlanc inhaled for courage. She inhaled as deeply as her cocaine-clogged nostrils would allow. They wouldn't allow deep enough.

"He's a—"

The phone rang.

Regina answered it and then socked the cordless over to Kim. "It's for you. Jay."

"What's taking so long?" said Thomas.

Regina Hartwell paced around the apartment and tapped her foot to show LeBlanc that she thought Kim was taking too long.

Kim glanced at Regina. Regina glared. Kim bowed her head. "Soon," she said and hung up. The bones in her forearms felt like shaking rocks. Her jaw ached from the stone tightness. She reached for another cigarette.

Hartwell yelled. "Tell the bastard not to ever phone here again. Tell the sonofabitch you're never going to see him again. Tell the—"

In her mind, Kim heard Justin yelling too. "Tell the cunt . . ."

"Tell the—" yelled Regina.

"I'm going back home," said Kim. She lit another cigarette. The flame on the lighter quivered as she did. "To my parents," she clarified so that Regina would understand she didn't mean to the apartment that Regina paid for. "I don't want your money anymore."

Regina's heart pounded. She jammed her hands deeper into her pockets. No one could see her fear. She felt like her heart was going to explode out of her chest. "You can't do that."

"I don't want Jay, either. If I go home, as soon as I go home, my parents will see that I need help—"

"I can help you," Hartwell panicked.

"—that I'm messed up." LeBlanc wanted a line, one more line of coke. "My life didn't start out this way—"

"No!" Regina yelled. "No. You can't go back there!" Her voice rose and filtered through the walls. But no one was next-door to hear.

Kim just bowed her head. It was easier that way. Just split apart and not feel. She'd done it for years. Just stuff another drug in and not feel. She was good at it. She placed the cigarette to her lips. Not feel, and she could do what anyone told her. Not feel, and she could listen to anyone for hours.

She did.

Regina argued, begged, pleaded with Kim for almost two hours, and Kim just listened.

By 3 p.m., the temperature had risen to ninety-two degrees and the pavement was hot. Kim and Regina sat on the concrete balcony near Regina's apartment door. Their legs dangled through the second-story protective railing, and their faces peered from behind the iron bars.

Kim and Regina simply spoke softly and smoked and stared down at the courtyard below. Regina's hurt wouldn't leave. She didn't know what to do. Her money could no longer buy Kim's love. It scared her. Left again by a woman she adored, it scared her shitless.

Ryan Watson was on his way to work when he walked out of his apartment and passed by LeBlanc and Hartwell. "Hi," he said.

"Hi," they returned.

He noticed the drinks in their hands, their faces flushed red, the tears they'd cried.

Watson hurried away.

Hartwell watched the green grass below, and she sipped on her toddy. She thought about what she could do.

Kim LeBlanc knew what she was going to do. She was going home to her parents. She had every intention of doing that. Kim pulled on her cigarette. She had as much die-hard, split-second intention as any cokehead.

An hour and a half later, LeBlanc walked with Hartwell from the Château parking lot into the apartment building. At the same time, Kyle Blake walked down the back stairs of the Château, headed for his car, and he heard Regina's voice. It was raised.

Blake knew that voice well. Many times he and Hartwell had called to each other as he had stood below her window and twirled his baton. Now he practiced in his mind as he walked and looked up to see Regina and Kim. LeBlanc's head was bowed. Hartwell scolded her, something about her Jeep.

Kim was embarrassed, like a child being chided by a parent in front of her friends. Blake ducked to the right so as not to embarrass her any further.

Yelling at Kim, that was the last time Kyle Blake ever saw Regina Hartwell.

Finally, Kim got up and said, "I'm going home." Her voice was soft. Her heart wasn't.

Regina felt the hardness, and it terrified her. It terrified her that she might never see Kim again.

"I'm leaving Justin, too." But that wasn't enough for Regina. Nothing seemed to be enough.

"What the fuck took you so long?" Kim claims Justin Thomas bitched as he climbed into Kim's Jeep later. The oak leaves were green over their heads. "Y'all were doing coke, weren't you?"

"No," she said, her head down.

They wound back down Gillis Street, crossed Ben White Boulevard again, and turned right at the Ramada Inn.

"I don't believe you."

She pulled her Jeep up as close to her apartment door as she could.

"You better not be lying to me. 'Cause if you're lying to me, I'll—"

"She's driving me up the wall, Jay. She won't let me breathe. She won't let me sleep. She won't let me do anything. She's got to know when I pee. She's got to know when I fuck."

Thomas's jealous breath grew fast.

"She's got to know everything I'm doing every minute of the day. She's got to be with me every minute of the day."

His fists tightened. He wanted to be with Kim every minute of the day.

"Regina threatened to cut me off if I don't stop messing with you."

"Look, quit fucking with her," he ordered.

LeBlanc still remembers her response.

"Help me, Jay. Help me get out of this situation." Kim climbed out of her Jeep and flicked a cigarette onto the ground. She inched up to Justin's hazel eyes. "Get her out of my life."

Thomas fell onto the futon and flicked on the TV. LeBlanc curled up close to him and lay her head on his shoulder. "Please, Jay." She kissed him.

"Let's just get the fuckin' money and we'll leave, you know what I'm saying? We'll blow this Popsicle stand," said Justin. "We'll go someplace else. We'll go to Mexico for a year or so. We don't need to stay here—"

The phone interrupted.

"We'll get the fuckin' hell out of Dodge, you know what I'm saying?" To the moon and back for his girl.

His girl answered the phone.

"What ya doin'?" Regina Hartwell said.

"Just watching TV."

Thomas angrily rolled over and flipped channels.

Kim kept talking to Regina. Thomas started talking to the air. Hartwell chatted, and Thomas talked louder. Hartwell kept speaking, and Thomas spoke more. Kim covered the phone hoping his voice wouldn't be heard.

"I'm a gangsta," yelled Justin to make sure Regina heard. "I'm a gangsta of—"

"That Jay?" Regina yelled.

"Yeah," Kim moaned.

"You fucking told me—what's he saying?"

"He's just joking around. He's talking about being a gangster or something."

"Put the sonofabitch on the phone."

Thomas grabbed the phone. "Look, would you fuckin' quit calling over here and arguing? Quit your goddamned yelling. Quit your goddamned screaming, you know what I'm saying? It's fuckin' pointless for y'all to fight and argue if y'all can't talk right. There just ain't no fuckin' sense in y'all communicating."

"I can have you fucked off," said Hartwell.

Thomas laughed. LeBlanc was terrified. She was listening on an extension. But Justin had dealt with real threats before, drug-family threats. Regina Hartwell was just talking out the side of her mouth. And he knew that. Still, Regina's silly little threats irritated the hell out of him. "Just fuckin' leave it alone." he shouted. "Just fuckin' leave it alone."

"If you hurt Kim," Hartwell screamed, "I'll have you—"

"Don't call if you're going to argue and threaten me." And Justin hung up.

Kim stayed on the line.

"I can have the sonofabitch thrown in prison," Regina yelled to her.

The screaming voices raced through Kim LeBlanc's head like a child lost at a traveling circus, carnival barkers bellowing in every ear. She felt caught, and she felt like screaming, too.

"I can have the bastard killed. You know I can do it. He knows I can do it."

Caught. Trapped. Kim hung up, only to hear Justin yelling at her, too.

"I ain't letting nobody send me to prison. Especially not

some coke-snorting lesbian bitch. Ain't nobody sending me to prison!"

"She's just blowing hot air, Jay. You know, Regina. She's always making stuff up, especially when she's all jealous and protective."

"I don't care. Ain't nobody sending me to prison. And I'm gonna make damn sure of that, with or without you. I'm gonna kill the fuckin' cunt. Are you in this with me? 'Cause I can do it with or without you."

Kim just wanted one more eight ball of coke. Just one more line. Just one more jump at freedom.

"Can you handle this?"

His words knocked Kim back into a moment of consciousness. She nervously glanced around her home. She sped through the options of living without Regina, of living without an apartment, without money.

In spite of herself, in spite of all the drugs she had snorted up her nose to clog up her mind, memory, and feelings, Kim heard her stepfather's voice. *You're only good for one thing, you use that one thing, and it gives you power, and you'd better use that power of yours, because you can't take care of yourself. You can't take care of yourself. You can't take care of yourself. You—*

"I can take care of you," said Thomas. "I can set you up, just like Regina."

"Yeah, I can handle it," Kim said. Yeah, Regina could be a bitch, controlling, obsessive, possessive, but she'd never killed anybody. Had them thrown into jail, yeah. Threatened to beat them up, yeah. Threatened to have them killed, yeah. But ever actually killed anybody, no way. But Justin . . .

He tossed her her car keys.

Kim felt even shakier than usual.

"We're going to Del Valle."

"Why?" She picked up her Marlboros and walked out the door.

"I've gotta get some stuff from the house," he said.

Kim didn't like Del Valle. She didn't like being with Justin's family, out in the country, away from Austin.

Regina Hartwell frantically dialed Anita Morales's number. She was crying, hysterical, and furious. It was around 8 p.m.

"Hello?"

Damn, thought Regina. She wanted Anita, not Carla. "Anita there?"

Morales was standing outside as Carla Reid handed her the phone. She looked up at the sky. It was cloudy, the sun hadn't yet gone down, and it looked like rain any minute.

"What you doing?" said Regina.

"Nothing."

"Get away from Carla. I don't want her to hear." Regina waited. "Are you alone?"

"Yeah. What is it?"

"You better not tell anyone this, but I need somebody I can talk to. Who do you know in narcotics?"

"I know lots of people. Why?"

"I want to bust that fucking bastard, Justin. I'm sick and tired of him. And this time, he's crossed the line. He's demanding that Kim spend more time with him, and she's already spending way too much time with the motherfucking sonofabitch."

Morales had never heard Regina so angry. She sounded as though, if she had a gun and Thomas were standing right in front of her, on the spot, she'd blow him away. "You'll have to talk to the investigators yourself," said Anita.

"There's an ounce to an ounce and a half of crystal meth coming in from Moreno, California. It's supposed to arrive via UPS tomorrow at Justin's house in Del Valle or my house. I'm not sure which."

Morales walked inside her apartment and started jotting notes to herself.

"But at this point, I don't think the bastard would dare send it to my house. I gotta talk to you about this in person. There are things you don't know, and I don't want to tell you over the phone." Hartwell cried.

Anita Morales looked at her watch. She really needed to get off the phone, but she couldn't let her friend down. "Who does Justin answer to?"

"A man named Rashon. Justin used to run with an East L.A. gang, and he's killed before."

"Do you want to come over here?"

"No, I'm too fucking mad to drive."

"Do you want me to come over there?"

"No, I'll be okay. Look, I'll page you at work tomorrow. Now promise me you won't say anything until I see you tomorrow."

"I promise you."

"No, say, 'I promise, Regina.'"

"I promise, Regina."

"I love you."

"I love you, too."

Justin Thomas walked up the stairs to his father's bedroom and grabbed his old Army duffel bag. In the heat of the Texas June, he crammed it full with a black trench coat. Excited, he tossed in some face paint, too.

Kim thought he was playing GI Joe, but she didn't think much beyond that. She couldn't think on much of anything, not for very long. Cocaine. Crystal meth. Nicotine. And when she did think, she simply wondered where her next high would come from.

Around 9 p.m., darkness finally settled in, and Brad Wilson walked up to his Château apartment across from Regina

Hartwell's. He noticed that her door was open. "Hi, Regina," he shouted.

"Hey," she answered back and came out. "I'm sorry for all the noise we made this morning."

He stuck his key into his door, then turned around to glance at Regina. "What are you talking about?"

"The noise, this morning," she repeated.

"Oh, I wasn't home. I didn't hear anything."

"Kim and I got into a huge fight. Then they left."

"Who's they?"

"Kim and her boyfriend."

Wilson didn't know Regina well. He'd only lived at the Château for about a month, but he thought Kim LeBlanc and Regina Hartwell were lovers. He was a bit confused by the reference to a boyfriend. He opened his door.

"What are you doing?" she asked.

"Packing. We're going to New Orleans tomorrow." He stepped inside.

"Like to have a drink?"

"Sure."

"What do you like to drink?"

Wilson really looked at Hartwell now. Her hazel eyes, painted pretty with perfect shadow and liner, seemed sad. He knew she'd been crying earlier. Ryan Watson, his roommate, had told him that. "I like wine," he said.

"Good." Regina smiled that big grin of hers. "I'll go to the store and get a bottle." She was so sweet and outgoing. "Then we can just sit and talk."

Kim LeBlanc and Justin Thomas left Del Valle and drove the twenty miles back to Austin and Kim's apartment. "One person can't stab and dispose of a body by himself," he told Kim. "You know what I'm saying, you need more than one person." Thomas got on the phone and dialed some of his friends, his "posse," he called them.

Under the late-night cover of charcoal sky and rain, LeBlanc drove through the heavy construction on Highway 71 and dropped Thomas off at Jim's restaurant, a coffee shop in rustic Oak Hill.

It was almost like going home, like she'd told Regina. Kim could look across the highway and see World Gym. It was also getting closer to her Dripping Springs house with her mother and stepfather. And it was getting closer to her old high school of Lake Travis.

In fact, at Jim's, Kim recognized two of Justin's posse— Bryan Frnka and Michael Mihills. She'd gone to high school with them both. She wondered how Justin knew them, but she didn't ask questions.

Thomas was somewhat nervous. "Regina's threatened to turn me in to the cops because she thinks I'm a drug dealer."

They all chuckled.

Regina Hartwell plopped herself down on Brad Wilson's living room couch with a bottle of red wine for him and a big, plastic cup full of ice and some kind of liquid for herself. He realized that she'd gone to get the wine just for him. His cats crawled near her. He opened the wine.

"Kim's boyfriend is named Justin," said Regina.

She and Brad had never just sat and talked over drinks before.

"He lives in Del Valle, home of Mexicans and white trash." Hartwell made a face. "He treats her like shit, white-trash shit. He's a drug dealer. Sonofabitch. Asshole. Jerk."

Her voice was controlled, but so much openness and so much emotion took Wilson aback. He watched her as she sipped from her big, plastic cup. This wasn't her first drink of the evening, that was obvious. She was too outgoing, too upset.

"I'm going to cut them out of my life. I'm going to get a job and get my life straightened out. I hate that fucking asshole, Justin. I hate him. He's fucking up Kim's life. I know enough about him to have him thrown in prison."

Wilson didn't believe Hartwell. To him, Regina didn't seem the type to have someone thrown in prison. But she didn't seem the type to party all night either, and he'd heard that she did that. He thought about the Marilyn Monroe posters in her apartment.

"I've made the decision. I'm going to stop seeing Kim." Tears welled in Regina's eyes. "I really love her."

To Brad, Regina seemed so very much like Marilyn Monroe—like a down-home girl who wanted to be in love and have a stable life, but who was charmed by the celebrity life. Brad sipped on his wine.

"I really care about her."

Hartwell didn't seem cut out for a fast-paced life. But she would have loved to have known that Brad compared her to Marilyn Monroe.

"I hate seeing Justin manipulate Kim," she said. "The way he influences her."

Too nice, just too nice, Wilson thought, *like the type who could get caught up in, and swayed by, almost anything.*

"But I'm tired of the off-and-on thing—the way Kim leaves me for him and then comes back and spends the night with me."

Brad suddenly wondered if Kim had feelings for Regina, but that she just didn't want to make a commitment. He didn't say anything, though.

Regina took another drink. "I'm ready to give up hoping that Kim will come back to me. That's so fucking hard. I love her so much. But the hoping, the waiting, the trying to convince her, it's just tearing me up. I'm going to try to just cut them out of my life. That's what I want to do."

"Well, yeah," said Wilson. "That sounds like a good idea, since this is tearing you up. I think that's a really good idea."

Hartwell heard her phone ring, and her heart leapt. She jumped up to go answer it. She prayed to God that it was Kim calling.

Minutes later she came back. She took another swallow of liquid. "You know my mother was killed by a hangar door." Her eyes watered over again. "I'm still really, really upset about that. I was so close to her. A lot closer to her than to my father."

"Yeah," said Brad, "I know what it's like not to have a mother. Mine died a few years ago, too."

"Yeah?" said Regina, and she smiled weakly. "I never really had the father I wanted. He's not supportive of me and my lifestyle. He doesn't agree with my sexuality. He's gotten mad at me a bunch of times about that. We hardly ever speak. We're not very close. I feel so alone in the world." She took another gulp from her plastic cup. "I really love Kim. I mean really, really love Kim."

Wilson watched Regina Hartwell. He noticed a few tiny bruises on the right side of her face. He noticed some bruises on the right side of her thigh, too. He pointed to them. "What happened?"

She shrugged and stood up, stuffed her hands into her pockets, and wandered around the room. "Somebody threw an ashtray at me."

"This morning?"

"Uh-huh." She didn't look him in the face. "I have fainting spells sometimes, too. I find myself waking up on the floor."

"You should see a doctor."

"I don't have any insurance." Hartwell sat back down and slurped more on her drink. Her phone rang again, and, again, she prayed it would be Kim as she ran out the door to her apartment.

Brad pondered the situation. He'd heard Regina had money, loads of it, dump-truck loads of it, inherited just recently, but she hadn't mentioned any money to him. She just seemed antsy, like she'd been doing . . . something.

She walked back in and paced around the room. She picked up her cup and sucked the last drip out of it. Regina looked so very down, so rejected. Then she brightened. "Need someone to take care of your cats while you're gone? I can do it."

"Yeah."

"Good. Drop off your key tomorrow." And she was gone. It was about 11 p.m.

When Kim LeBlanc picked Justin Thomas up after the meeting with his posse, he was pissed. "The chicken-shit bastards didn't have the guts to go through with it," he griped. "They thought I was fuckin' crazy, and blew me off. Can you believe that? Me, fuckin' crazy? They're the fuckin' crazy ones."

Thomas still griped and planned as they walked back into her apartment. He griped as he fell onto Kim's bed. He griped about his friends. He griped about Regina. He planned Regina's death.

Kim poured herself a few tablets of Valium and swallowed them down. "Go to sleep," she said. "It's just the cocaine." She climbed into bed. "Regina's just blowin' hot air. Go to sleep. It's just the cocaine. Go to sleep. In the morning, it's going to be different." She drifted off into a Valium-induced dreamland.

Regina Hartwell sat with Jeremy Barnes. They were in his bedroom, on the floor, music playing, lights low. It was their ritual. They had watched TV for a bit, and then they talked.

"Kim and I had a big fight," said Regina. "She and I had sex, and then she went home and had sex with Justin." She only looked at the floor. "I'm tired of Justin, and I want to get him out of the way. I want to turn the sonofabitch in to the cops. I'm going to talk to Anita about it. I've already talked to her some, but we're going to talk about it more tomorrow."

She took a drag from her cigarette. "I want to change my life. I want to go back to school."

"Oh, Reg," smiled Jeremy, "remember when you were in school? You were so happy then."

"I want to get off of drugs. I want to get right with my family. My dad. My stepmom. I need to totally change my life."

Barnes talked about his life, too—changes he wanted to make, his dysfunctional family. Hartwell talked about her own dysfunctional family. He knew he came from one; she felt that maybe she came from one, too.

Their emotions roller-coastered. They laughed, and they cried.

"I would die for her," said Regina. "I would die for Kim. I really would."

"I don't like her, Reg. She's just a user. But I respect your feelings for her. I know what it's like to love somebody everybody hates. I won't do that to you."

They held hands and talked to God. "Jesus, give us the wisdom and the knowledge to know what to do and the strength to be able to follow through with it," Jeremy prayed for Regina.

"Help me to be with my parents and that everything will work out and that I won't have to lose Kim, that we can be friends later on," Regina prayed.

Barnes had seen his dear Reg happy in the past; he had seen her down in the present. He believed she was about to turn herself and her life around. He cried for joy.

Their prayer together was an answer to his prayers. Barnes knew that, in Hartwell's mind, her hope of being a couple with LeBlanc would never end. Hartwell was too obsessed. But if they could just get Justin Thomas out of Regina's life, that would be great. It would be a start. It would help.

Regina Hartwell laughed some more, she wept again, and two hours after sitting down with Jeremy, she went back to her apartment.

* * *

Jeremy Barnes tried to sleep, but he couldn't. He tossed, and he turned. He wondered if he should phone his parents to see if they could help get Regina some help. He wondered if Regina's words and prayer were sincere or if she'd been bull-shitting him, again.

The front of his mind was sure. Regina's words were sincere.

Barnes tossed and turned more. He thought about his belief that life on Earth is a pathway, that you have to be careful to walk on that pathway or if you don't, you fall into the cactus and get thorns in your butt. Kim and Justin, he knew, were thorns in Regina's butt, and she was trying to pull the thorns out and get back on the pathway—that's what Jeremy believed.

Regina's heart was so true to him that night that Jeremy knew she was really and truly sick and tired of it all. She was sick of people using her. She was sick of all of her money being dwindled. She was scared that she wasn't going to have enough money to do the things that she wanted to do.

Jeremy prayed some more.

But the next morning, it wasn't like Kim LeBlanc had said. It wasn't much different. It was still raining off and on. It was still humid. It was still hot. Justin Thomas was still hot. And Regina Hartwell was still lonely. She dreamed of how it felt to have her hands around Kim's waist. Of the touch of Kim's skin against her own.

Kim rolled over to see Justin get out of bed, quickly. She watched through slowly blinking eyes as he threw on a purple T-shirt and blue, denim pants. Then she rolled back over and fell back asleep. She had had way too much Valium.

CHAPTER 17

It's hard always loving someone you can't have. Your mother. Your father. Your lover.

Justin Thomas shut the door to Kim LeBlanc's apartment and walked over to his cousin Josh Mollet's house.

Intermittent thunderstorms steadied the temperature near eighty degrees. Ninety percent humidity, however, provoked an easy, morning sweat. Inside, Justin Thomas was a firestorm. Antsy, unable to sleep, full of rage fueled by drugs and revenge, he walked quickly.

Thomas was on a mission. His adrenaline was ready. He and Kim had talked about it. He'd planned it through the rainy night before, toyed with it through his crystal meth mind. Another noontime drizzle and drop in humidity did nothing to cool him. He was ready to carry it out, a good soldier.

Kim LeBlanc woke and went into her usual routine—get up, snort cocaine, lose conception of time, history, reality.

It was Thursday, June 29, 1995.

* * *

Regina Hartwell rolled over on the faux-leather couch she'd bought with Jeremy Barnes and stared at her coffee table. She was crazy about that coffee table. She knew it was ugly. Jeremy had told her that enough times, almost every time they'd played cards at that table, but she still loved it.

She and Trey Lyons had decorated it together. They'd covered it in tacky black-and-white shelf paper. It'd been fun. They'd laughed a lot that night, drunk a few beers, smoked a few cigarettes. She'd done her infamous French inhale. They'd done a little coke.

Coke. She reached under her couch to see what was left of her stash. Not enough. She stared at her posters of Marilyn Monroe. Marilyn would understand. She knew what it was like to be alone. Regina looked at her photographs of Kim. She and Kim had had a good time together at that coffee table too—doing a few lines together.

There was just something bonding about getting out the razor blade, the mirror, tapping the amber-colored vial against the glass. They'd always grin at each as the pearlescent white crystals poured out. Then getting the razor blade and chopping the crystals into fine powder, listening to the scrape of the razor blade over the mirror, God, there was something wonderfully bonding about that. It was as good as being in love.

It made Regina Hartwell feel strong and not so alone in the world. She patted the couch for Spirit to jump into her arms. She held him tight. She wanted right then to get up and go look at the photographs of her mother and her father on their wedding day, holding each other tight. That, too, made her feel not so alone.

But the rich, white, blood-money, trailer-trash girl from Pasadena, who knew how to paint a perfect red bow across her lips and make them smile, just didn't have the energy. Pulling on her Garfield boxer shorts was about all the energy she could muster that morning after.

She reached for her cordless phone and knocked over a few empty beer bottles as she did. A last sip of beer dribbled into the green, marble ashtray. She thought about wiping it up with her purple T-shirt. But, nah, it didn't matter. Jeremy would clean it up for her. Marlboro butts swam, then sank in the yellow liquid.

Ebenezer walked by and sniffed at the old beer. He rubbed his bare-haired tail against Regina's white leg. She scratched at the tattoo on her ankle. In the past, the tattoo had been a broken, pink triangle. But she didn't like that, so she'd gotten another design cut on top of it. Now, the tattoo just looked smudged.

She scratched again and dialed Anita Morales's pager number. She pressed in her number but didn't sign the page with 911, as she always did. It was something that would haunt Anita.

Regina Hartwell drifted back to sleep, in and out of consciousness. The leftover pain from drugs was much easier than the leftover pain from love. Your mother. Your father. Your lover. She didn't know how she'd live without Kim. But Regina would take care of it. She'd get Kim back . . . some way. Regina was strong, she told herself. She was in control, she told herself. She could be tough, she told herself. She could do it, she convinced herself. She could do anything by herself. She'd show 'em.

She opened her hazel eyes. They widened in fear. She'd show 'em. She was tough. She could do anything. "What up, Jay?" she said calmly.

The knife blade flashed. She glanced at the photo of Kim. God, it hurt when someone betrayed you. Justin Heith Thomas stabbed Regina Stephanie Hartwell deep, until the blood gurgled through her lungs and filled them to overflowing.

It took Regina Hartwell less than twenty seconds for every year of her life to die.

It took Justin Thomas less than thirty minutes to kill her in her purple T-shirt and Garfield shorts with "Eat Your Heart

Out" stamped on the material, carry her body to the bathroom leaving a thin trail of blood in the hallway, dump her body in the bathtub, and turn on the shower. He would never forget her short, dark, wet hair and her open eyes as they stared face-up at him.

He drained her body of blood like a mortician, cleaned himself up, and moved the black recliner he'd given her over the pool of dark, red blood spilled on the pale, gray living room carpet. Thomas tossed her 110 pounds into a maroon comforter and hauled her corpse to her Jeep like a sack of dirty sheets.

Kim LeBlanc was ready for another line of coke, but Thomas was knocking on her door. He wore a bloodied, purple T-shirt and bloodied, blue, denim pants. He stood silent in the doorway, then dropped Hartwell's wallet onto the floor.

"It's done," he said.

Kim fell to the ground and cried. She wanted to ask him if he had an eight ball of coke.

"I stabbed her. The bitch wouldn't die." He pointed toward the parking lot. "I've got her Jeep. She's in it. Get me some salt." Justin strode toward the bathroom.

LeBlanc went into the kitchen, got the salt, and followed her boyfriend into the bathroom. "Why do you want salt?"

"She cut me."

Kim looked down and saw a slash in the webbing of Justin's right hand, between his thumb and forefinger.

"Did the bitch really have AIDS?" he said, and motioned for her to pour the salt onto his bleeding hand.

"I don't know," she answered, and poured the salt on his wound.

"I walked in the front door, and she said, 'What up, Jay?' You know what I'm saying? Stupid bitch. I said, 'Hi, Regina,' and I went and sat down by her couch. And when I looked in her eyes, she knew what was coming, you know what I'm saying? She knew she was gonna die. Then, I stabbed her."

He shook the blood from his hand into the sink. "It took the bitch a lot longer to die than I expected. That little cunt was a lot stronger than I thought. Then I dragged her into the bathroom and picked her up and put her in the tub."

Kim felt herself easing out of her body. Separating. Floating to the ceiling. Hanging there like a helium balloon. This didn't seem real. She wondered if it was. "How did you carry her body down the stairs and get her into the Jeep without anybody seeing?"

"Adrenaline. A lot of adrenaline pumping, you know what I'm saying? And I killed her and wrapped her in the comforter from her own bed. The fucking bitch was a lot heavier than I expected. And the apartment, goddamn, it was bloody. Blood on the walls. Blood on the carpet. Blood on the sink." He didn't notice the blood on Kim's sink. "Get me a garbage bag." He pulled off his clothes and stepped into the shower. "Put my clothes in the bag."

LeBlanc crammed his bloody clothes into the garbage bag. She also tossed in Hartwell's wallet.

Regina's machine answered the phone. "Call me," said Anita Morales, finally responding to Regina's page of almost four hours earlier. Anita had been on a police investigation, and it was now close to 3 p.m.

Close to that same moment, Jeremy Barnes checked his messages and found a call from Hartwell. "I'm throwing a little get-together. Can you clean my house by the end of the weekend?" She sounded very happy. "Everything's going to be all right. I'm going to look for a job and go back to school.

I'm glad we can talk and be together. I'm really glad that I have you as my big brother. I love you."

Thomas climbed into Hartwell's Jeep. LeBlanc climbed into her own matching Jeep. Thomas drove south toward Ben White Boulevard, then onto Highway 71 East. Kim followed. She was close behind as he spotted the small, gray water tower with "Garfield" painted on its tank in big, black, block letters. He was almost home.

At the Rainbow Cafe & Grocery, they turned onto Caldwell Lane, drove a ways, took a right onto Whirlaway Drive, and then a left onto Justin's father's property. Trees were thick and green, their undergrowth, in places, ten feet tall.

Thomas drove beneath the trees, then made a quick U-turn and parked under a metal shed of a carport, a distance from the house, obscured by the gentle rolls of the terrain.

He got out of Hartwell's car and walked around to the passenger door. LeBlanc got out of her car and watched Thomas shove something in the backseat. She watched it flop down to the floor. It was Regina's dead body, wrapped in the maroon comforter from her bed.

Pam Carson phoned Regina Hartwell. What she really wanted to do was run to Regina and be hugged and say, "You were right." Marion Casey had broken up with her, and Pam needed Reg. No one understood like Regina did. In terrible, rotten, lonely times, no one could comfort away the hurt the way Regina did. The phone rang and rang. Only the machine answered.

Kim LeBlanc needed coke.

She searched the side pockets of her Jeep and found one of her hidden stashes, a quarter bag. She did that for herself—hid her drugs. That way, she wouldn't do them all at once and they would be there when she really needed them. She really needed them then. It was 3:30, maybe four o'clock, a pleasant mid-seventies temperature. But the heat was rising, and Kim felt it.

She climbed back into her Jeep and jammed it into gear. She drove the few yards on up to the Thomases' three-story home. There, Kim could sneak a taste of drugs before anyone got home or Justin found out.

The drugs brought out the chatterbox in LeBlanc, and she started asking questions. "How'd you get over to Regina's?" she asked Justin as he climbed the stairs into the living room.

"Josh. And his friend Carlos. They took me."

"What are you going to do with the body?"

"Chop it up. Put it in a garbage can. Fill it full of concrete. Sink it in the river."

Kim sneaked another hit.

Thomas picked up the phone.

"What are you doing?"

"Calling Robbye." He meant Robbye Cellota, their former boss at World Gym.

Drugs. Kim didn't feel like sharing. She went to another room.

"Want to buy a Jeep?" Justin asked Cellota. "Know anyone who wants to buy a Jeep?" Moments later Thomas hung up. "Robbye said he'd check around and call back. We need to buy concrete, a trash can, a lock, and chain. You know what I'm saying?"

"Wal-Mart," said LeBlanc, "they should have concrete." She tried to brush the grains of cocaine from her nose blistered red from too many rails of speed.

A half-hour later, LeBlanc and Thomas sped back onto Highway 71 East and headed to the town of Bastrop and Wal-Mart.

As Anita Morales got off from work, something told her to stop at Hartwell's apartment. Everyday she passed Regina's

apartment as she drove home from work. *You'd better stop.
You'd better stop. You'd better stop,* said the voice inside her.

No, I'll just call her when I get home, Anita decided. She
stared at the Château as she drove by its high, concrete wall.

You'd better stop.

It's a decision Anita Morales would always regret. She
didn't stop.

Kim LeBlanc and Justin Thomas stopped at a convenience
store. Kim got out. Justin stayed in the Jeep. He always did.
Justin Thomas wasn't about to let his face appear on any
video surveillance tape. Kim LeBlanc walked in, used Regina
Hartwell's ATM card to get some cash, then walked back to
her car and handed Thomas the wad of twenties. He wrapped
them around his stash of cash and curled them all tight with
a rubberband. Kim LeBlanc wasn't allowed by Justin Thomas
to ever hold Regina Hartwell's money.

He thought about the thousands of dollars that were hidden
in Kim's Jeep.

But Wal-Mart didn't have concrete.

So LeBlanc circled her green Jeep Sahara around and
headed back west on Highway 71 to Austin and the Builders
Square. It was relatively new, and bright and shiny. It would
have anything and everything.

Thirty to forty-five minutes later, she swung into a parking
space in the Builders Square concrete sea of a parking lot, a
lot that was rarely full and radiated summer heat almost as
well as the sun. But the sun was sinking, just like Thomas
planned to soon sink Hartwell's dead body. Time was growing short. It was almost eight p.m.

Thomas grabbed eighty pounds of concrete. He and LeBlanc
asked an old man with blond hair about chain. They measured

out twelve feet of chain and snipped it off. They reached for three tumbler padlocks and a thirty-pound trash can made in Great Britain. They wheeled their goods toward the rear side of the store and checked out in the nursery. The total came to $37.83. They paid for it with $40 cash—Regina's money that they had just "pulsed" from the dead woman's account.

Moments later, Thomas and LeBlanc were headed back to Garfield and Justin's father's home. His father, aunt, and cousin all should have been home by then, back from working hard, sawing wood, making cabinets.

Thomas placed his new purchases in the garage. LeBlanc went upstairs to do more drugs. Justin counted the cash in her Jeep, then grabbed an axe, took off his shirt, and started whacking old tree stumps. But soon, he got nervous and went inside.

"Got to wait until dark to do it," he told Kim. "Don't want anybody to see me." He seemed shaky. "I think somebody saw me." Cocaine and crystal meth make a user paranoid. "Over there. From that house over there." He grabbed the phone and called Cellota again.

He hung up. "Robbye can't get rid of her car. Says it's too short notice. Fuck," said Thomas. "Just fuck it." He glanced out the window. It was dark. He looked toward the house from which he thought someone had been watching him. He couldn't see through the darkness to make sure no one was there.

"Fuck the garbage can. Fuck the chain. Fuck the concrete. You know what I'm saying? I'll just blow up the whole fuckin' thing. Regina. The Jeep. Everything."

Justin Thomas grabbed a five-gallon gas can from his father's carport and walked down to the shed that hid Hartwell's Jeep. "Follow me," he yelled as he got in. "We're going to the gas station up the road." Then he turned Regina's stereo up really loud and swerved onto the pavement.

Kim got into her Jeep. She followed Thomas back onto

Highway 71. He turned east, towards Bastrop, away from Austin. They passed a Fina station, then a Phillips 66 station. Thomas didn't pull in either. He made a quick left onto County Road 1209. Kim followed. They came to a stop sign where the road split into a T, and Thomas gunned Hartwell's Jeep into the weeds. By then, he was shaking. He couldn't drive anymore.

LeBlanc drove into the weeds, too.

"You stupid . . . What are you doing?" yelled Thomas.

"Following you, like you told me to."

"You weren't supposed to follow me all the way into the weeds." He climbed into Kim's car.

She reversed, went back down the county road to the highway, and pulled into the Phillips 66 station.

"Go in and pay for the gas," Thomas ordered. "I'll fill the car and the gas can."

LeBlanc followed the former infantryman's commands. She paid for the $12 worth of gas with cash from Regina's account, got in her Jeep that Regina had matched with her twenty-fifth birthday purchase just four months earlier, and drove back down County Road 1209.

That time, LeBlanc stopped near the stop sign. She wasn't about to pull off into the weeds and be berated again.

Thomas got out and disappeared behind some trees. Two minutes later, an explosion fired the wet, night sky. The leap of flames singed the brows over Thomas's hazel-green eyes. He ran. "Go. Go," he yelled as he jumped into Kim's Jeep. "Let's get the hell out of here! Let's go! Let's go!"

Kim slammed the car into reverse and raced backwards, halfway to the highway. Finally, she spun the car into drive and nearly wrecked it.

Their hearts beat faster than any cocaine or crystal meth could ever cause. But Justin Thomas, he didn't feel anything, nothing, nada. Except disbelief. *This stuff,* he whispered in his head, *it can't be going on again.*

CHAPTER 18

"There." Justin Thomas pointed to a convenience store.

Kim LeBlanc pulled her muddy Jeep into the parking lot and jumped out. It was still drizzling.

Thomas waited in the car with the music playing loudly.

LeBlanc came running back to the car. She handed the $200 she had gotten from the store's ATM to Thomas.

He took it and wrapped it in a rubberband. He stared at the cut on his hand. It was oozing blood. "Shit," he said. "Let's get someplace fast so we can take care of this." He wiped blood from his hand. "I could use some pot to calm my nerves. You know what I'm saying?"

"I need some coke," said Kim.

Her hands shook hard on the steering wheel. They shook so hard as she raced her Jeep up Interstate 35 North that it felt like her wheels weren't simply out of alignment, but that they had been knocked out of whack in a major wreck. Kim LeBlanc zoned out to try to forget how badly she needed a line, to forget how her body was shimmying and shaking, to forget that she'd just helped burn Regina to a crisp.

She drove past a Motel 6, she crossed Town Lake, passed a

Holiday Inn, the state capitol, the University of Texas, the LBJ Library, Robert Mueller Airport, a Ramada Inn, another Motel 6, a Super 8 Motel. She was oblivious to it all. She was almost out of Austin—Justin Thomas wanted out of Texas—when she swerved to the right and pulled in to the Heritage Inn.

"You go on and check in," Thomas said. Again, he was going to make sure he wasn't on any videotape. "I'll go make the phone calls." He peeled a few twenties off of his rubber-banded roll and handed them to her.

It was 10:39 p.m. when Kim LeBlanc signed her name to the signature card, guest number 26901. She used a fake Kentucky driver's license for identification. The name on the license was Kim Derrick, the name she had used for seventeen years of her life. The photograph on the driver's license was of Kim Derrick with chin-length, blonde hair combed straight back, dark, unplucked eyebrows, and no lipstick.

Her real driver's license featured a photo of Kim LeBlanc with short, brown hair, big, brown eyes, perfectly plucked eyebrows, and bright, red lipstick.

Thomas was in the Jeep when she returned.

"Checked in," she said.

"Everything's cool," he said. "I've got some coke and pot lined up."

She and Thomas went up to their room for a moment, a double that cost $45 a night, then left to pick up the drugs and run by the grocery store. They bought black hair dye and little, bitty rubberbands. Back at the motel, LeBlanc shaved off Thomas's shaggy, wavy, light brown hair so that only a Mohawk was left.

"Lots of people in California want a Mohawk," he said.

She dyed the Mohawk black.

'Wait here in Austin for me," Thomas said. "Pulse out as much money as you can from Regina's account and send it to me."

Regina Hartwell as she looked in high school
in Pasadena, Texas in the late 1980s.

Regina Hartwell, four years after moving to Austin, Texas in 1988.

The radical changes Hartwell made to her hair and makeup can be seen in this 1994 photo.
(Photo courtesy of Ynema Mangum)

Kim Derrick LeBlanc, 16, at the Lake Travis High School 1993 Junior Prom in Texas.

While in high school, LeBlanc was a popular cheerleader and a member of the National Honor Society.

During 1994, Regina Hartwell tried to woo Kim LeBlanc, who had dyed her hair black, with trips. They took a Bahamian cruise in August *(top and bottom left)*, and for New Year's Eve, they flew to New York City, where they rode in limousines and stayed at the Plaza Hotel *(top and bottom right)*.

The Chateau apartment complex in Austin, Texas where Hartwell was murdered. Her apartment window is on the second floor, next to the bicycle. *(Photo courtesy of the Travis County, Texas District Court)*

Regina Hartwell was stabbed to death on the black leather couch in her living room on June 29, 1995. The photos on the coffee table and pedestal are of Kim LeBlanc. Next to the recliner is the bloodstain. *(Photo courtesy of the Travis County, Texas District Court)*

After Regina Hartwell's murder, but before her friends reported her missing, her bathroom was cleaned spotless except for one stubborn rust stain *(lower right hand corner)* that Kim LeBlanc frantically scrubbed, thinking it was blood. *(Photo courtesy of the Travis County, Texas District Court)*

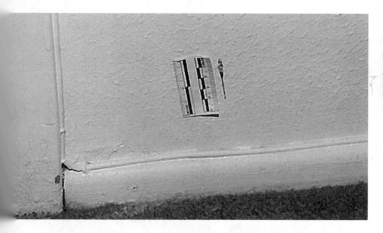

Police investigators found tiny drops of blood on the walls of Regina Hartwell's apartment, just enough blood to provide DNA evidence. *(Photo courtesy of the Travis County, Texas District Court)*

Justin Thomas carried Hartwell's dead body from her living room to her bathtub, where he wrapped her in a maroon comforter before hauling her body downstairs and loading her corpse into the back of her Jeep. (Photo courtesy of the Travis County, Texas District Court)

Police investigators found drops of Justin Thomas's blood in the bathroom trash at Kim LeBlanc's apartment. Regina Hartwell paid the rent for the apartment. (Photo courtesy of the Travis County, Texas District Court)

Justin Thomas originally planned to dump Regina Hartwell's body in the Colorado River, which flowed behind his family's home. Instead, he hid her body in a shed on the property before deciding to burn her corpse. *(Photo courtesy of the Travis County, Texas District Court)*

After putting out the blaze, firefighters found Hartwell's burned body in the back seat of her Jeep. *(Photo courtesy of the Travis County, Texas District Court)*

A trail of scorched grass ran from an upside down five-gallon gas can to the Jeep. *(Photo courtesy of the Travis County, Texas District Court)*

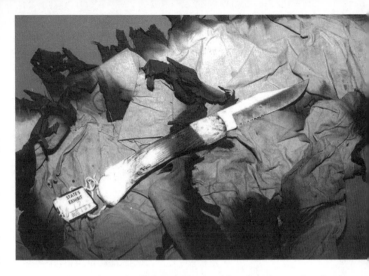

Underneath Hartwell's burned body, police found a single-edged lockblade knife wrapped in blue cotton cloth.

In the dark of night, no one spotted the charred license plate to Regina Hartwell's burned Jeep. *(Photo courtesy of the Travis County, Texas District Court)*

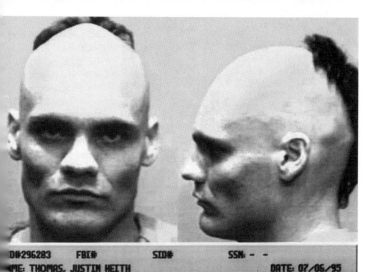

LeBlanc's boyfriend Justin Heith Thomas, 24, was arrested for the murder of Regina Hartwell on July 6, 1995. *(Photo courtesy of the Austin, Texas Police Department)*

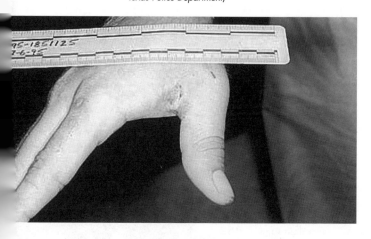

The cut webbing on Justin Thomas's right hand was oozing pus when police photographed it for evidence. *(Photo courtesy of the Travis County, Texas District Court)*

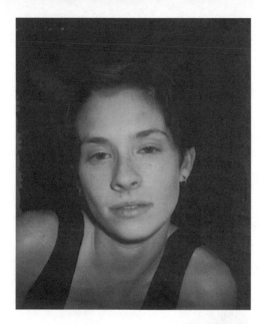

Police photographed LeBlanc on July 5, 1995 during an interview regarding the disappearance of her friend Regina Hartwell. *(Photo courtesy of the Travis County, Texas District Court)*

Justin Thomas being escorted to court by a Travis County, Texas Deputy Sheriff in August, 1996. *(Photo courtesy of Tom Lankes/Austin American-Statesman)*

Gregg Cox, lead prosecutor, and Gail Van Winkle, chief prosecutor, for the Justin Thomas trial.

Justin Thomas's Texas defense team of Jim Sawyer, K.C. Anderson, and Patrick Ganne loved to dine at Austin's Paggi House, where red wine was their preferred drink. *(Photo courtesy of Kelly Anderson)*

In June of 2000, Justin Thomas was extradited from Texas to California to finally face charges in the murder of Riverside County, California drug dealer Rafael Noriega. *(Photo courtesy of the Riverside County, California Sheriff's Department)*

The Honorable Terrence Boren, Superior Court Judge in Marin, California was part of a judicial strike force brought in to alleviate the backlog of cases in Riverside County, California. Justin Thomas was the first such case to go to trial. *(Photo courtesy of Judge Terrence Boren)*

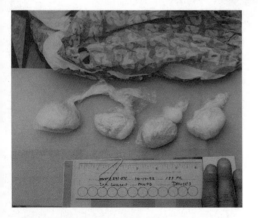

A battle over crystal meth was the reason for Rafael Noreiga's murder. *(Photo courtesy of the Riverside County, California Superior Court)*

Justin Thomas was caught with shanks while incarcerated in the Riverside County Jail. (Author photo)

Noriega's remains were discovered in the hills outside of Riverside, California, on October 17, 1992, more than one month after he had gone missing. (Photo courtesy of the Riverside County, California Superior Court)

By the time Noriega's body was found, his body was so badly decomposed that his skull was visible. (Photo courtesy of the Riverside County, California Superior Court)

Bullet fragments were removed from Noreiga's chest. *(Author photo)*

Attorney Darryl Exum fought to keep Justin Thomas off of death row, despite the fact that Thomas begged for the death penalty. *(Photo courtesy of Heather Chavez)*

"Where?" she said.

"Probably California. I want to see my kids. I miss them. Shit, it's a fuckin' crime we can't get more than $300 a day out of her account. You know what I'm saying?"

Liz Brickman, a party friend of Regina Hartwell's, phoned Regina and left a message. "I thought we were going out tonight. What's happened?"

Kim LeBlanc and Justin Thomas spent the night doing drugs.

Anita Morales paged Regina. There was no reply. She tried again. Regina was supposed to help her move into her new apartment.

"I want to go home," said Justin.

Kim rolled over on the bed and did another line.

"Let's go to Garfield. We can stop and get some cash on the way," he said.

Justin Thomas and Kim LeBlanc left behind a room full of bloody towels and sheets.

At 12:02 p.m., Kim LeBlanc withdrew $200 from Regina Hartwell's checking account. She withdrew the money while standing at an HEB grocery store.

Justin Thomas's body relaxed as LeBlanc drove up to the ramshackle house on stilts by the Colorado River. It was home. It was family. He stared at the boots and shoes that lined the outside wall, placed very neatly there so that no one could track dirt and mud into the house. Jim Thomas, with his gray hair and beer belly, was a tidy man. Justin smiled down at his dad's shoes. And there were aunt Bonnie's—Momma B's. There were J. R.'s. He was always a good wrestling partner.

Justin slipped off his shoes and walked upstairs.

Kim followed behind him and headed straight for the bedroom, straight to do another line of coke.

Jim Thomas stared. He'd never seen his handsome son bald with an irregular line of a skunk's tail of hair down his head. He'd never seen his son with hair dyed black instead of its natural, beautiful, light brown color. He'd never seen his son with eyes so sunken, cheeks so hollow.

He looked at Kim as she closed the bedroom door behind her. Her body was too skinny. Her eyes were black with circles of exhaustion. She hadn't eaten anything but ice cream in God-knows-when. Those girls were just no good for his boy.

Bonnie walked in from the kitchen. She held a beer in one hand and a cigarette in the other. "You look like you've been 'round hell and back," she said.

Justin walked over and kissed her on the cheek. "That's what I love about you, Momma B, you're always honest with me. Where're my cigarettes?" Justin followed Kim into the bedroom. He shut the door and locked it behind him. He sat on the bed and counted their money. There were two pounds of drugs in her Jeep.

Bonnie stared at Jim. He got up and got a beer.

Sunday, July 2, was warm and sunny, just like a Texas Fourth of July weekend should be. A breeze shimmied in and out of the trees that lined the banks of the Colorado River and the Thomas property.

Jim Thomas and his family sat out on their second-story deck, drinking, smoking, and looking at that translucent, blue Colorado River. If only everything could be that clear. The summer wind was soft on their handsome, suntanned faces.

"I want to do some shooting." Justin stood by the deck railing.

Everybody just listened to the wind. Jim thought there was no better place on Earth than that little piece of property on the banks of the Colorado.

"I want to shoot from up here," said Justin.

"No," answered Jim. The slowly rustling leaves seemed to whisper to each other.

"Come on, Dad. I want to shoot from up here."

Jim cherished the serenity of his property. "Well, you're not gonna do it from up here."

"Well, whatever," said Justin, and he walked inside, banging the screen door behind himself, and brushed past his aunt Bonnie.

Jim Thomas tried to ignore his son's anger. He lit a cigarette and sipped on his beer.

Justin packed up three guns and walked out the door.

Bonnie watched her nephew climb over a barbed-wire fence. "Where's he going?"

Jim took another swallow of beer. "Across the river."

She watched Justin wade the Colorado. He carefully balanced his loaded guns above the water, then disappeared in the trees on the other side.

Twenty or thirty minutes later, Justin returned. Blood dripped from the gash in his right hand.

"Shit, how'd you do that?" said Bonnie, concerned.

The white tissue and red meat of his hand shined in the sunlight. "Snagged it when I jumped the fence." Justin pinched the cut together with the thumb and forefinger of his left hand.

"You need stitches. Let's get you to the doctor." Bonnie headed inside to get her truck keys.

"Nah," said Justin.

Jim told Justin he needed stitches. J. R. told him he needed stitches. Everyone told him he needed stitches.

Justin was adamant in his no.

So he and Bonnie went into the bathroom. She washed out the gash with peroxide and alcohol. She coated it with bag balm, an antiseptic farmers use to sooth the chapped udders of milk cows, then butterfly-bandaged the gash. That still didn't stop the bleeding.

Kim LeBlanc went to buy drugs and max out Regina's ATM card. She did that everyday after Regina was stabbed to death, sometimes standing at the ATM machine just at midnight, poking the card in and out of the slot, waiting for the stroke of the day to end so she could press the buttons one more time and get another day's worth of money and drugs.

Jim Thomas grabbed Justin as he walked by. He just couldn't stand it anymore. "Son, we gotta talk." He couldn't believe he was saying that. In fact, it took every ounce of gumption in Jim Thomas to say it.

He inhaled deeply so that he drew himself up to his entire six feet. He reached for a beer. Jim Thomas wasn't much at communicating—not orally, not any which way. He drank down half his beer. It had always been one of his limitations—keeping things all bottled up. But he also knew he just couldn't live like that anymore. "It's time you go. I want you out of here."

"But, Dad—"

"No, arguing. I'm sick of your comings and goings." Jim's insides tore up as he spoke.

"But, Dad—"

"I'm sick of your bullshit. I want you out of here."

"Dad?"

But Justin Thomas knew there was no arguing, just like he knew there was no arguing about shooting his guns from the deck.

Justin pulled Kim aside and told her. They started pulling out their clothes, piling them in the middle of the floor of Jim's bedroom, readying them for the washer and escape. Justin counted the money again.

At 5:31 p.m. on Monday, July 3, Kim LeBlanc withdrew $200 from Regina Hartwell's account. She did so at a Bank One ATM machine on Ben White Boulevard, the road between her apartment and Justin Thomas's home in Garfield.

Twenty-four hours later, on Tuesday, the Fourth of July, LeBlanc went to Hartwell's apartment and helped file the missing-person report on her dead friend.

"What happened?" Justin Thomas demanded, on her return to Garfield.

She looked like hell. "It went fairly well," she said.

But Justin looked rather hellish himself, with his Mohawk growing smaller and smaller by the day, as he worryingly chipped away on it.

"We filed a missing-person's report. Anita was really understanding and everything." Kim lit a cigarette. "But Anita said you'd probably come up as a suspect, you know, since you're in my life and the new person in my life." She puffed.

Thomas peeled off a few bills from his rubberbanded roll of dough, enough for two eight balls of cocaine, and handed the dollars to Kim, and LeBlanc left again for Austin and a drug run. While she was gone, he counted the money again. He'd probably counted it twenty or thirty times over the past few days.

On Wednesday, July 5, the heat of the day was just winding down as APD Detective Hunt and Bastrop County Sheriff Deputy Nelson drove onto the Thomas property in search of Kim LeBlanc. Minutes later, Justin Thomas walked into the yard, handcuffed, and trailed by deputies.

Bonnie Thomas stared in shock through the windshield of her white Dodge Ram truck. She, too, had just driven through the Thomas gate and into the yard, Jim Thomas with her. "What's going on?" they shouted, tired from work and confused by the chaos and cop cars.

"He's agreed to go with us for questioning."

It was the last time Bonnie and Jim saw Justin for days. It was the last time they saw him free, ever.

Kim LeBlanc's bones vibrated in her as Detective Hunt drove down the winding road from Whirlaway. Her arms felt like an out-of-whack tuning fork that couldn't stop being struck. "I have way too much coke in me, and I need some serious help," she said.

"I don't really care what you've been doing," he replied.

She gripped her arms trying to stop their ringing. LeBlanc wanted her mother there to take care of her, to hold her 'til she was quiet. She closed her eyes and she vaguely remembered she was supposed to meet her mother at the Circle K. Her pager went off.

"Would you call and answer it?" she said to Detective Hunt. "I think it's my mother."

She gave the detective the number, a pay-phone number, and Hunt dialed it on his police cellphone. Kim's mother answered. "I have your daughter," he said. "She's going with me to the police station to talk with me about Regina Hartwell, who is missing." He turned north onto Interstate 35.

"We found 'em," said Hunt to Carter over his cell phone. "We're escorting them in to Homicide."

Kim closed her eyes again; it was better that way.

Detective Hunt exited the interstate and drove up to Austin Police Department headquarters. The University of Texas football stadium was just blocks away, the school Kim should have been attending, cheering the Longhorns to victory.

She didn't know where she'd be spending football season. At 6:41 p.m., she was placed in a small, gray, cramped, windowless APD interview room. It was claustrophobic, awfully claustrophobic for a coked-out, sexually abused child. In the ceiling, hidden in a vent, was a video camera. Kim didn't know it. Detective Hunt turned on the camera.

Kim was exhausted, weak, red-eyed, red-nosed, and frail like a newborn fawn. She'd been up for days.

"You do the interview," said Sergeant Reveles to Detective Hunt.

At 6:48 p.m., seven minutes after LeBlanc was placed in interview room two, Detective Hunt walked into the cramped cubicle. Detective Carter sat in. "This is Detective Carter," said Hunt.

Carter noted LeBlanc's red, runny nose, her sniffling, her red, tired eyes, her thinness—a drug addict. He left to get her some water and brought it back.

Detective Hunt questioned Kim for a few minutes. "Do you want to talk to the police?"

Carter left the room.

At 6:51, Kim LeBlanc requested an attorney before being questioned further. At 6:52 p.m., she was told, "You may leave any time." At 6:55 p.m., LeBlanc was obstinate, insisting that all questioning cease, and asked again for counsel. At 6:56 p.m., she said, "I want to talk to my mother," and again asked for counsel.

Hunt eventually left her alone.

Kim got up to leave, too, but the door wouldn't open. "I'm caught," she mumbled. She sat back down in the chair. LeBlanc rocked back and forth, as though trapped in the windowless cubicle, as though she thought she was going to die if she didn't get another line of coke, a rope to escape with.

"I'm caught," she mumbled again, and she pulled her knees up to her chest, wrapped herself into a fetal position, and moaned. She was shaking flesh and bones.

At 6:58, Hunt told her, "You are not under arrest."

Kim LeBlanc's mother and stepfather arrived at the Austin Police Department. Cathy LeBlanc seemed nice enough, but she was very quiet. Ken LeBlanc did all the talking.

The couple appeared concerned about their daughter, but acted strangely, almost as if they weren't surprised by what was going on. To the police, what reaction they did have came across as feigned, exaggerated. Her parents wanted to talk to Kim, badly.

"She's not under arrest. You can talk to her."

David Carter walked into the interview room where Justin Thomas sat. "I'm Detective Carter. I need some identifying information."

"Uh, what's going on here, you know?" said Thomas.

"We're investigating a missing-person case and felt that you may have some information that could assist us."

Carter left the room to monitor the interview with Kim LeBlanc.

"We're going to get you out of this, baby." The LeBlanc family was alone in the interview room. Cathy was small and slim. Kim was short and emaciated.

Ken was big-boned and big-bellied. He dwarfed his step-daughter. "Tell them what they want to know," he said.

Kim shook even harder from too little cocaine and too much fear. "He's in a gang in California," she said. "He killed a man in California. He's killed someone before. He's danger-ous." She rocked back and forth.

"Just say he did it."

Her mother watched, her shoulders slightly hunched.

"Just tell them he did it," said Ken. "He did it. We'll get you out of here. It's going to work."

"No, no, no. You don't understand," cried Kim.

"Just say he did it."

At 7:16 p.m., Kim LeBlanc knocked on the inside door of interview room two and invoked her right to an attorney.

Ken LeBlanc sat outside the room with Bastrop County Deputy Sheriff Nelson. Cathy LeBlanc sat in the interview room with her daughter. Kim LeBlanc requested an attorney again at 7:39 p.m. and 7:40 p.m.

Milliseconds later, Kim cried. "Take me home. I want to go home where we can talk with a lawyer about Regina."

"Kimmie, don't worry," said her mother, a legal secretary.

"The room's not bugged. That would be a violation of your constitutional rights."

The videotape ticked 7:41 p.m.

Twice more, in the next sixty seconds, she repeated her request to be taken home so that they could talk with an attorney about Regina's death.

Detective Carter performed a quick computer identification and criminal check on Justin Thomas. He located a California driver's license and some U.S. Army data.

He talked with Sergeant Reveles.

"It's clear these people were witnesses, maybe suspects, to a homicide."

"Don't wait much longer to interview Thomas," said Reveles. "You do it," he said to Carter.

Justin Thomas had been sitting in interview room one for a long time. Detective Hunt had thought it best if no one interviewed him until they learned what Kim LeBlanc had to tell them, and if they didn't turn on the videotape until the interview was started.

Now, the videotape was running, and Detective David Carter was with Thomas. So was Detective Mark Gilchrest.

"This is Detective Gilchrest," said Carter to Thomas. "Do you know why we are talking to you?"

"No."

"We're investigating an apparent murder."

Justin Thomas was cold, uncaring, nonchalant.

Detective Carter was tall, firm, professional. He read Thomas his Miranda rights, verbatim, from a standard form.

"Do you understand the warning? Would you sign the form and talk to us?"

Thomas signed the form.

"Do you know who I'm referring to when I say we are investigating an apparent murder?"

"Well, I know that Regina is missing."

They talked politely about Justin, where he worked, what he did.

"How long have you known Regina Hartwell?"

"Two, three months."

Carter noted that Thomas was evasive, even with non-specific questions. "When was the last time you saw her?"

Again, Thomas was vague.

"Were you involved in the murder of Regina Hartwell?"

Thomas began to fidget.

Detective Carter stared. There was an open wound in the webbing of Thomas's hand, smooth and clean, as if cut by a knife. "How'd you get that?" He pointed to the unbandaged gash between the thumb and forefinger of Thomas's right hand. It obviously needed stitches. A tendon appeared to be visible. Pus oozed at the edges.

Thomas lifted the hand toward his face and studied the cut. "I got it helping my dad mend a fence."

"Yeah," said Carter. "It's the kind of wound one would expect to get stitches for."

"Nah," said Thomas, "it's fine. Just rinse it with salt water."

Thomas was trying to display his toughness, thought Carter. But the detective knew such wounds weren't unusual when one used a knife to stab or cut another person.

"Where have you been? Who have you been with? What have you done since June 29?"

"I bought a trash can for my dad. I bought a tow chain, too."

Thomas was now too specific; that bothered Carter.

He stretched out his legs. "Wal-Mart," Justin said. "We went to Wal-Mart." He stretched out his arms and hands. He was aloof.

Carter left the room to check again on Kim LeBlanc.

* * *

"Justin told me that he had stabbed her and that he had her Jeep and her body inside of the Jeep." LeBlanc wept. "Regina took advantage of me against my will," said Kim to Detective Hunt. "Justin knew about it, and he killed her for that reason. He was trying to protect me."

"How did he get that cut on his hand?"

"A hammer. A hammer from a gun."

It was dark when the Crime Lab team taped black paper over the windows so that they could do a Luminol luminescence test for blood. Jeremy Barnes was back at the Château and standing in Hartwell's apartment.

Jeremy was asked what cleaning products he had used as Luminol reacts to bleach.

Brad Wilson was there, too. Jeremy and Brad were perhaps the last two people to see Regina alive, the last two people other than her murderer.

The Crime Lab team turned out the lights. Hartwell's phone rang nonstop. In the darkened apartment with the continually ringing phone, blood glowed from the chair, the walls, the carpet.

Again, Jeremy Barnes freaked. To him, blood looked like it was everywhere, coating the chair, flooding the carpet, dripping from the walls. The Crime Lab team saw footprints on the living room carpet near the recliner, drops of blood by the window, drops of blood next to a closet door. *This is somebody else,* Jeremy told himself. *This is somebody I don't know.*

A quarter-sized bloodstain was found near the bottom of the shower curtain; a three-to four-inch-long smear of blood was found on the shower rod. Jeremy could not, would not, believe that it was sweet, dead Regina's blood. He just couldn't.

* * *

Later that night, Regina's friends gathered in Barnes's apartment—they needed to call Mark Hartwell. But no one had his number; no one knew him, really.

Regina's friends ran back to her apartment, grabbed a black, plastic garbage bag she had used for a file cabinet, and ran back. Each quickly pulled a handful of papers out of the bag and sorted through them, looking for her father's phone number.

They found it.

"You want to call him?" said Ynema Mangum, looking at Anita Morales.

"I can't."

Ynema, the young, American Indian woman, to whom Mark Hartwell had once commented about her heritage, phoned him.

Regina's stepmother answered the phone.

"Mrs. Hartwell, this is Ynema Mangum." She tried to sound calm. "Uh, I hate to tell you this, uh, but we believe Regina has died."

Words of response couldn't come out of Dian's mouth. The thoughts were there, but not the words. She'd recently suffered an aneurysm. Finally, she relayed to Ynema that Mark Hartwell was at work and that she would go get him. "Ten minutes," she chaotically uttered. "Call back, fifteen."

Ynema Mangum called the Hartwell residence again and Mark Hartwell answered.

She told him what they thought had happened. Ynema, like Dian Hartwell, felt she wasn't using the right words. "Regina, didn't suffer any pain, but you do need to bring her dental records to Austin."

He cried, and Regina's friends wept with Mark Hartwell.

* * *

Carter conferred with Wardlow, Nelson, and Dukes, who were also monitoring both interviews.

Kim LeBlanc wrote out a statement. "Regina Hartwell and I had a relationship that began on July 4, 1994 until January 1, 1995." She sweated. She ached and hurt. Her bones still rattled, and her heart still pounded, too hard. "May of 1995, I met Justin Thomas. He and I had a relationship since then. He knew a lot about things Regina had done and the role she played in my life and was very concerned about that.

"Then Thursday morning, late morning, he left to go to her apartment to take care of something that I asked him to do. I asked him to get her out of my life. I could not handle her being a part of my life anymore. I asked him to help me kill her. When he left to go over there, he did not say what he was going to do, but we had an understanding of what he was going to do."

Kim made a pen change to the statement. She changed "kill her" to "help me out of this situation." She signed the statement.

Three and a half to four hours after Kim had walked into interview room two, the video camera was shut off.

Detective Carter walked back into interview room one. With his blue eyes cold and hard, he stared at empty-eyed Justin Thomas.

"We know what happened—how you wrapped her in the comforter, put her in her Jeep. . . . It's time for you to tell Detective Gilchrest and myself your side of the story."

Thomas shifted in his chair, as if withdrawing. "I guess I'd better have a lawyer," he said, calmly.

The interview was over. Carter and Gilchrest exited the room and left Thomas there by himself.

* * *

"Regina's life was like tragedy here and tragedy there. And she liked these people who had tragedy in their lives, like Marilyn Monroe and Madonna. Then what happened? Her life ended in a way that we will never forget, no matter how hard we try," said Anita Morales.

She and her friends laid flowers at Regina's door and lit Mexican votive candles.

Texas Ranger Rocky Wardlow and APD detective John Hunt obtained a consent to search a 1993 Jeep, 1995 Texas license number KCD 33S, registered to Mary C./Kenneth D. LeBlanc. The Jeep was located at the home of Justin Thomas on Whirlaway Drive in Travis County, Texas.

Kenneth D. LeBlanc and Kimberley Alex LeBlanc signed the consent in similar, sloping-to-the-right-scrawls. Cathy LeBlanc signed in an upright cursive that looked almost like printing.

At nine minutes past midnight on the sixth of July, Texas Ranger Rocky Wardlow and APD detective John Hunt received a consent to search Kim LeBlanc's apartment on Southway Drive, Apartment 118, Austin, Texas.

Ken, Cathy, and Kim LeBlanc signed the consent, then Kim turned over her apartment key to Wardlow.

Carter, Gilchrest, Wardlow, Hunt, and Reveles all conferred. Wardlow and Carter then went to Carter's office to type out a probable-cause affidavit, and Carter phoned and woke Municipal Court Judge Phil Sanders.

"Could you review a PC for us?" said Carter.

"If you come over to my house," replied Sanders, groggy from sleep.

Carter and Wardlow immediately left for the Sanders residence, where the Judge met them in his bathrobe, at the front door.

Sanders read the affidavit, which said, in part, that "numerous witnesses, who were friends or neighbors of Regina Hartwell, told investigators that an argument occurred on or about the 28th of June at Regina Hartwell's apartment. The argument was said to be between Regina Hartwell and her former girlfriend Kim LeBlanc. The same witnesses identified Justin Thomas as being the current boyfriend of Kim LeBlanc.

"Kim LeBlanc advised police officers that her boyfriend, Justin Thomas, arrived at her apartment in Regina's Jeep. Justin Thomas told Kim that he had stabbed Regina with a knife that he had kept in a box."

Judge Sanders asked the officers a few questions and approved the warrant of arrest for Justin Thomas for first-degree felony murder with a $100,000 bond. It was 1:45 in the morning.

Approximately fifteen minutes later, Carter and Wardlow were back at APD headquarters. Carter, Wardlow, Gilchrest, and Deputy Nelson then walked into the interview room where Justin Thomas sat. "You are being charged with murder, and we have a warrant for your arrest."

Thomas did not react. He simply stood, and the four officers walked him to booking.

As Wardlow booked Thomas, he noticed the gaping wound in the webbing of Thomas's right hand. Thomas's clothes were confiscated and sent to the DPS Crime Lab. Thomas was placed in a jail cell.

Kim LeBlanc went to Whataburger with her parents.

CHAPTER 19

Jim Thomas and his sister Bonnie were at work creating wood cabinets when their boss brought a phone to Jim. "It's your son . . . from a correctional institution."

"I've been arrested for murder," said Justin.

Jim's face went pale, and his knees buckled.

The hurt on her brother's face pained her so, Bonnie's heart fell to her feet.

Jim simply went back to his saw, went back to work, and wept.

Jim Thomas, Bonnie's big brother, the sweet, strong, silent man who never showed any emotion, who didn't know how to express himself, cried. He wondered what had gone wrong with his one and only child.

"J. R.," Bonnie Thomas stood at work with a phone to her ear, "the police are probably gonna come to search the house."

J. R. was at the Whirlaway home, recuperating from poison oak.

"You tell them that it's not your property and that you can't give nobody permission to search it."

"Yes, ma'am," he said. "There's a black car pulling up. Yes, sir," Bonnie heard her son say.

Then the phone went dead. Bonnie stood there listening to a dial tone. There was nothing to do but hang up and rout some more wood.

A few minutes later, Bonnie was called back to the phone. She wiped her brow of sawdust.

"There's cops all over the place," J. R. panted. "Man, I'm scared. Can you, uncle Jim, somebody come home?"

Bonnie was out the door.

J. R. was sitting under a tree when Bonnie drove up in her full-sized Dodge Ram truck. This was the second time she'd driven up to the Thomas dream home to find the yard filled with police cars. This was getting old real fast, but Bonnie was polite. She walked up to Ranger Wardlow.

Wardlow looked at Bonnie with her gray hair, blue eyes, tattoos, and tanned, firm legs. She almost always wore shorts in the summertime. She lit a Parliament 100 cigarette. "Can I come with you?" she said.

"Yes," he answered politely.

Bonnie respected him. "What are you looking for?"

"Just a few certain items. When we see them, we'll know them, and we'll be on our way," Wardlow responded. He eyed everything as he walked.

Several men were loading Kim's Jeep onto a DPS wrecker.

"Do you mind if we look in your truck?" he said.

Bonnie obliged, and officers quickly confiscated a bright, shiny, new piece of chain found in the bed of her truck. There was a locked padlock on the chain.

"Who'd you get the chain from?" said Wardlow.

"Justin," said Bonnie, in her slow drawl.

"When'd you get it? Why do you have it? How'd you use it? And is it used?"

"Yeah," she said, puffing softly on her cigarette. "My brother's truck broke down, and we had to use the chain to tow it to the shop. After we towed it in, we threw the chain in the back of my truck."

Bonnie followed Wardlow into the house as several other officers scooped up three-quarters of a row of shoes lining the garage wall of the house. A pair of Regina's boots was with them. One-hundred fifty dollar boots, Bonnie had estimated. Wardlow pointed to a new thirty-gallon trash can, and it was gone—taken into custody.

Bonnie dropped her cigarette to the ground and walked upstairs with the Texas Ranger. They walked into Jim's bedroom. Piles of clothes were on the floor.

"Whose clothes are these?" he asked.

Bonnie pointed them out. "Justin's. Kim's. Jim's." The clothes were just as Justin and Kim had left them two days earlier as they had prepared their laundry for their departure from Austin and the Jim Thomas house.

Wardlow took Justin's and Kim's clothes into possession. He left Jim's neat like he would have wanted. Wardlow was always polite and neat.

A deputy sheriff walked up to Wardlow. He whispered into his ear. "Drug paraphernalia. Turn the search warrant over to me."

Wardlow backed his body away from the deputy. "No. We came here to get what we came to get. We're gonna get it, and then be on our way."

"I can have some black-and-whites out here in fifteen minutes," said the deputy.

"No," replied Wardlow, again. "I got what I came for, and I don't want to bother these folks anymore."

"Turn the search warrant over to me," said the deputy, his moustache twitching.

Wardlow looked the deputy straight in the face. "I said 'no'." And Wardlow walked out of the room.

He left the Whirlaway home neat as a pin. He took with him a 1993 Jeep Sahara, a tow chain, trash can, a bayonet-type knife, and a silver-and-black-handled, single-edge knife, both found under the house on stilts, a pair of black, men's lace-up boots, one pair of black, men's Reeboks, one pair of men's White Force tennis shoes, a green, nylon bag containing some of Kim's and Justin's clothing, a red duffel bag full of Kim's clothes, a brown-leather billfold with a silver chain, a green canvas duffel bag, a silver lighter, some cigarette butts, and Kim's black leather backpack purse, which was much like Regina's favorite purse.

The purse had been found in one of the bedrooms. In the purse were a receipt from the Heritage Inn, several ATM receipts, an ATM card with Regina Hartwell's name on it, a Builders Square receipt, Kim's Texas driver's license, and Kim's fake Kentucky driver's license in the name of Kim Derrick, which stated she was over twenty-one.

Ken and Cathy LeBlanc tried to stir Kim from her sleep. "The police want to talk to you again."

They picked her up and tried to dress her. They tried to get her out into the sun on that Thursday, July 6. It was a cloudy morning, a clear afternoon. The high was only 87 degrees, but Kim LeBlanc passed out in the heat. She fell on the concrete and skinned her knee.

That's all she remembered of that day.

But she did return to APD headquarters. "How did Justin get from your apartment to Regina's?"

She wasn't really sure—he might have walked to a friend's and gotten a ride from there.

The Regina Hartwell murder investigative team rode non-stop throughout the city for the next twenty-four hours.

Around three, 3:30 p.m., on the day Justin Thomas was incarcerated, the day Kim LeBlanc fell and scraped her knee, Dukes met Wardlow at LeBlanc's South Austin apartment and searched it with the DPS Crime Lab.

Kim's multicolored, childlike panties were found in the bathroom and photographed laying just in front of the commode. Traces of blood were also found in the bathroom. It was on tissue paper in the trash can by the toilet. The blood matched the DNA of Justin Thomas. The toilet-paper holder was empty.

Blood was also found on the floor, on towels, and on an Acuvue contact-lens case.

Pam Carson glanced at the parking lot at Carla Reid's and Anita Morales's apartment and wondered why Kim's car wasn't there. If Regina were missing, as Carla had told her when she'd phoned Pam at 10:30 that night at work—"Regina's still missing, and we need you to talk to the police, missing persons, tonight"—then Regina's little partner in crime should have been gathered with everyone else, worrying like everyone else.

Carson was furious with Hartwell for making everyone worry so. *I'm gonna chew Regina out when I see her and get her away from Kim and Justin,* she thought as she had driven up Interstate 35 from San Antonio.

It was close to midnight as she knocked on Carla's and Anita's door. Kelli Grand answered it. She was holding a glass of red wine, as was Carla. Anita was holding her usual rum and coke.

"Where's Kim?" said Pam.

"She's down at the station talking to the police. Go make yourself a drink."

"Call Fran in Houston," said Carson. "I have her number in the car."

"We'll do that," said Morales. "But first, make yourself a drink."

"Call—"

"We'll do that later. Are you finished making that drink?"

Pam Carson fixed herself a White Russian and noticed that everyone was scribbling notes.

"Sit quietly and listen," said Reid. "Regina's Jeep was found in Bastrop. It was burned to a crisp. There was the body of a 5'2" Caucasian woman found in the backseat, unrecognizable. It was Regina."

Pam rushed out the door and vomited over the wrought-iron railing. Carla walked out and wrapped her arms around her.

The following morning, Cathy LeBlanc spoke with APD's Detective Dukes. She recalled talking to Regina Hartwell on the Wednesday before the murder. Regina had told Cathy, the woman she called Mom, about the morning fight with Kim and Justin. Cathy also told Dukes that she was going to take Kim to Houston for drug rehab. She was trying to save her one and only child.

Mark Hartwell drove from Houston to Austin—Dukes had also spoken with him that morning. He was on his way to Austin to identify the burnt, black body of his one and only natural daughter. His brother Joel Hartwell, a law-enforcement officer in Harris County, rode with him. Joel Hartwell hadn't seen his niece in a year.

Mark Hartwell had in hand Regina's dental records from ages five through thirteen. They showed that he had taken his daughter to dentist appointment after dentist appointment, that she'd missed a few, and that she'd been recommended for orthodontia. The records showed where her permanent retainer fit in her mouth, the one that had survived the flames set by Justin Thomas.

At 2:30 p.m., Mark Hartwell turned over to APD his dead daughter's dental records. Detective Carter and Texas Ranger Wardlow sat with Mark and Joel Hartwell while Detective Gilchrest transported the records to the Travis County Medical Examiner's office, just a few blocks away.

Within fifteen minutes, Gilchrest returned, and he and Carter stood alone in an adjoining office. "Dr. Bayardo confirmed it," said Gilchrest. "It's Regina Hartwell."

Carter turned away; it was time to advise Mark Hartwell that his daughter was truly deceased.

Mark Hartwell was devastated.

However, Regina's father composed himself. The officers and Hartwell brothers discussed sending Regina's remains to Houston, and Carter and Wardlow put Hartwell in contact with the Bastrop County morgue that held his daughter's body.

"I want to see Regina's apartment," said Hartwell.

"There are no police holds on it," replied Carter.

Mark Hartwell dialed the Château office number and spoke with the apartment manager. Shock splashed over his face as he and the manager proceeded to argue. Hartwell turned to Carter. "She won't let me into Regina's apartment."

Wardlow reached for the phone. "All police holds have been dropped," he told the manager. Wardlow listened, and confusion covered his face. "I don't know what you're talking about," he said.

Carter got on the phone. The Château manager shouted, "Mr. Hartwell cannot take anything from that apartment until he shows a will or paperwork!"

"He is the sole next of kin," said Carter.

"I'm liable," she yelled, "for Regina's belongings! Others have more right to that property than he does!"

"Let me remind you," said Carter, calmly, "you just said you were responsible for the property. Therefore, the property better not be disposed of without Mr. Hartwell's knowledge."

"Are you threatening me?" screamed the manager. "You better not be threatening me!"

Joel Hartwell took the phone, talked at length with the manager, and finally came to an agreement.

Jeremy Barnes watched Mark Hartwell, the father he'd heard so much about. He had to reconcile the images in his mind. From what Jeremy had understood from Regina, Mark Hartwell hadn't paid much attention to his daughter like Jeremy thought a parent should.

But right then, Mark Hartwell looked like he was about to burst into tears. Hartwell stared at the yellow police tape that still marked off his daughter's apartment as they walked into Brad Wilson's apartment. They needed to use the phone.

To Jeremy, though, Mark Hartwell seemed surprisingly obsessed at the moment with Regina's money—the money in the bank, the insurance on the Jeep, the insurance on the tires.

Barnes passed it off. It was just a strong man acting maturely, taking care of business, and, most of all, trying to keep his mind off of his daughter's death. Mark Hartwell was just a big, ole country hick, just a guy, and Jeremy Barnes liked him.

Mark let Jeremy go into Regina's apartment and take anything he wanted to remember his friend. Jeremy took the Wile E. Coyote pen he'd given Reg for her twenty-fifth birthday, and he took his best friend's favorite shorts—a pair of too-big yellow Gap shorts. They made him smile.

Detective Carter and other members of the investigative team spread out across the capital city—Builders Square to question the manager about the receipt in Kim LeBlanc's purse, First Interstate Bank to check the ATM receipts in Kim LeBlanc's purse, convenience stores and grocery stores to check the video surveillance tapes of the ATM withdrawals in Kim LeBlanc's purse, and the Heritage Inn to check the receipt in the purse.

Detective Carter also fielded anonymous pay-phone calls from Hartwell's friends, all of whom stated they would be killed if they identified themselves. They gave Carter details of the murder, and more.

Kelli Grand phoned APD. "Kim's behind the whole thing," she said. "She knew she was going to get lots of money if Regina died. Kim had to have been there and told Justin to kill Regina. Regina would never let Justin in her apartment by himself. Kim and Justin were inseparable."

"Do you have any personal knowledge of Kim being present or having any part in planning the murder?" said Detective Gilchrest.

"No. I just know it. And I know the bank teller at First Interstate bank, and he told me about the accounts Regina used. Look, all of Regina's friends know that Kim was the cause of Regina's death, and it looks like the police made a deal with Kim to get to Justin."

Gilchrest felt like Kelli Grand was trying to use him to get information rather than trying to give information.

Hope Rockwell tried to avoid the police and would only talk to them briefly over the phone.

Anita Morales stood in Regina's apartment and sketched the homicide scene. She had to keep busy, she had to think, to save, to rescue Regina. It was her only way to cope.

The worse thing I've ever done? thought Anita. *Ignoring my friend's drug problem because it was just something that I didn't want to see, deal with, or be involved in. I could have done more for her. I just convinced myself that, since Regina seemed okay she was okay.*

Morales couldn't cry. There was too much to do. Friends to call. A funeral to prepare for.

Mike White got a phone call from Morales telling him that Regina had died. He closed his blinds, sat in his room, didn't go to work, and cried for a day.

Amy Seymoure's father closed the door to his office. "Honey, Regina has been murdered."

The breath slammed out of Amy, as though she'd been smacked into a brick wall. She collapsed onto the floor and sobbed. Her tears fell heavily, like a summer storm.

"She didn't go out without a battle," Amy said. "Regina was a fighter."

It wasn't enough.

Jeremy Barnes didn't know what to do, how to feel. At times he thought, *Jeremy, you're exaggerating. This is stupid. Just get over it. This is the way it is, and you can't change it.*

Other times, he beat his head against the wall because he missed his friend Regina so very much. He thought she was so beautiful when she took off her mask of makeup, when she was just her natural, gorgeous, country-girl self. He wept as he thought about how they country danced together, two-stepped across the dance floor.

"Son, did you ever think that maybe God let her die when she did because she prayed with you and she believed in her

heart that she wanted to become good and get away from all
that stuff, that she was really trying? So God took her home
then so that she wouldn't slip and fall again?" Jeremy's mom
said that to him when she went to stay with him and comfort
him for a week.

Thank God for moms. Regina was finally with hers. "She
just needed to let go of all of that superficial life so that she
could for sure go home—to Heaven. I pray that's how she really
felt, and I have to believe that's how she felt because I loved her
so much," said Jeremy. Then he cried some more.

On Monday, July 10, 1995, Detective Carter watched the
DPS Crime Lab team as they searched Regina Hartwell's and
Kim LeBlanc's formerly matching Jeeps, each parked at DPS
headquarters in Austin.

Kim LeBlanc's Jeep was set inside the DPS paint shop so
that the lab crew could do a Luminol test in the dark. Blood
glowed on the passenger door and passenger seatbelt. It
matched the DNA of Justin Thomas. But Justin Thomas's
drugs and money, which he'd stashed in Kim's Jeep and in-
ventoried time and again since Hartwell's murder, were not to
be found.

Burned CDs were found in the chalky-white Jeep. Ash remains of Hartwell's, piled in a compressed heap, sat in what
would have been the backseat. Mixed in the ash were burned
remnants of an XL black, denim shirt, reeking of smoke, and
remnants of what appeared to be fatigue pants, burned black.

Also in the pile of compressed ash were flesh and bones.

The following day, Carter contacted the Riverside County
Sheriff's Department about Justin Thomas. Hours later,
he got a return call. Thomas was a suspect in a drug-and

gun-related murder. "The victim was a known drug dealer, and his body was possibly set on fire," Carter was told.

Hartwell's body was cremated twice. First in the car fire, then by the mortician. Still, her ashes weren't at her July 14, 2 p.m. memorial service at the Pasadena Funeral Home in Pasadena, Texas.

Regina's father, her stepmother, Dian, her grandparents, uncle, and cousins were there. Amy Seymoure and some of Regina's friends from high school went. They all stared at, and studied, a poster of photos of Regina.

Ynema Mangum, Anita Morales, and Carla Reid had made the collage of memories. Ynema had enlarged the photos on a color copier. Anita and Carla had pasted them on the board. It was their salute to their beloved friend.

To the contingency from Austin—twenty-five friends or more including Anita, Carla, Ynema, Pam Carson, Kelli Grand, Jeremy Barnes—Regina's family members seemed stunned at the appearance of the girl in the photos. The girl with the bright red lipstick, the perfectly plucked eyebrows, the black hair. Some didn't recognize which person in the pictures was Regina. She had changed that much.

Mark Hartwell walked up to Jeremy and leaned over to him. "Jeremy, I just want to let you know that this is for you and Regina." Hartwell then sat down, and the music started. He looked over at Jeremy and smiled. Jeremy burst out laughing.

So did Anita. The music was the song "New York, New York."

If Regina were here right now, thought Jeremy, *she'd fucking drop dead of embarrassment. She'd say, "My God, what in the hell is this country bumpkin doing?"*

Jeremy, Anita, and Carla sank their heads in their laps, hoping that people would think they were crying. They knew Regina was up in Heaven, laughing and dancing. *Hell,* they thought, *if she's still doing drugs up there, she's doing a great big line right now.*

Another song was played. Amy Seymoure gave the eulogy. Pam Carson read a poem. Anita finally broke down and cried. Ynema stared at the stained-glass window over the memorial, and she felt a sense of peace—everything was going to be okay. It made her feel much better.

At the moment Regina had died, Ynema had been landing in Florida, lightning flashing around the tips of her plane's wings. She believed it to be Regina's call for help.

Suddenly, the lights flickered in the funeral home. Everyone knew that it was Regina saying hi.

Over the next few months, Ynema's career blossomed, and she believed Regina had a part in that. Regina would do something like that from her grave, she was that generous, Ynema felt.

Regina was buried next to her mother.

"Hey, let's go do an eight ball of coke."

"Yeah, in honor of Regina!"

It sickened Jeremy Barnes to hear Regina's drug-using, Regina-using friends from Austin.

"Let's go to Manuel's."

"An eight ball of coke for Regina."

"She'd want us to do that!"

Barnes's grief exploded inside. *Y'all are a bunch of losers,* he screamed to himself. *You don't even know the real Regina. It's people like y'all who really fucked up her life in the first place. She probably wouldn't even be dead right now if it weren't for you.*

Anita Morales pulled him away from the crowd.

Hartwell's girl friends went back to Austin and to Manuel's.

Kim LeBlanc's high school friend Amanda Dexter was there to celebrate Regina.

Kelli, Regina's favorite server, said to Pam, "You should have seen Kim on the New York trip. She just threw a fit and sat in her room the whole time. We wanted to go out and do stuff, and Kim just threw a fit and sat in her room.

"And Regina would go out by herself and go on foot and went to all these fabulous stores and bought all these clothes and would just come home with bags and boxes of clothes and hold them up and Kim would either nod or shake her head. And whatever Kim didn't like, Regina would take back. Kim was being a big baby. Nothing was good enough for her. She wouldn't socialize with anyone there. She just walked all over Regina."

Jeremy Barnes didn't go to Manuel's. He went to his apartment.

He called Regina's apartment, time and time again, before her phone was disconnected, just to hear her voice on the answering machine, one more time, one last time.

Anita Morales phoned, too. Time and time again. She was there when Jeremy cleaned Regina's apartment for the last time.

A friend of Jeremy's helped. He scrubbed the toilet and turned to Anita and said, "I saw Kim here with Regina at eleven o'clock the night before she died. I came by to say goodnight, and they were here watching TV. Then the next morning when I was going to work at 7:30, I saw Kim's car. It was parked next to Regina's."

Morales phoned the police and relayed the information. No one recalls getting that call.

Barnes found CDs in Hartwell's apartment—heavy music like Led Zepplin. He didn't think they were hers. Regina liked lighter music—Madonna, Reba McEntire, the Oak Ridge

Boys, the Pet Shop Boys, dance music. He thought they were Justin Thomas's.

Jeremy couldn't take it anymore. The residents of the Château loved to gather in the evenings, down by the pool, drink, and talk about the murder of Regina Hartwell. Jeremy Barnes moved out.

But every night for the next two weeks, he returned to Regina's apartment and sat by her door, with flowers and Mexican votive candles, and wept. He wished he'd never let her leave his apartment that Wednesday night, that he'd called her back on Thursday, or gone over to her apartment on Thursday. He wished he'd pushed harder, sooner, for Regina to get away from Kim and Justin. He wished.

Due to the widespread allegations of murder, drugs, guns, and gangs outside the jurisdiction of APD, Detective Carter notified the federal authorities about Justin Thomas.

He also entered known information about Thomas into the National VICAP—a clearinghouse for violent offenses and repeat offenders involved in the likes of murder and sexual assault.

CHAPTER 20

K. C. Anderson sat down and looked her client straight in his hazel-green eyes. Even seated, Justin Thomas looked almost giant-tall in comparison to the petite Anderson, and he was as bald as a skinned chicken since his Mohawk had been shaved off.

But even with his new skinhead look, Thomas had a gentle demeanor. Anderson glanced down at her notes. To the young attorney, Thomas didn't appear to have one iota of a mean or menacing presence. He was sweet-natured, friendly, and surprisingly open.

"I don't want to know yet what happened," Anderson said, concerned that Thomas was going to tell her that he had done it. "Let me tell you where we're at."

A bright, animated, smiling, young woman with plenty of stories and plenty of energy, Anderson didn't show her excitement and nervousness over this, her first murder case in ten years of practicing law. As the daughter of the late legendary horse-racing announcer Chick Anderson, she had a lot to prove.

Anderson had been on vacation when she was appointed by the court to represent Thomas against the charge of murder. She arrived home, found and read the affidavit, talked to a television-reporter friend who was familiar with the case, and immediately thought, *My God, this is a book. It has everything. It has drugs. It has sex. It has lesbians. It has murder, loyalties, mixed loyalties, betrayals. It is a microcosm of the seamy side of life.*

Anderson and Thomas talked for thirty minutes, maybe an hour. She reassured him that someone was there for him and that she would file the motions he wanted her to file. Justin seemed intelligent, on top of things. K. C. Anderson never saw any other side of him. Not then, not ever.

Kim LeBlanc spent the four weeks following Justin Thomas's arrest in inpatient drug rehabilitation in Houston. As part of Kim's rehab, she finally claimed to her mother that Kenneth Dwain LeBlanc, Cathy's husband of almost eighteen years, had raped her.

On August 1, 1995, Ken moved out of the Dripping Springs house he shared with Cathy and ran to Baton Rouge, Louisiana. A week later, on August 8, 1995, Kim's mother filed for divorce in the 200th Judicial District Court of Travis County, Texas, the Honorable Jon Wisser presiding. Wisser normally handled criminal cases.

Cathy was forty-two years old. Ken was fifty-two years old. She was represented by the law firm that had employed her for more than a decade.

"The marriage has become insupportable because of discord or conflict of personalities between Petitioner and Respondent that destroys the legitimate ends of the marriage relationship and prevents any reasonable expectation of reconciliation," said the original petition for divorce.

As part of the divorce settlement, Cathy received her three-year-old Pontiac Bonneville, her retirement funds, her bank accounts, some Wal-Mart stock, the Dripping Springs house less $10,000 to Ken, the adjoining lot, another lot in another subdivision, and her clothing and personal effects.

She was also ordered to pay off all existing credit-card debt jointly incurred by herself and her soon-to-be ex-husband.

Ken received his brand-new 1995 Mazda truck, his retirement funds and bank accounts, and absolutely no financial obligations to his stepdaughter Kim LeBlanc, with the exception that Kim and Cathy would be covered by his medical insurance. He was not civilly sued for rape. However, according to prosecutor Gregg Cox of the Travis County District Attorney's Office, Ken LeBlanc didn't deny Kim's accusation.

On October 25, 1995, the final divorce papers were mailed to Ken in Baton Rouge. By then, his stepdaughter was about to be released from a supervised home, still a part of drug rehab. Through the help of a twelve-step program, Kim had survived suicidal days.

Cathy sold the Dripping Springs home to pay for an attorney for Kim.

Justin Heith Thomas never left jail, and the next thirteen months were rough. Dawn told him that their daughter, Harlie, was not his. "You're a liar," he told her. "You're just doing this to hurt me, to break any ties with me."

Jim Thomas phoned K. C. Anderson to ask her a few questions. "This is my first murder case," she admitted. "But I'm certainly associated with very skilled lawyers, and I'll be able to handle it. But it won't hurt my feelings if you want to look around and hire another attorney."

Thomas mentioned names of attorneys with whom he wanted to talk. He conveyed to Anderson that he was puzzled by Regina Hartwell's murder and that he felt responsible.

"How about Patrick Ganne and Jim Sawyer?" said Anderson. She was married to Ganne, but she also believed he and Sawyer were the best criminal attorneys in Austin.

Jim Thomas, though he seemed poor, said he had access to some money—he owned land in Oregon.

"If that's all you have," asked Anderson, "would you feel better if you didn't spend it and went with a court appointed attorney and lost, or would you feel better if you did spend it and got a hired attorney and lost?"

"No, question," said Jim, with softness in his voice, "I'd much rather spend everything I have and know I've done everything I could." His hurt revealed itself in his tenderness.

Anderson stayed on the case until Thomas found a way to hire Ganne and Sawyer; that happened a year later, just before the trial began.

On September 28, 1995, at 4:36 p.m., the Travis County Grand Jury filed an indictment in the 147th Judicial District Court of Travis County, Texas against Justin Thomas for the murder of Regina Hartwell. At the time, Hartwell had been dead almost three months.

The indictment stated "that Justin Thomas, on or about the 29th day of June A.D. 1995, and before the presentment of this indictment, in the County of Travis, and State of Texas, did then and there intentionally and knowingly cause the death of an individual, namely, Regina Hartwell, by stabbing Regina Hartwell with a knife, a deadly weapon, that in the manner of its use and intended use was capable of causing death and serious bodily injury.

"And The Grand Jury further presents that on or about the 29th day of June A.D. 1995, and before the presentment of this indictment in the County of Travis and State of Texas, Justin Thomas did then and there, with intent to cause serious bodily injury to an individual, namely, Regina Hartwell, commit an act clearly dangerous to human life, to wit: stabbing Regina Hartwell with a knife, a deadly weapon, that in the manner of its use and intended use was capable of causing death and serious bodily injury, thereby causing the death of said Regina Hartwell, against the peace and dignity of the State."

* * *

On November 20, 1995, K. C. Anderson filed eight motions including those for discovery, to suppress evidence, for production of evidence favorable to the accused, and for investigative and expert assistance fee in indigent case.

On December 30, 1995, Thomas set a small fire in the jail. Three months later, he got fed up with the slowness of the legal process and, on March 29, 1996, filed his own handwritten motion for discovery and inspection "to insure [sic] proper representation."

Dawn Thomas divorced him.

On April 11, 1996, at 4:06 p.m., the Travis County Grand Jury filed an indictment in the 147th Judicial District Court of Travis County, Texas against Kim LeBlanc for the murder of Regina Hartwell.

The indictment stated "that Kim LeBlanc, on or about the 29th day of June A.D. 1995, and before the presentment of this indictment, in the County of Travis, and State of Texas, did then and there intentionally and knowingly cause the death of an individual, namely, Regina Hartwell, by stabbing Regina Hartwell with a knife, against the peace and dignity of the State."

The following day, an arrest warrant was issued and bond was set at $50,000. On April 18, 1997 Kim LeBlanc turned herself in to the Travis County Sheriffs Department. Quickly, she was released on personal bond.

Not long before his trial was scheduled to begin, Justin Thomas's financial arrangements for new attorneys were

finalized by his father—one hundred acres of Oregon property
to be deeded over to Patrick Ganne and Joe James Sawyer, an
old law school buddy of Ganne's. Jim Thomas was also to build
them some fine wooden cabinets.

On June 26, 1996, Ganne and Sawyer filed motion after
motion. That continued well into July.

On July 16, 1996, Judge Jon Wisser, the same judge who
had granted Cathy LeBlanc's divorce, granted Kim LeBlanc
immunity from her testimony. Anything she said in court
could not be used against her and could not be used to gain
evidence against her.

Two days later, Ganne filed a motion to compel disclo-
sure of any agreement with co-defendant Kim LeBlanc.
Eleven days later, Ganne and Sawyer filed another motion
to declare LeBlanc an accomplice.

Thomas's trial was postponed.

Justin got a new girlfriend, a high-school-aged runaway
whom he met through his cellmate. They communicated
through jail windows by gang-style hand gestures. She was
there in the courtroom the day the trial started, and she was
there everyday, often in cutoff blue jean shorts. August in
Austin is always hot and miserable.

August 13, 1996 was no different. Innocents and criminals
alike could step into the day and break into a frying sweat in
ten seconds flat. But in the District Court 331st Judicial District of Travis County, it was black and chilly.

Closed, black mini-blinds covered two long walls of the
courtroom and kept sun and sound at safe distance. Air con-
ditioning blew too strong.

A khaki-clad Travis County Sheriff's deputy ushered Justin
Heith Thomas into the courtroom. Thomas wore dark slacks,

a white shirt, and a tie. He looked at his attorneys, Patrick Ganne and Joe James Sawyer, street-fighters who were dressed like TV evangelists. They wore sharp, expensive suits, silk ties, gold cufflinks, and gold watches.

Ganne, a Navy Reserve pilot with a luncheon taste for good wine and good cigars, was perfectly tanned. Sawyer had piercing, dark eyes, salt-and-pepper brows, a tight butt, stained teeth, and also a taste for good red wine. Time and time again, around the Travis County Courthouse, Sawyer was described simply: "slick." He was even known to refer to himself on occasion, including in this trial, as a "slick dog."

Sawyer and Ganne stood to the left of the state's attorneys, lead prosecutor Gregg Cox and chief prosecutor Gail Van Winkle. Cox, a slight, but determined, young man, walked with the unafraid confidence of a strong, wiry bull terrier.

Van Winkle, with tightly curled brown hair, was smart, erect, and had a dancer's posture. She, too, was determined, so much so that some thought she was unfeeling. She was not. She was simply controlled, like a dancer. It was her father's teaching. A law professor at the University of Houston, he was theoretical and brilliant. Over dinner, he never gave his children a straight answer. It was good training for a lawyer.

Retired, but visiting, Judge Larry Fuller called the attorneys to attention. Thin, with slicked-back, graying hair, he ran his courtroom like a saloon—loose, freewheeling, with humor, with respect for the customers, criminals, and jurors alike. He motioned to prosecutor Cox.

Cox looked at the jury pool, his eyes dark and intense. "The most important thing is that you only accept evidence from the witness stand." His voice was calm and methodical. "The testimony of witnesses or through exhibits that are entered into evidence." He seemed at ease, trustworthy. "What we, as lawyers, say in the case in opening statements and closing arguments is not evidence, and you're not to consider it as such."

His words went uncontested by the defense. "When you're looking at a witness who's testifying, you don't have to believe everything that witness says. You don't even have to believe anything that witness says." He was reassuring.

"You can determine a witness's credibility by looking at things such as their demeanor when they testify, the motives they may have to testify a particular way, any biases they have, their opportunity to observe, or the reasonableness of their testimony. Your most important tool in this case is going to be your common sense."

Those were some of the last words prosecutor Gregg Cox spoke that went uncontested by the defense. Time and again, the defense objected during the selection of the jury. Sawyer and Ganne watched carefully the reactions to their objections.

Then Sawyer stood. He straightened his cuffs and cufflinks. He looked at the jury pool, and he talked about his father, the sharecropper. Dramatically, he talked, like a Pentecostal preacher.

He talked about the movie *Body Heat,* about how a beautiful woman can manipulate a man into murder. "You're dumb. I like that in a man," he quoted. He closed with, "If you're going to . . . hold it against the lawyers for objecting, you're depriving the defendant of a fair trial, aren't you? If you just hate the lawyer and think, *'God, that slick dog, I don't like him,'* are you giving the defendant a fair shake? Probably not."

The man who had just called himself a slick dog sat down.

The prosecutors and defense lawyers picked their jurors. Ten of the jurors were college graduates. Several of them had advanced degrees. Three of them were engineers, and two were attorneys—a young, practicing attorney and mother of two, and a young Texas A&M University graduate who had recently taken the bar and was awaiting the results.

Outside the presence of the jury, the attorneys argued whether there was "a deal" between Kim LeBlanc and the state. The defense asserted that there was a deal and the proof was in the indictments. Justin Thomas's indictment noted use of a deadly weapon, and Kim LeBlanc's indictment, in the defense's view, made no mention of a deadly weapon.

Prosecutor Gregg Cox angrily argued that the indictments were equal. "My charging decision is not any sort of any agreement with anyone!" Cox shouted.

"Yes, it is," said the defense. "A fix is a fix."

"There have been no discussions of any deals whatsoever," said Cox.

"I know that they think they don't have a deal," said the defense. "The word 'deal' means something different to the state than it does to me. I accept that."

Judge Fuller overruled the defense, and Court recessed for lunch.

At 2:05 p.m., court reconvened, again outside the presence of the jurors, so that the defense attorneys could present their objections to the state's motions *in limine.* Patrick Ganne wanted the freedom to ask witnesses about motivation, bias, and prejudice. The state wanted the Judge to rule before the defense could ask such questions.

"And my response," said Ganne, "is that I think . . . [Cox is] trying to gain a strategic advantage by interrupting the flow of questioning so as to allow us to approach the bench, get the ruling, seek permission, get the ruling to go into it, and warn his witnesses at the same time that the hammer is about to drop on them."

"Judge," pleaded Cox.

"You've been watching TV, Ganne," said Fuller.

"Your Honor," Ganne continued, "what he's trying to do is interfere with trial strategy. If I'm going to an improper area, I'm sure that the way to stop it is for him to object, for you to make a ruling. If that's what it comes to."

"I'm asking before he gets into stuff that he knows is probably objectionable, that we approach the bench and talk about it," said Cox.

"I'm not going to do that," replied Ganne. "I'm not going to knowingly, intentionally ask inappropriate or objectionable questions."

"My God, Ganne," said Judge Fuller. "You expect to sell that to the Court? You talk about taking advantage of the elderly."

The arguments proceeded, and Judge Fuller added, "Probably ought to open this Court with a prayer before we bring in the jury. You want me to rule on that?"

Again the arguments continued, and Ganne stated, "What we're asking is that when a witness is passed, we don't want to be running up to the bench every five minutes."

"Well, I don't think this means every witness, surely," said Fuller. "You're not going to be doing this to police officers." Fuller looked at Jim Sawyer. "What did you whisper? I read lips, too." Fuller sustained the defense's objection.

More arguments continued briefly; then prosecutor Van Winkle read the indictment against Thomas.

"Justin Thomas, how do you plead?" said Fuller.

"Not guilty."

Opening statements began before a packed courtroom, so packed that one could no longer see that the gallery chairs were dirty orange, like a Halloween gone bad, that the carpet was tan, the walls yellow ochre.

There were reporters. There were Mark and Dian Hartwell. There were observers. There were friends of Regina's, well-dressed, bright, young, flamboyant Gen-Xers who chattered and hugged each other often.

Gregg Cox stood. In a soft, smooth voice, he made a brief opening statement—Justin Thomas stabbed Regina Hartwell after she threatened to turn him in to police for dealing drugs. "She was jealous of Justin, and you're going to hear evidence Justin was jealous of her; his girlfriend being such close friends and accepting money from Regina."

Thomas and LeBlanc "then came up with a plan of chopping up the body, putting it in a trash can with some cement, wrapping a chain around, dropping it in the Colorado River. They went into town, went to Builders Square, and purchased the trash can, two bags of cement, a chain, and a padlock. And they drove back to Bastrop.

"In the meantime, Justin had called a friend to ask to get some help in getting rid of her Jeep. When they got back out there from Builders Square, they figured they couldn't get rid of the Jeep very quickly. It's going to take some time. And his family had come home. And Kim's going to tell you they found out what had happened, and they told him to get that body out of there and they didn't want this going on.

"So she said that Justin came up with a new thing."

He burned Regina's body.

The jurors glanced at Thomas. In slacks, shirt, and tie, he looked like a handsome University of Texas football player. Patrick Ganne wanted them to see Thomas as a dumb, ole farm boy. And he wanted them to see Kim LeBlanc as a Jezebel.

"What I anticipate you're going to hear within the next two

to three days is state-sponsored perjury," said Ganne. "I hope the words shock you. Because they were meant to."

He accused LeBlanc of murder. "What she is is a person who goes not by her own name," said Ganne, his piercing, blue eyes staring right at the jurors, "but she changes her name when it is convenient for her to do so, who sells her body, who sells her sexuality for money."

He told the jurors that Regina Hartwell had bought Kim LeBlanc a matching, identical Jeep Sahara "as a symbol of their wedding" and that Kim had murdered Regina because she believed she was going to inherit $3.7 million from Regina.

"Follow the money," announced Ganne. "Follow the money. You'll find your guilty party."

Ganne looked intently at the jurors. "The prosecutor further has not told you that he's kissed [Kim LeBlanc] on the lips, that is that he's made a deal with her."

"Who we gonna blame," said Ganne, "the people who've been involved for a number of years or the guy who just comes on the scene looking dumb? 'I just love a dumb-looking man. They can be used and become useful at times.'"

Ganne closed, "So I look forward to spending the next few days with you as we navigate these treacherous shoals of falsehoods. The truth will come out. It's so evident that it just cries."

The jurors didn't know that Ganne's and Sawyer's usual, admitted defense tactic was "the bitch did it."

At 2:40 p.m., the first witness took the stand for the prosecution, Bluebonnet Volunteer Fire Chief Terry Duval. He painted the picture of Regina Hartwell's burning. As the photograph of her flaking, crispened, black corpse flashed before the courtroom, stomachs turned.

Even Justin Thomas didn't want to look, despite the fact that he was no stranger to the gruesome. If Hartwell's tar-baby black corpse had been someone from his California days, back when Thomas "took care" of business, he wouldn't have thought twice about staring at that grotesque photograph.

Regina was different, however. She was someone he'd spent time with, had fun with, developed a relationship with. But Thomas showed no reaction.

Regina's friends, in tears, shoved open the court's swinging wooden doors and ran for the restrooms to vomit.

"What? What?" asked Anita Morales. "Tell me what's going on." Anita, not allowed in the courtroom because she was scheduled to testify, sat in the hallway. She was furious that she couldn't listen to the trial. No one, she thought, loved Regina as much as she. Anita sat back down and waited.

Witnesses came and went quickly. Bastrop County Sheriff Deputy John Barton told of seeing the body and calling for a homicide investigator. Joy Parrot, an employee of Regina's childhood dentist, told of turning over Regina's dental records to Mark Hartwell.

Joel Hartwell, Regina's uncle, testified more about Regina's dental records, as well as her inheritance. He, rather than Mark Hartwell, took the stand so that Regina's father could sit in the courtroom and listen to the complete trial.

"Mr. Hartwell," said prosecutor Gail Van Winkle to Joel Hartwell, "I believe you testified you came to Austin with your brother and you were present at a probate hearing. Is that correct?"

"Yes, I was," said Joel Hartwell.

"Who received Regina's estate?"

"Her father."

He pointed out Mark Hartwell, the man wearing glasses and a white shirt and tie.

The prosecution then called to the stand Deputy Robert Gremillion of the Bastrop County Sheriff's Department. He stated that he was at the scene of the fire, had helped collect evidence, had seen the knife wrapped in blue cloth under Regina Hartwell's body, and had escorted her burned Jeep from the fire site to the the county's sullyport, a holding area for prisoners that was also used as a holding area for vehicles.

Jim Sawyer watched Gremillion. "Now," said Sawyer as he cross-examined the deputy, "were you surprised—I'm just asking you about you personally—were you surprised to find a knife—may I approach the bench, Your Honor?—wrapped, I take it the cloth seemed to have been wrapped around it to preserve it or protect it, wouldn't you agree?"

"I would think," said the deputy.

"Surprised to find that knife there under the body?"

"No," said Gremillion.

"Well, let me ask you this," said Sawyer. "If she had been shot to death, if that turned out to be the evidence, would you have been surprised to find a gun wrapped in a cloth stuck under the body, a dead body of a person you find in a Jeep?"

"Not really," answered the deputy.

"Not really," Sawyer repeated, incredulously. "So let me see. You think it's kind of not unusual that someone lights a fire that can be seen a mile away and leaves a weapon wrapped in a cloth under the body in a Jeep that's being burned?"

"In my opinion, yes, they're going to leave [a weapon], especially being a wood handle like that, near the source of ignition, the highest temperature," said the deputy.

"Why not leave it out without being wrapped, and away from the body, so it would burn with the rest of the car?"

"Maybe his thinking was that it was more fuel around it with the cloth," answered Gremillion.

At 4:30 p.m., court recessed until 9:10 the following morning.

CHAPTER 21

On Wednesday, August 14, 1996, day two of the trial of Justin Thomas, Deputy Gremillion briefly took the stand once again. He stated that as soon as he was on the scene of the fire, he had smelled fuel, and, the closer he had moved toward the Jeep, the stronger the smell had gotten.

Detective David Campos, in charge of CID at the Bastrop County Sheriff's Department, then testified about transporting the slightly charred knife to the Texas Department of Public Safety Lab on July 7, 1995 and releasing evidence, including the scorched, blue cloth and trash can, to APD Detective Doug Dukes on July 10, 1995.

Officer Timothy Pruett stepped up to the stand next to tell of the missing-person report he had taken on Regina Hartwell. He had noticed dried blood on a statue, he said, but Regina's friends had not seemed concerned about it. They had been concerned, however, that her dog had been unattended and that her makeup had been in her apartment.

Kim LeBlanc, he said, had been worried too, but she had not talked a lot. LeBlanc had admitted, however, that she had been on Hartwell's bank account and could have used Hartwell's ATM card anytime she'd wanted.

The following day, July 5, 1995, stated Pruett, he had

received a computer message from APD Homicide telling him to contact them. He also had received a call from Ynema Mangum telling him that a great deal of money was gone from Regina Hartwell's account. At 2 a.m., on July 7, he had written up a report for Homicide.

As Officer Pruett exited the courtroom, he stopped near Anita Morales. He apologized to her.

Eighteen minutes after Officer Pruett had begun his testimony regarding the missing-persons report filed by Anita Morales, Ynema Mangum, Kim LeBlanc and Jeremy Barnes, Barnes was called to the stand.

He stared at Thomas. Justin didn't look the same as Jeremy had remembered. Before, Thomas had looked presentable. In court, to Jeremy, Justin Thomas was deadly frightening. There was nothing in his eyes. They were empty.

Gregg Cox turned to Barnes. "Did Regina have a motor scooter of some kind?"

"Yes," said Jeremy, "she did."

"And are you aware of an accident that occurred with that scooter?"

"Yes."

"Who was driving when the accident occurred?"

Barnes didn't want to look at Thomas, but he couldn't take his eyes off of him. Never before had Jeremy believed in the death penalty. Then looking at Justin, testifying in the face of the man he believed had stabbed to death Regina Hartwell, he believed in an eye for an eye, a tooth for a tooth. "Justin Thomas."

"When did that happen?" asked Cox.

"It was before they went on their trip," answered Barnes.

He testified about seeing an upset Regina the night before she died, about Regina leaving a message on his machine the next day, about cleaning up her apartment, about thinking the blood in her apartment was from a nosebleed, about searching for Regina, and about finding Kim LeBlanc in Regina's apartment scrubbing the rust stain with liquid detergent and crying, "I'm trying to get this blood off."

He told the jurors about cleaning out the apartment again with Kim and Anita Morales and about making the missing-person report. He told of his conversation with the Bastrop County Sheriff Deputy and of the subsequent arrival of the Austin Police Department. To the court, he pointed out Justin Thomas. "He's wearing a light, cream shirt with a tie, a pair of khakis."

"Did you ever see Mr. Thomas with a Mohawk?" asked Gregg Cox.

"No."

"Did you ever see him with his hair dyed black?"

"No, not that I remember."

More officers took the stand. APD Detective John Hunt testified about his arrival at the James Thomas home and his encounters there with Kim LeBlanc and Justin Thomas, about his transporting Kim to APD, and his cellphone conversation with Cathy LeBlanc.

He then stated that he had spent approximately five hours with Kim LeBlanc, and that during that time she had been "cooperative but hard to understand because she spoke so softly and quietly and was so detached."

He also said that Justin Thomas had not been handcuffed at the Jim Thomas house.

Under cross-examination, Hunt admitted that LeBlanc had tried to leave the interview room and that she had mumbled, "I'm caught." He also stated that at 7:16 p.m. on July 5, 1995, after being alone with her parents for fifteen or twenty minutes, LeBlanc had knocked on the door of the interview room and invoked her right to an attorney.

Next, Detective Douglas Dukes testified to going to the Regina Hartwell apartment on July 5, 1995 and spending several hours there "holding up a wall." He told of witnessing the Luminol test done by the Texas Department of Public Safety Crime Lab team, and of seeing a large piece of carpet glow with the Luminol.

He stated that on July 10, 1995, he had gone to the Bastrop County Sheriff's Office, met with David Campos, and received and transported some evidence, including the five-gallon gas can.

Dukes also said he had been present at the search of Kim LeBlanc's apartment and that on July 5 he had conducted the interview of Brad Wilson.

Texas Ranger Rocky Wardlow stepped up to the stand. He told the court about searching Regina's apartment and meeting Kim LeBlanc on the night of July 5, 1995. "She looked extremely tired," said Wardlow. "Weak. Frail might be another word that might be used."

The jurors were shown a police photo of LeBlanc, taken that July night. In the Polaroid shot, Kim wore a dark-colored tank top. Her hair was short. Her red, drugged eyes were half-shut. Her swollen nose and lips were chapped scarlet.

He said LeBlanc had been cooperative and that he had gotten a consent to search from her parents. He stated that he had booked Justin Thomas. Wardlow was shown a mug shot of Thomas—hollow-cheeked, hollow-eyed, and Mohawk-coiffed. "Yes, ma'am," said Wardlow to Van Winkle, that accurately depicted Thomas on July 5.

He testified to having seen the cut on Justin Thomas's hand.

He stated that he had searched the Thomas home the following day and obtained weapons, a trash can, bags of cement, a new chain with a locked lock on it, Kim LeBlanc's purse containing receipts and a fake Kentucky driver's license, and Kim's Jeep.

And, he had searched Kim LeBlanc's apartment. There, blood had been found. On September 21, 1995, he had obtained an evidentiary search warrant for blood, hair, and saliva samples from Justin Thomas, which had been taken in Wardlow's presence.

Elmer Ballard, assistant manager of Builders Square, took the stand next for less than nine minutes to verify the authenticity of the hardware store receipt found in LeBlanc's purse.

On that second day of trial, at 3:31 in the afternoon, Kim LeBlanc entered the courtroom. In shock, everyone stared. Unlike her police photograph, which had been displayed earlier in the courtroom, Kim looked healthy and alive. Her dress was conservative and nice. She looked sweet, innocent, like a University of Texas sorority girl.

"Is your attorney in the courtroom?" asked Cox.

"Yes, sir," said LeBlanc, softly.

"And who is that?"

"John C. Carsey."

John Carsey was a former University of Texas basketball star who made 6'4" Justin Thomas look small.

"John, will you raise your hand," said Judge Fuller.

Carsey glided his hand into the air like a player on well-oiled wheels.

"Your Honor," Ganne interrupted, urgently, "1 think he ought to be identified for whom he works."

"What?" said Fuller.

Carsey was also the son-in-law and law partner of Roy Minton, Austin's most notorious attorney. Minton, a University of Texas alum, had represented the publicly traded Freeport McMoran for another wealthy and influential U.T. alum.

Minton, and anyone affiliated with his law firm, was an attorney with clout among D.A.s, U.T. supporters, and judges. His close ties to prosecutors and judges, pointed out one local magistrate, were symbolized by the location of his offices, across from the D.A.'s office and across from the courthouse.

"It doesn't matter where he works," said Fuller.

But to Ganne and Sawyer it mattered. They believed the Carsey-Minton-D.A.-judge connection was why their client was on trial by himself rather than with his co-conspirator, Kim LeBlanc—LeBlanc had the attorney with the bigger clout. On top of that, they believed, LeBlanc had the Caucasian-beauty clout—*Beauty and the Beast* the defense attorneys dubbed the case.

Finally, the beautiful twenty-year-old Kim LeBlanc, protected by immunity, got into her testimony. She talked about how she had met Regina Hartwell. She told the court that, no, Regina hadn't bought her her Jeep—she'd had her Jeep since she was seventeen years old, since before she had met Regina. But Regina had given her a multitude of other gifts.

LeBlanc spoke of the diamond ring and of the $5,000 mutual fund Regina had set up for her.

"Did she tell you this was your money?" said Cox.

"Yeah, it was in my name, is what she told me."

"And did she deal mostly with you, as far as the financial things like that, or did she deal with someone else?"

"No," said Kim. "She dealt with my mother."

"Okay," replied Cox. "Did your mother and Regina know each other?"

"Yes."

"Did your mom understand your relationship with Regina?"

"I really—" Kim stuttered and stalled, "I think she did. She had to. We didn't talk about it other than at my home about it, but she knew that I cared for Regina a lot and that I spent the majority of my time with her."

"Okay. Now, did Regina ever talk to you about putting you in her will or giving you any kind of inheritance? Was anything like that ever discussed?"

"No."

"Did you ever feel uncomfortable accepting all these monies, gifts and so forth from Regina?" said Cox, his voice calm.

"Yeah, ah, in the beginning, because I've never been around anybody with a lot of money, and in the end because I realized I wasn't a lesbian. And, yeah, that was the source of a lot of discussions between her and I [sic]." Kim's voice sounded deep and older than her years.

"Why did you continue to take money from her?"

"Because I didn't want to go back home."

"Were there problems in your home life?" said Cox.

Kim paused. "Yeah," she spoke softly, but firmly. "There were. There were problems."

"So you didn't want to live with your parents," said Cox. "Is that correct?"

"No. My father [sic] was a very sick man."

"If you had not accepted money from Regina, would you have been able to live on your own in the current state that you were in?"

"No, I wouldn't have. Today I know that anybody can live on their own, but at this time I had never lived without my parents or without somebody taking care of me, and so I was definitely convinced that there was no way I would be able to make it without her money. I would either have to go home or I would have to stay with her."

LeBlanc was business-like and detached as she talked

about Regina Hartwell, her once friend and provider and lover, as she talked about their drug use, as she talked about Justin. Her coldness turned off many in the courtroom.

They just didn't know that that's the way sexual abuse victims cope—by detaching, by going outside themselves, by leaving their bodies so that they can no longer feel. No one had ever told them that.

Kim told them, though, what it was like to use drugs.

"By the time that you knew Regina, what sort of drugs were you using?" asked Cox.

"When I knew Regina I was doing Ecstasy."

"What is that?"

"It's a, well, it's a drug that . . . I really don't know what it is. It's a pill," she laughed. "I probably should have known what was in it, but it's got heroin in it. It's got a little bit of cocaine in it. It's got . . . it's a pill that looks like a vitamin C pill, and you take it and it makes you feel like—lowers your inhibitions and makes you feel sexual. It's a very relaxing kind of drug."

"Okay," Cox responded. "Were you using cocaine when you first met Regina?"

"No."

"Okay. Did Regina use drugs?"

"Yes."

"What sort of drugs did she use?"

"Ecstasy, mushrooms, cocaine."

"Did you use cocaine with her in the beginning?"

"No, sir."

Kim LeBlanc talked about partying with Regina at Manuel's, Club 404, and Oil Can Harry's.

"At some point," said Cox, "during this time that you were having this relationship with Regina, did the nature of the relationship change in any way?"

"I don't understand the question," said Kim. "Did it change?"

"You were dating in the beginning, you said."

"Right," LeBlanc answered.

"Okay. Was that always the case?"

"Yeah," she said. "We were always, I mean, when I say I was dating Regina, I didn't go out with anybody else, ever. That would have been bad."

LeBlanc told the court about meeting Justin Thomas, about snorting crystal meth with him, about Justin, Kim, and Regina doing drugs together, and about Justin's drug dealing.

"Now, did Regina—was she interested in this drug dealing?"

"Yeah," answered Kim. "Mainly because she was concerned about me being involved with Justin if she wasn't there."

"Did she get herself involved in it somewhat?"

"Yes, she did. She was always real protective, and she wanted to—she wanted Justin and her to work together to sell it in Club 404, and she wanted to become a part of it between [sic] the guy in California also, and she wanted to become more part of it so she could be there in some way to protect me."

"Now, she wanted to sell in Club 404. Had that ever happened before?"

"It happened once," said Kim.

"Okay. Could you tell the jury about that?" said Cox.

"Regina and I and Justin went into Club 404, and Justin had some packets of crystal meth in his—they come in little Ziplocks—and put them in his sock, and we walked in and Regina knew everybody there, and so she would get one of her friends and then they would come over, they would give her the money and Justin would give them the drugs, but it didn't last very long."

Cox glanced at Thomas. "Did he like doing that?"

"No."

"Why?"

"He didn't want people to know what his face looked like."

She talked about seeing a shipment of crystal meth for Justin arrive at Justin's father's apartment in South Austin.

She told the court that the shipments had stopped after they had gotten back from Cancun because Justin's California connection, a man named Rochon, had thought it too dangerous. By then, she was hooked on drugs and needed them daily, said LeBlanc, but Thomas couldn't get the drugs she needed.

"And so Regina and I—I started to hang out with Regina more and doing more cocaine with her because she had cocaine dealers around Austin that she knew."

"What would y'all do during the day?" said Cox. "I mean, is that all you did?"

"We went shopping, sometimes. We['d] usually wake up, call Diva, get drugs. She liked to drive when we would get the drugs. We'd do some drugs, we'd drive around, either hang out at Diva's or, you know, go to the mall, but mainly what we ended up doing was coming back to her house and staying in her room and just doing them there in her room."

"Was Justin around you all during this time?"

"No."

"Where was he usually?"

"He was usually in Del Valle."

"At his father's place?"

"Yeah," she answered.

"Was Regina paying for all the drugs?"

"Yes."

"Did your appearance change at all because of the drug use?"

"I lost about thirty pounds."

"How about Regina?"

"She lost probably like fifteen. She was starting to lose a little weight. She was more, she was more bigger-boned than I was, much stockier. So she didn't lose weight the way I did, but . . ."

"Were you eating much?" asked Cox.

"I ate a lot of ice cream."

"Do you have any idea what you weighed in June of 1995?"

"Eighty pounds."

"What do you weigh now?" said Cox.

"Hundred and twelve," said Kim.

She talked about her fights with Regina Hartwell.

"When you would fight about money, what was that involving?"

"It was involving—" she paused, "she would take offense if she offered to do something for you and you said, you know, 'You really don't have to do that, you know, I appreciate it but, you know, you don't have to.' She would get really offended at that. I would say it to be polite, you know, that is what I was always taught, to be polite to people so that they wouldn't just think you were just, you know, taking advantage of them, but she took that to, she took offense to that because she thought that you were not accepting a gift from her, and if you weren't really excited then you were offending her."

"Did your fights ever get physical?"

"No."

"Did you ever hit Regina?"

"No."

 Did you ever threaten to kill Regina?"

"No."

Cox paused for a very, very long time. "Now, you said that Regina—I'm sorry—Justin was spending most of his time out at Del Valle. Had y'all stopped dating or . . ."

"No," said Kim, "we hadn't stopped dating. It's just when Regina and I were done doing our drugs it was usually at night time because we used all day long, and then I would tell her that I was going to see Justin in Del Valle and I would go see Justin in Del Valle, and when I'd wake up there I always wanted to go back in town because I didn't like being in Del Valle. But he didn't like to go back in town. So I would usually just go back to town by myself, and then Regina would call and then we'd go get drugs and start it again."

LeBlanc then pointed out on a map of South Austin her apartment, Justin's cousin Josh's house, and Regina's apartment.

Just over an hour into LeBlanc's testimony, the court recessed for the day. It was 4:25 p.m.

CHAPTER 22

With each passing day of the trial, the jurors bonded. They couldn't talk about the case, so they talked about themselves—what they'd done with their lives, what they liked to do, who they were, their beliefs, their morals.

They talked over breakfast snacks they brought to share each day—sometimes coffee cakes, sometimes doughnuts, one time breakfast burritos. It was their special time together, like husbands and wives who make a point of sharing morning coffee and conversation. Often, Judge Fuller joined them.

"How are you?" the amicable judge always made a point to ask. He was a man who wore Wrangler jeans and mowed his own ten acres of land. "Are you comfortable?" He was the type who got asked for help, as if he were an employee, as he shopped in Wal-Mart. "Is there anything you need?" It proved to the jurors beyond a reasonable doubt that he cared. It proved to them that he cared about them as human beings—something that mattered in a case that so destroyed humanity and human kindness among friends. All of that made them comfortable in making a very important decision together.

* * *

Gregg Cox looked at Kim LeBlanc and subconsciously squeezed the pen he always kept in his hand.

"Now, toward the end, in the last week or two before her murder, did you ever have arguments with Regina about Justin?"

"Yes," said Kim, "I did."

"Okay. Why? What was the reason you argued?"

"The reason was mainly because she didn't want me going out with a drug dealer and she and him [sic] started to really not get along, at all."

"So did he sort of feel the same way about her?"

"Yeah, he didn't like the idea that she paid for my rent and she was in my life. It was a different situation."

"Was he jealous of her at all?"

"Yeah. She could buy me things he couldn't. She could do things that he wasn't able to do."

She talked about her last argument with Regina—how she had told Regina she was going to go back home. She talked about her last phone conversation with Regina, during which Thomas and Hartwell had argued, Regina had threatened Justin, and Justin had said Regina had said—

"Hearsay," objected the defense.

The jury was sent out of the courtroom.

LeBlanc was questioned further, and Judge Fuller said, "I'm going to allow her conversation as to what happened but not as to . . . I think that's all right, whatever she told him, and I think whatever he told her. And the Court will allow that. But, listen, before you frame those, file those cases away," he said to Cox, referring to Cox's legal backing for the ruling, "let me look at them up here. That's my ruling, but I might as well get educated. If that's all right." He turned to LeBlanc. "Do you understand?"

"No," she answered.

"Well," replied the Judge, "you don't have to."

"Cool," said Kim.

Judge Fuller laughed.

The jury returned to the courtroom, and Cox continued his questioning of Kim LeBlanc about the telephone argument between Hartwell and Thomas.

But LeBlanc's answers weren't revealing what Cox wanted. He looked to Judge Fuller. "Judge, I don't think she's understanding your ruling from earlier. May we approach?"

"I'm trying," said Kim, urgently. "I really am."

"I know you are," comforted Judge Fuller.

"I think," said Jim Sawyer, his voice sandpaper rough, "the proper procedure, simply, the attorney—"

Cox interrupted.

"—may I finish?" Sawyer interrupted, too. "I think the attorney should frame his question and the witness should answer if she can. Clearly, if she can't, another question is in order. I don't think we need huddles and instructions. I object."

"What did he say?" asked LeBlanc.

Judge Fuller looked at her. "It's lawyer talk."

Soon, the questioning resumed, and LeBlanc continued telling the court about Justin's and Regina's telephone argument, Justin's anger, and Kim's and Justin's trip to Del Valle to get the duffel bag, trench coat, and camouflage paint.

"Did he ever specifically say he was going to kill her?"

"He did in my apartment."

She told about their trip to Jim's coffee shop, the Valium she had taken to sleep that night, seeing Thomas leave the next morning, and his return to her apartment.

"What did you notice about him?"

"I noticed that he had blood on his arm and on his upper body. I didn't look at his lower body. I just looked at his upper body."

"Did he say anything to you?"

"No. He did, yeah, eventually he did. He said that it was done."

She talked about seeing the cut on Justin's hand, how Thomas described Hartwell's death, about the burning of the corpse, about their run to the Heritage Inn, about scrubbing the rust stain in Regina's apartment, about making the missing-person report, and about going to the police station.

"What did you tell your parents and the police about Regina?"

"I had told them that she had taken advantage of me against my will, and that Justin had known about it, and was, and had killed her for that reason because he was trying to protect me."

"Was that the truth?"

"No."

"Why did you say that?"

"I thought I really loved him and I wanted to protect him."

"If you wanted to protect him, why did you tell them anything?" asked Cox.

"Well," said LeBlanc, "because I thought that I was going to spend the night in jail, and my parents were telling me that they already knew everything anyways, and that pretty much what I was doing is I was admitting to how much I knew in order to keep myself out of prison because they'd already known everything and that, you know, I could either go along, I could either tell the truth or I could pretend like I didn't know anything, but they already knew."

"Okay. Why did you put this particular twist on it? Why did you say that Regina was bad to you?"

"I wanted to protect Justin, and my stepfather was in the room, and I had just gotten done with several weeks of cocaine use and got kind of confused between who did what to me against my will. It was what was on my mind in that room."

"Did you think that by making it sound like Regina had done something to you that they would go easier on Justin?"

"Yeah."

Cox neared his final questions for Kim LeBlanc. "Are you still in drug treatment at this time?"

"I am no longer in a treatment facility," said LeBlanc.

"I am maintaining a program through therapy, meetings, you know, the whole nine yards."

She often curled up with her twelve-step books while in her attorney's office.

"You have a job now?" said Cox.

"Yes, I do."

"Without saying where you work, what line of work are you in?"

"I'm in early child care."

A gasp filled the courtroom. Then the room went silent with shock. Even Justin Thomas looked up, stunned.

Thomas believed Kim didn't like kids. She had refused to discuss children with him.

"Are you afraid of Justin Thomas?"

"Yes, I am."

"Are you telling this jury the truth?"

"Yes, I am."

"And just briefly, first of all, let me ask you, do you see the person that you know as Justin Thomas, the person that committed this murder, in the courtroom?"

"Yes, I do."

"Could you point him out and identify for the jury by something he's wearing?"

"Point him out?" said Kim.

"Yes. And describe something he's wearing, please."

"He's right there. Justin Thomas."

"What's he wearing?"

"What's he wearing. He's wearing a white shirt, burgundy tie with—"

"That's enough," said the Judge. "Let the record reflect . . ."

Court recessed at 10:35 a.m.

Jim Sawyer stared at Kim LeBlanc. "Ms. LeBlanc, Jim Sawyer is my name." His gravelly voice was nice, polite, easy-going, respectful. "When I'm asking you questions, if I ask you one that confuses you or you simply don't understand it, if you'll let me know, I'll rephrase it so that it's clear to you before you answer it."

"Yes," said LeBlanc.

"And if you feel the question is unfair, if you'll simply let me know, I will try and rephrase it so that you can deal with it fairly. Is that an agreement?"

"Yes, sir."

Sawyer, a man who, like Thomas, had gone into the military because of troubles on the street, ended his politeness.

"First of all, when you were finally indicted in this matter, in April, I think, of this year—is that right?"

"I believe so."

"So about three or four months ago, the State of Texas didn't oppose you being released on a personal bond, did they?"

"That is correct."

"So you haven't been down at the jailhouse waiting on trial, have you?"

"No, I only spent about one day in the jail . . . in a holding cell while I was indicted, I had to walk through—"

"And then it was these prosecutors that took you in front of Judge Wisser and got you the immunity for the testimony that you would give here?"

"I was with John Carsey and the prosecutor."

Sawyer didn't mention that it was the same Judge Wisser who had granted Cathy LeBlanc her divorce.

"And then Judge Wisser gave you a grant of immunity that you understand means basically anything you told the jury today and anything that it might lead to, that that evidence could never be used against you in any other proceeding?"

"My understanding of it was that what I said here would not be used against me at my trial."

"No one had explained to you that any evidence that might

be uncovered as a result of that testimony could likewise not be used against you?"

"That is not my understanding of it."

"It would be a benefit if that were true, wouldn't it, ma'am?"

"Yes," said Kim, "it would be a benefit."

"Has it been explained to you, ma'am, that a statement that a person gives while under the influence of drugs can't be used against them as evidence? Has that been explained to you?"

"Cannot be used against me?"

"Yes."

"No, that has not been explained to me."

"If it is true that that in fact is the law, that is, that the statement which you give while under the influence of drugs can't be used for any purpose because you're not of clear mind, why then, you would have realized a secondary benefit today, wouldn't you?"

"Realized a secondary benefit of what?" asked Kim.

"I'm going to object," said Cox. "He's asking her legal conclusions about issues that have not been litigated."

"Oh, no," said Sawyer. "I think I'm asking her about her understanding of the deal that doesn't exist."

Judge Fuller interrupted. "But, as I understand, she does not recognize what she said."

Sawyer looked straight into Kim LeBlanc's brown eyes. "But it's your contention today that there has been no deal between you and the State of Texas?"

"That is correct," answered Kim.

"But you understand, don't you, that it's going to be up to the prosecutor to make a recommendation about what would be appropriate punishment in your case. You know that, don't you?"

"I don't know who makes a recommendation to who."

"You know that there's going to be a recommendation, don't you?" said Sawyer.

"No, sir, I do not."

"You don't understand that there is a possibility that someone might grant you probation instead of sending you to trial?"

"No," Kim said angrily. "I was told that I needed to be honest because I'm going to go to prison. That's what I was told."

"And so," said Sawyer rather facetiously, "you're up here just testifying out of the goodness of your heart, not trying to gain anything from it."

"Regina was my friend."

"You're here because of your friend and the terrible feelings you now have about her very terrible murder," Sawyer whined. "That's why you're speaking to the jury."

"That is correct."

"It's not because you think that your performance in this trial and the punishment this man might receive, if he's convicted, would influence the State of Texas in how it might treat you. You're not even thinking about that, are you?"

"No, I am not."

"You're a truth-teller, ma'am?"

"When I'm sober."

"Yeah, sober." Sawyer's voice was sarcastic.

"When I'm sober," said Kim, "I am a truth-teller."

"You only lie when you've had drugs."

"Well," she answered, "when I'm on drugs, it's more than likely probably a lie."

Sawyer shook his body to let the jury know his disgust. "But never," he said, "under oath in the presence of the jury."

"I'm doing my best," said Kim. "It's kind of fuzzy, but I'm trying to remember everything as best as I can."

"Doing your best for yourself or for the truth, ma'am?"

LeBlanc was getting tired. "I'm doing the best I can because I'm really nervous and they told me just to tell the truth."

"In the belief it would set you free?"

Sawyer pressed more. "And you mentioned the man who helped conceive you. Did you ever know your father?"

"Yes, I did."

"For how long did you know him?"

"I've known him for twenty years now."

"Is he the man you told the jury was the sick fella the other day, yesterday?"

"No, sir," replied Kim. "That is my stepfather."

"And in what way is your stepfather sick?"

Kim paused for a very long time. Finally, she got the words out. "My stepfather has a fetish for teenage women."

"Are you one of them?" said Sawyer.

"Yes," answered Kim, "I am."

"And when did you first have sexual experience with your stepfather?"

Again, she took a very long pause. "When I was fourteen."

"And did he rape you on that occasion?"

An eternity seemed to pass in that summer courtroom before she spoke. "Yes, um, he did."

"How long did that experience with your stepfather go on?"

"For about four years." Kim began to cry. Her voice weakened so that she sounded like a very frightened, little girl. "This is really not," she choked. "I don't understand why this is being asked. I'm sorry. I don't understand why this has anything to do with this," she wept.

"When did you leave home?"

Kim composed herself. "I believe I was eighteen." Her voice returned to her mature-beyond-her-years sound.

"And," said Sawyer, "had you reported this relationship be-

tween you and your stepfather to law-enforcement authorities
by the time that you left?"

"No, not to any law-enforcement authorities."

"You just told your mother."

"No," LeBlanc said, as though that was the most ridiculous
idea in the world, "I didn't tell my mother."

"You didn't tell anybody?" said Sawyer.

"Oh, no, I did tell people."

"Friends?"

"Yes, close friends." She emphasized the word close.

"Your friend Tim, for example?"

"Yes, my friend Tim, for example."

"Did you have sex outside of that relationship with your
stepfather?"

Cox motioned firmly with his pen. "I'm going to object
to relevance at this point."

"Sex," said Sawyer, "is relevant in this case whether we like
it or not. It's going to be unpleasant, I'm sorry, but I'm going
to keep asking."

"Well, maybe," drawled Judge Fuller, a bit bored. He'd
heard too many sex stories.

"If the Court says no," said Sawyer, "I'm going to stop. You
run this court, Judge, but I don't care if the State likes it or not."

"And the Court is not happy, of course, with these kinds of
trials, but I think that's really true." Judge Fuller had presided
over many trials of child sexual abuse. "The whole . . . the jury
must decide in this case. . . . I just . . . the jury's got to make
this decision on truth-telling, and what weight, credibility. And
unfortunately, reluctantly, but the Court's going to allow it."

Sawyer didn't show his grin. "Outside of that relationship,
when did you begin having sex?"

"It was not a relationship," stated Kim, "and I began having
sex when I was about, I believe, fourteen or fifteen."

"So by the time you left home you had learned at least some

of the advantages of sex, that is, it influences affection and what people might do for you."

Kim's old high-school newspaper was covering the trial.

"That is what my father taught me."

"Not only your father. I'm sure you must have learned that with your boyfriend. That you find them affectionate and re-inforcing and you need to get sex in return instead of just verbal affection."

"I thought that was all I was good for, yes."

"Certainly," said Sawyer, "one thing you thought you were good for was sex. By the time you were eighteen, that was certainly fixed in your constellation of thoughts, wasn't it?"

Kim LeBlanc had met Regina Hartwell in that gay bar six weeks after her eighteenth birthday.

"The subject of sex?"

"The subject of sex and the fact that it was one way you could affirm yourself," said Sawyer.

"Yes."

"Had you had sex with a woman prior to the time that you went to the Club 404 and met Regina?"

"While under the influence of Ecstasy I did experiment once with a close friend of mine."

"And did you find that to be a pleasurable experimentation while you were under the influence of Ecstasy?"

"I found anything to be a pleasurable experience under the influence of Ecstasy."

"So, by the the time you're eighteen, it didn't really much matter if it were a man or a woman in terms of being able to achieve a sense of sexual pleasure, at least while you were under the influence of drugs."

"True," she said a bit weepily.

"Now, you had been . . . how old were you when you met Regina?"

"Eighteen."

"And you had not been able to that point to get away from your stepfather. You were still having to live at home."

"That's true."

"And the reason for that is you simply didn't have the money, the means to get away."

"That is correct."

"And for whatever your own personal reasons might have been, you hadn't gone and reported it to the police so he could be yanked out of the house."

LeBlanc glanced at her mother. "That is correct."

"And that's a state of affairs in your state of mind when you met this woman at the 404 with your friend Tim. Isn't that true?"

Kim looked down. "That is true."

"Now, it became readily apparent to you immediately after meeting Regina that she was attracted to you."

"No, I didn't think she liked me that first night, but she was nice."

"One of the things that you are sensitive to is whether or not someone is attracted to you. Would you agree that's a fair statement?"

"When I was using, yes, that would be a fair statement."

"Is it true when you're sober, you know when a man or a woman is attracted to you?"

"I don't find power in that today." Her voice was calm, detached, mature.

"I'm not asking about the power. I'm asking about the perception."

"No."

"You don't know," said Sawyer incredulously. "But when you're under the influence of drugs you do know."

"When I'm under the influence of drugs that was what I was concerned about, what I was like on the outside."

"The word you used just a moment ago was power. Sex was power, wasn't it?"

"People finding me attractive gave me some power."

"And using sex only reinforced that power, didn't it?"

"Yes, it did."

"Do you remember if it was about two weeks [after you met Regina] before money began going from her hands to yours?"

"Yes, I believe so," said Kim.

"Now, one thing you told this jury yesterday—I want to revisit with you to make sure I understood you—is that in that year that this woman gave you money and established a trust fund for you and gave you rings, one of which you described as an engagement-type ring, in all of that time, . . . you never had sex with her?"

"Is that a question?" asked LeBlanc.

"Yes."

"No," she answered.

"No, you never did. Never even experimented while you are under the influence of Ecstasy."

"After we had broken up, I believe it was probably a week and a half before she was murdered, she and I were in her room doing a lot of cocaine and we experimented."

Sawyer leaned in. "Realizing the delicate nature of it, how far did the experimentation go?"

"We were both naked, and at this time I thought she had HIV. And so she told me that, you know, make sure that I didn't touch her."

"Bodily fluids," said Sawyer.

"Yeah," said LeBlanc. "And so, she had, like, a vibrator, and I used that on her."

"But this was the very first time in all of these gifts and transactions that you even came close to sex with her."

"That's true."

CHAPTER 23

Carla Reid sat in the courtroom taking notes, every day. And every day, she wept for Regina Hartwell.

Justin Thomas sat alert, his head up, watching, listening. He didn't look afraid.

Jim Sawyer watched Kim LeBlanc. "If we were to compare the arguments you had with Regina in the spring of 1995 to the arguments that you had in the fall of 1994, were they the same or were they getting worse?"

"Well, the fall of '94, Regina and I's [sic] arguments were mainly about if her friends liked me and if I was flirting or looking at somebody too long. And in the spring of '95, they were pretty much the same, and they were also about money."

Sawyer smiled to himself. "Money, in fact, became almost the central issue in the arguments that you began having with Regina during the spring and early summer of 1995. She was growing tired of the amount of money and the amounts of money that you were taking. Isn't that true?"

"No."

"It is true, is it not, ma'am?" Sawyer sounded like he were straight from television.

"No," Kim repeated.

"Were you spending the same or more money, in the spring of '95 than the fall of '94?"

"I believe in the spring of '95 I had a job," Kim answered.

"Were you spending more of her money or less of her money?"

"More because she was paying my rent."

"She was paying your rent," he repeated for the jury. "She was giving you gifts. When did you get the engagement ring?"

"Valentine's Day."

"So Valentine's of '95, that early spring of '95, she gives you the ring. Nice ring?"

"Yes, it is a nice ring."

"When did she put the tires on your Jeep?"

"I believe it was before my birthday."

"When is your birthday?" he asked.

"My birthday is May 17th."

"Nice tires on that Jeep?"

"Yeah," answered the country girl from Dripping Springs. "Thirty-one by 10.50s."

"If I understood your testimony from this morning and yesterday, you were increasing the amount of drugs you were doing—greater intensity of usage—late spring, early summer, of 1995."

"Yes, my drug use was increasing."

"She was paying for those drugs."

"Yes, she was."

"Money became at least a feature in your arguments?"

"Yes, they were [sic]."

"Do you remember late May, early June 1995, any discussion about a fifteen thousand dollar withdrawal from her bank accounts?"

"I remember she came over to Tim and I's [sic] apartment and said that somebody had taken a lot of money out of one of her accounts."

"Well," Sawyer drawled, "let's narrow the range of suspects. There are only a number of people that could take money out of her accounts, right?"

"That's true," answered LeBlanc.

"She was one of the them."

"That's true."

"And she was claiming she didn't do it."

"That's true."

"Who were the others?"

"Who were the others?" Kim repeated.

"Yes," answered Sawyer. "Who were the others?"

"To my knowledge, Regina is the only one, or I'm sure her trust officer could."

"What about you?" He looked LeBlanc straight in the eyes.

"I'm not Regina Hartwell," she said.

"No, no, no. When did you acquire the capacity to take money out of her accounts?"

"When she handed me her Pulse card."

"When did you get that Pulse card."

"Probably before, gosh, probably only took her like a month to let me use it. She would give it to me and told me I could go to Diamond Shamrock and Pulse out such and such amount."

"Regardless of what authority she gave you, you had the Pulse card before the time that the fifteen thousand dollars came up missing, didn't you?"

"Yes," answered Kim LeBlanc, "I did."

"And, in fact, she thought you were one of the people who might have taken the money, and she confronted you about that, didn't she?"

"No, she did not."

"She never accused you at all?" said Sawyer, with a huge look of questioning on his face.

"Never accused me of that," said Kim.

"There was never any argument about that money."

"No."

"Just the other money?" he added, as he stared seriously at Kim.

"What other money?" she asked.

"Just the money that you argued about."

"Yes, but it's not the way that you're making it sound."

"I don't want to make it sound," he replied, innocently. "I want you to tell the jury." He motioned toward the jurors. "What money was it that you argued about?" He looked at LeBlanc for an answer.

"I argued about, we argued, one of our biggest arguments was the fact I wanted to sell my CD player to go get an eight ball of coke, and she told me that she was going to pay for it, and that if I sold my CD player, she would get really pissed off at me."

"Did she get pissed off at you on a regular basis during the early spring, early summer?"

"She was kind of moody," Kim understated.

"Trip to Cancun wasn't exactly a roaring success was it?"

"No, it was not."

"In fact," said Sawyer, "if you were to put it on a scale from zero to ten, it was about a minus one, wasn't it?"

"Depending on your scale," answered LeBlanc.

"Well, depending on your continued beneficence from her, it certainly wasn't a good trip as far as the two of you went in terms of your relationship, was it?"

"No," said Kim. "I thought she was dying."

"Thought she," and he emphasized she, "was dying?"

"Yeah."

"In a sense she was, wasn't she? She was very close to being dead, wasn't she?"

"Of AIDS, I thought she was dying." Kim said the word dying strongly and tersely.

"Was she emaciated?" said Sawyer.

"Was she what?"

"Emaciated. Was she losing a great amount of weight?"

"She lost some weight, a lot of bruising."

"A lot of bruising."

"Yeah."

"Where was the bruising coming from?"

"Her legs," answered Kim. "It was on her arms."

"Spontaneous bruising?"

"She didn't say she ever knocked into anything."

"Big bruises. You told the jury yesterday that you lost upwards of thirty pounds and that she lost about fifteen pounds during that last run beginning mid-spring of '95 to the day that she got killed. Remember that?"

"I remember that, but I did not lose thirty pounds. At the time I probably weighed 105. I weigh more now than I ever have."

"In the two weeks prior to the trip to Cancun, you worked up a pretty intense relationship with Justin, didn't you?"

"Yes, I did."

"It's pretty fair to say that his feeling on his part was that he had fallen into a bed of roses where you were concerned. Isn't that true?"

"Fallen into a bed of roses?" questioned LeBlanc.

"Fallen into a bed of roses," the attorney repeated. "He was pretty crazy about you, wasn't he?"

"He seemed to like me, yes."

"Pretty enthusiastic in his response and approach to you, wasn't he?"

"Yes."

"Certainly always there for you physically, wasn't he?"

"Yes," she answered softly.

"Concerned about you, wasn't he?"

"Yes."

"Protective of you."

"Jealous, yes," she said.

"Jealous. Insanely jealous?"

"No," Kim replied, "I would not say insanely jealous."

"Possessively jealous."

"Yes."

"Able to control his jealousy enough to stay at the apartment and let y'all go off to Cancun."

"Yes."

"You came back from Cancun, things were fairly low ebb between you and Regina now, aren't they?"

"Yes."

"I mean really low ebb. Something is about to happen to you, isn't it? If you lose her and her money, you're almost back to where you started, aren't you?"

"Yes."

"Except for one big difference. You are now a full-blown cocaine addict, aren't you?"

"Yes, I am."

"I mean, it's pretty safe to say that what you are is obsessive, about June of 1995, about the need at damn near any cost to have cocaine."

"Yes."

"And the tab," he continued, "the money to buy that cocaine is in danger now of being shut off, isn't it?"

"Yes."

Sawyer looked toward Gregg Cox. "You told Mr. Cox—he was asking you if you had an argument the night before the murder with Regina. Remember that?"

"Yes."

"That argument was really the last argument you were ever going to have with Regina, wasn't it?"

"Yes, it was."

"You told Mr. Cox that you went back to your apartment, you went to sleep with Justin, and that it was Justin who was saying, 'She has got to be killed, and I'm going to kill her,' right?"

"That's what he said the day before, yes."

"And the truth of the matter is, it was because he thought, according to you, that he was going to be turned in for drug-dealing. Is that right?"

"No, I didn't tell him that."

"So he was just going to kill her because he was protective of you?"

"No."

"He was going to kill her because he was half nuts from doing drugs and just thought, 'You know what, I'm going to go over there and I'll do her in.'" Sawyer innocently glanced over at his sometimes sweet-faced client. "Is that what it was?"

"No," said Kim.

"He was going to kill her to try to stop her from doing something?"

"Yes."

"And he brooded on that that night, I presume, when you all were asleep."

"I don't know what he said when we were asleep. I was taking Valium," said LeBlanc.

"Never had any part in his drug-dealing, did you?"

"In his drug-dealing?"

"Yeah. That's something he really carried on by himself or with Regina, but not involving you. That's true, isn't it?"

"I was there, but I'm not—I don't have a very good mind for drug-dealing."

"One thing we know you could do, according to everything you told Mr. Cox, regardless the time of day or night, you knew how to drive that Jeep if it was there to get where you need to go. That is the truth, isn't it?"

"That is the truth."

"That's what you did sometime that night, isn't it? You left your apartment," his voice grew in flamboyance, "you went over, and you, not anyone else, you, went over, went in that apartment where you knew you could go and you killed Regina. You killed her sometime early that morning, didn't you?"

"No, sir."

"You knew that she died of a stab wound, didn't you?"

"Excuse me?"

"You knew she died of a stab wound, didn't you?"

"Yes, I did."

"The truth begins, doesn't it, when you got him, when you got him and told him that you had killed her. That is when the rest of your story starts to become true, doesn't it."

"No."

"Have you ever met Jim Thomas, for example? Have you ever met his father?"

"Yes, I have."

"I want you to look at the jury now and tell me if it is your testimony to them under oath, in the light of our Lord, that that man does drugs and did them with you."

Jim Thomas was not in the courtroom.

"Jim Thomas," answered LeBlanc, "in the light of the Lord, did drugs with Justin Thomas and I."

"Did they also list themselves in this cause as helping you get rid of the body? Did they know there was a body there on the property?" asked Sawyer.

"I don't know that they knew about the body," answered LeBlanc, in contrast to Cox's opening statement.

"You think there's a chance they could have known there was a body?"

"I don't know," she said.

"Did you tell them there was a body?"

"No, I did not."

"If the jury is to believe you, here's what happens. You wake up, and here's Justin saying, 'Look, man,'" and Sawyer whistled in the courtroom, "'I did it. Ha-ha, she's dead,' and you went right along with it."

"I did not stop it."

"Not only didn't stop it, [if] the jury is to believe you, [a] couple of days after the murder, you," and he emphasized you, "not Justin, you proceed on your own in your Jeep—you're the mobile person—and go over to Regina's apartment."

"Yes."

"And you're there for the purpose of examining what you think is going to be this slaughter den—as you told them, blood, everywhere—and you said you didn't see any, remember that?"

"Yes, that's true."

"When Jeremy [Barnes] came in while you were industriously scrubbing away on the sink board, remember that?"

"Yes."

"And you said to him, 'I'm cleaning up blood. I'm cleaning up blood.' You remember saying that?"

"I do not remember."

"You don't remember saying that?"

"No," said LeBlanc, "I don't remember anything after Jeremy came in."

"Because you were so freaked out," said Sawyer.

"Probably," she answered.

"And because of all that cocaine in you?"

"Probably."

"Knowing there was going to be a [a missing-person] report filed, why were you there cleaning up evidence of a crime somebody else committed?"

"Probably because I was trying to protect Justin."

"Because you loved him."

"Yes," answered Kim, "I did."

"Love him more than you loved Regina?"

Kim LeBlane took a very long pause. "I don't know," she said.

"Hard to say," said Sawyer. "Must be difficult to love two people so much at the same time, is it?"

"I wouldn't say that I loved Regina the way I loved Justin."

"When, you cleaned up dope and the paraphernalia to try to protect her . . . you knew she had been burned to a crisp— her body had been—in her own Jeep. Is that true?"

"Yes, I did."

"Because you were there."

"And you sat there with [Regina's friends] while they were smoking cigarettes and talking about her—'My, God,'" and Sawyer began to mimic a shaming crying and whining, "'she's missing. This is terrible.' And you participated in that, didn't you?"

"Yes, I did."

"But it must have been the dope that made you do it. If you had been sober, you would have piped right up and said, 'You know what? That dirty rat, Justin, killed her. She's dead. She's burned to a crisp out in a field in Bastrop County.' That's what you would have done, isn't it?"

"If I was sober," said LeBlanc, "it never would have happened."

"Because you would have called the police and intervened."

"Because I never would have stayed with Justin."

Sawyer looked at Judge Fuller. "May I approach, Your Honor?"

"Yes."

"This knife here," Sawyer showed Kim LeBlanc the single-edged lockblade knife with the slightly scorched wooden handle, "you ever see it?"

"No," Kim answered quietly.

"Complete surprise to you?"

"Yes," she whispered.

"Do you know this was found under her body?"

"No, I didn't know that." Her voice was barely audible.

"Great, big, old bowie knife, isn't it? Isn't that what this is? Not something a little, ole girl would carry, is it? You know girls who carry knives like that?"

"Not personally," said Kim.

"You wouldn't hang around with that kind of company would you?"

"I used to sell knives, so I have hung around with people that have owned knives."

"Where did you sell knives, ma'am?"

"I sold cutlery for Cutco."

"Cutco."

"Uh-huh."

"Knives that were sharp with long blades?" he asked seriously.

"Yeah," LeBlanc answered. "To cut chicken with."

It was an answer that kept Sawyer laughing for months.

"Let us switch forward. Let's go to the police department. When you get there and, you know, when you're asked specifically about that cut on his hand, you don't tell them anything about Regina cutting him, did you?"

"No, I did not."

"You know, it's crazy that you didn't hesitate to say he killed her, did you?"

"No, I did not."

"So here we are. Let me see if I understand how you do this. He did it. Killed this woman, he wrapped her up, he took her out, he burned her. Do you think it's important to spare him that last indignity about that cut in the web of his hand?"

"He told me specifically not to tell anybody where he got that cut from."

Sawyer laughed in Kim LeBlanc's face. "So if he had said, 'Don't tell them I killed her,' you'd have done that, too?"

"I was under the impression," said Kim, "that they already knew exactly what had happened since they had the Jeep and they knew exactly what had happened. My mother had instructed me that right now it was just up to me to tell the truth as best I could because they knew already."

Judge Fuller looked over at the jurors, then back at Sawyer. "Can we quit?" It was noon, and he knew his panel was hungry and needed a break.

"Yes, sir," said Sawyer. He liked his lunches, too.

Judge Fuller turned back to the jurors to let them know that testimony would continue after lunch, but that the defense first needed time to study Kim LeBlanc's statement to the police.

As Kim LeBlanc and her mother left the court, Regina Hartwell's friends glared at them. But the investigator protecting Kim stopped. "Y'all are being really hard on Kim," she said, "and she's all you've got."

Court didn't reconvene, however, until 10:10 the next morning, Friday, August 16, 1996. Despite Judge Fuller's constant attempts to keep his jurors at ease, they were not as comfortable that day.

They were forced to move from the dirty, but large, 331st District Court in the courthouse's newer annex to a smaller room in the main courthouse. Judge, witness, and jurors sat almost elbow to elbow.

Kim LeBlanc was on the stand for her third day in a row. Regina Hartwell's friends still glared at her.

Jim Sawyer looked at her.

"Ms. LeBlanc," he said, "you gave a statement. You remember giving that?"

"Yes, sir, I did."

"And in your statement, if I recall what you told the police, was that you had told Justin that you wanted this woman out of your life. You wanted Regina to be gone. Is that true?"

"That is what I said then."

And that was all Sawyer said, too. He passed the witness.

"Why did you tell the police that?" asked Cox, his voice gentle.

"I told the police that because I wanted to protect Justin."

"How did you think that telling [the] police that you wanted him to take care of this would protect him?"

"I would go to jail for him."

"You still told the police that he did the murder, though, isn't that correct?"

"I figured that would be quite obvious. I thought if I changed the motive to where it seemed more justified, then it wouldn't be as bad. I knew that telling them that he didn't do it would be ridiculous."

"So were you thinking they would go easier on him?"

"Yes," said LeBlanc, "I did, if he had a justified reason for it."

"What did you tell the police was your reason for asking him to do it?"

"I told them that Regina had done some things against my will, and that he knew about that."

"Was that true?" said Cox.

"Yes. She had not done things against my will and I had not told him that."

"Okay. Now, Mr. Sawyer was asking you yesterday about a fifteen thousand dollar discrepancy. Did you have any other access to Regina's money besides the Pulse card or her actually physically giving it to you?"

"No, sir, I did not."

Cox asked LeBlanc about Thomas's motor-scooter accident injuries. "Was there much blood?"

"No," she said. "But it's like when you scratch yourself and there starts to come, like, little droplets because it's a pretty good scratch, you know? It wasn't oozing down his legs, but you could see dark red. It wasn't much, but . . . I asked him if he wanted a paper towel."

"Did he accept it?"

"No. Well, can I go on with the sequence of events?"

"Yes."

"Okay. Then he grabbed the keys to her Jeep and left."

"I believe you testified yesterday that Justin had, at some point, told you how he got to Regina's. What did he tell you about how he got there?"

"He told me that Josh and Carlos had driven and dropped him off at Lamar."

"Who is Carlos?"

"Carlos is a friend of Josh's."

Sawyer focused his dark brown eyes on LeBlanc. "Did you believe that you were in Regina's will as an heir?"

"No," said LeBlanc, "I did not."

"You never held that belief?"

"No, I did not."

"You never told anyone that you were an heir?"

"No, I did not."

Cox held his pen in his right hand, as he often did. "Did you and Justin ever discuss Regina's money?"

"Once or twice about, before she ever—she was killed, he asked me if there was any way that I could go into a bank and since I looked somewhat like her and [sic] get her money, just extract millions of dollars from her bank."

"What did you tell him in response to that?"

"Told him that that was not possible, that I personally did not think I looked that much like Regina either, because she was much bigger than I was and, plus, the fact that people don't walk into banks and extract millions of dollars from the bank by looking like another person."

"Was that the only time you discussed it?" asked Cox.

"After the murder, he told me that it was a shame that we couldn't have gotten any of her money."

The prosecutor passed the witness one last time to Sawyer.

"You mean more than the three hundred dollars a day that you were maxing out everyday after her murder?" said Sawyer.

"More than . . . I'm sorry. Was that a question?" said LeBlanc.

"Yes," answered Sawyer.

"I'm confused," said LeBlanc.

"He was regretting you couldn't get more than the money that you were taking out everyday."

"Yes."

After fourteen minutes, Kim LeBlanc was finally excused from the witness stand.

As she walked past Anita Morales, who still sat daily in the hallway, Anita thought about the investigator's comment—"she's all you've got."

Morales stood up and walked toward LeBlanc. Everyone stopped. The hall fell silent as everyone expected her to tear into Kim, verbally rip her into tiny pieces.

"As much as it is hard for me to say," said Morales, "I want to thank you for having the courage to come and give your side, because without that we wouldn't be able to put him away. And I want you to know that I do appreciate this because I know you don't have to do it."

Tears welled in Anita's eyes. It hurt to look into the face of someone who had had so much to do with taking her best friend's life. Anita's friends led her away, and she wished that Kim LeBlanc had never come into Regina's life, that Kim LeBlanc had never set foot in Club 404.

But there was no changing the past.

Jeremy Barnes watched Cathy LeBlanc. No one spoke to her. He thought about his mother and his family. Some of his brothers weren't the salt of the Earth either, he told himself, and he knew his mother was a wonderful lady. She hadn't raised her sons to be thugs. He didn't think Ms. LeBlanc had raised Kim to be a thug or a drug addict or an accomplice to a murder either.

He tried to put himself in Cathy LeBlanc's shoes, to think of himself as a straight parent with a child in unspeakably horrendous trouble. He felt her hurt, how her heart must grieve.

He walked up to Cathy LeBlanc. "I just want you to know that I feel so sorry for you. I just want you to know that I know it's not your fault, and I cannot hold anything against you. I feel so bad for you having to go through this. I pray for your peace. If you ever need someone to talk to or need an understanding person, please call me. I'm in the book."

But he couldn't speak to Kim. He couldn't look at Kim. It didn't matter if she was all they had.

CHAPTER 24

At 10:24 a.m. on Friday, August 16, 1996, Detective David Carter took the stand. He testified about meeting Kim LeBlanc at APD headquarters, interviewing Justin Thomas, seeing the gash on Thomas's hand, and asking the suspect about it. "He told me that he got the cut when he was helping his father mend some fences."

Carter stated that he had observed the searches of the Jeeps and had spotted a piece of a denim shirt marked "XL" and a piece of burned fabric from perhaps fatigue pants. He also had tried to locate ATM machines that had been accessed with Regina's Pulse card after the murder, in hopes that there would be video of the transactions. There wasn't. And he had obtained blood samples of the deceased and Kim LeBlanc.

Patrick Ganne then cross-examined Detective Carter.

"Aside from the information that you received concerning ATM transactions, you received additional financial information concerning Ms. Hartwell, that is, other accounts that she had," said Ganne.

"Yes, sir."

* * *

"Okay. And one of those is that there are some documents, that Ms. LeBlanc was to receive a sum of money in the event of Ms. Hartwell's death."

"I was told about that, but I never saw any document to that effect," said Carter.

On redirect, Cox said, "And the money that you discovered that Mr. Ganne asked you about that would go to Ms. LeBlanc in the event of Regina's death was the $5,000 mutual fund?"

"I recall $5,000," answered Carter. "I don't recall a mutual fund or what kind it was specifically."

Next, Detective Mark Gilchrest testified to having taken Regina Hartwell's dental records to the Travis County Medical Examiner's office on July 7, 1995 and then, on July 10, 1995, having gone to the Heritage Inn with a photo of Justin Thomas. An employee there, Maria Lisa Davis, had identified Thomas and stated that the couple had checked out on July 1, 1995. She had not identified Kim LeBlanc, said Gilchrest, because he had not had a photo of her.

Court recessed at 12:15 p.m.

After lunch, Dr. Roberto Bayardo, Chief Medical Examiner for Travis County, Texas, sat down in the witness chair.

A veteran of more than twelve thousand autopsies, Bayardo stated that he had identified Regina Hartwell from her dental records, primarily from the permanent retainer she had worn and the two teeth that the retainer had still held.

State's Exhibit Number 73 was the retainer and the two teeth of the late Regina Hartwell. She had begun wearing a retainer just about the time her mother had died.

"She was severely burned, . . . partially cremated," said

Bayardo of Hartwell. "Some parts of her body were missing." But there had been a few clothes. "I found portions of a T-shirt. I found two purple-color pads, and there were also panties."

When he had opened Hartwell's body cavity, Dr. Bayardo had found her right chest cavity completely filled with blood, three pints.

Prosecutor Gail Van Winkle presented the jurors with Regina Hartwell's autopsy photos. Hartwell's guts resembled cooked, pink meat, perhaps pork or salmon, with bright, yellow fat on the side, like lemon or apricot chutney. Stomachs tightened.

Van Winkle introduced photos of Hartwell's lungs. Their absence of soot proved that Regina had died before she was burned. A single-edge blade, three-quarters to one inch in width had killed her, said Bayardo. And, yes, the slightly burned knife found under her body could have been the murder weapon, despite the knife being shorter than the wound.

A chest wall is elastic and can easily be compressed by a strong person, someone like a former football player and body builder, someone like Justin Thomas. So, yes, the wound and blade were consistent, Bayardo stated.

On cross-examination, Dr. Bayardo said that Regina Hartwell may have been asleep or near sleep when she had been stabbed, that perhaps she had been partially upright, and that the perpetrator would not have been covered in blood because the majority of Hartwell's bleeding was internal, not external.

The defense team wanted the jurors to believe that Kim LeBlanc had seduced the sexually dominant Regina Hartwell in the bathtub and that she had stabbed her when Regina was down.

Dr. Bayardo stepped down from the witness chair.

* * *

At 2 p.m., Anita Morales took the stand. She told the jury about Regina Hartwell paging her on the day of the murder, about being worried about Regina, about searching for her, and about paging Kim LeBlanc.

As she spoke, Morales leaned forward in the witness chair, as if anticipating the next question, ready to answer, as though she had things she wanted to say but couldn't. She did have things she wanted to say but couldn't. She believed with all her heart and soul that Kim LeBlanc had been present during the murder.

She testified about finding the blood and LeBlanc in Hartwell's apartment. She talked about filing the missing-person report and told how Kim had cowered away from Anita as she had tried to comfort the crying Kim. Not once did Anita Morales lean back in the witness chair. She was too angry.

Judge Fuller looked over at his jurors. They appeared worn— the autopsy photos had gotten to them. He gave them a break.

While the jurors were out, the prosecutors attempted to present Maximina Bautista, a housekeeper at the Heritage Inn.

Her testimony was a disaster for the prosecution. The Spanish-speaking witness was terrified about testifying. She only occasionally sneaked a look at Justin Thomas. Bautista did admit, however, having run into a man at the Heritage Inn with very short hair, so short that one could barely see it, and that his hand had been wrapped and that the bed sheets had been bloody.

The defense objected on the basis of inadmissibility and irrelevance.

Bautista became more frightened and got quieter.

Gently, Judge Fuller questioned her.

But it was to no avail. The witness was dismissed. Gregg Cox was irate. He'd worked hard to prepare that witness, and then she had frozen tighter than an iceberg. Cox shook his head in frustration and glanced over at Thomas. Thomas was wearing one of his knitted-brow Frankenstein's monster looks. Cox loved being the white-hatted good guy who put monsters like Thomas in prison. "Shit," said Cox, and he stormed out of the courtroom.

Anita Morales again briefly took the stand for cross-examination by the defense. Ganne pounded her, harassed her, and tried to infuriate her. Hartwell's friends cringed in the gallery, fearing she would blow. But she didn't. Two minutes later, Anita Morales was off the stand.

The parade of witnesses continued. Robbye Cellota, LeBlanc's and Thomas's boss at World Gym, testified. He said that Thomas had worked at World Gym for four to six months. Cellota had met Kim when she was a junior in high school when she had worked part-time, on weekends, in the gym's gift shop. In May of 1995, said Cellota, Kim had worked at the gym for eleven days as a receptionist.

He stated that he hadn't known about LeBlanc's and Thomas's relationship. Yet, when Thomas had phoned Cellota about the Jeep, Cellota had presumed it was Kim's that Thomas had wanted to sell.

No one questioned Cellota as to why he would make such a presumption when he had just testified that he hadn't known about the couple's affair.

After eight minutes, Cellota left the courtroom. Michael Mihills, one of Thomas's posse, took the stand.

Mihills, a very reluctant witness for the prosecution, talked about seeing Justin Thomas at Jim's restaurant the night before the murder. Justin was "somewhat, but not really nervous," he said. He told the jurors that sometimes he and Justin had smoked pot and done crystal meth together.

* * *

Judge Fuller looked over at the jurors for one last time that day. He thanked them for their duty. He apologized for sending them out of the courtroom and for the delays. He told them they'd be in Courtroom 216 on Monday.

"It's like going through the corral to the pen," said Judge Fuller of taking the witness stand in Courtroom 216. "You'll be disappointed in the jury room, but at least you'll be close to the cafeteria." He dismissed the jurors for the weekend.

Anita Morales, Carla Reid, Ynema Mangum, Pam Carson, and Mark and Dian Hartwell left together. They grieved and consoled each other that evening, as they did every evening, as Mark Hartwell took the time to embrace Regina's Austin family. He spent time with Jeremy Barnes, and he spent the night at Mangum's. She cooked for the Hartwells. Dian was kind, and Ynema gave her a handcarved wooden elephant that Dian had admired.

The Hartwells were grateful for the hospitality.

Mark Hartwell began referring to Regina's friends as "my girls."

On Monday, August 19, 1996, the trial, the photos, the heat, the different rooms, the tawdriness of it, were all wearing on the jurors.

Criminalists Ivan Wilson, Gary Molina, and Jill Hill each took the stand regarding the blood evidence. Wilson simply stated that, on August 14, 1995, he had received the victim's blood samples and refrigerated them.

Molina testified to having assisted criminalist Hill in the collection of evidence at the Hartwell and LeBlanc apartments and to having tested for blood at both apartments and on both Jeeps.

Molina said they had done presumptive and Luminol tests for blood. Luminol, he noted, is not a great test, but it is helpful.

Hill stated that, on July 5, 1995, at Regina Hartwell's apartment, they had spotted blood on the arm of the black, leather recliner.

"What did you do?" said Cox.

"I did a presumptive test called TMB. . . . It tells us it may be blood. It doesn't tell us if it's human blood, but it tells us it may be blood. If a presumptive test is positive we will collect that stain and then take it back to the laboratory for further analysis."

"And, just briefly, how is that done?"

"We will take a Q-tip and moisten the Q-tip with a little bit of sterile water. We will take just a tiny portion of the bloodstain on the swab. We will add reagents to the swab. If there's a color change to a blue color, that means that it is presumptive positive, and we will go further to collect that stain and take it back to the laboratory."

She then stated that they had done additional presumptive tests on the side of Regina's black cube-shaped table, on the top of the cube table, on the foot portion of the black leather recliner, and on a statue on the coffee table. All turned out presumptive positive.

Hill had also collected a knife from the kitchen, brushes that had been used to clean the apartment, and a portion of the carpet pad from in front of the black leather recliner.

She then marked on a diagram of the apartment, every place from which they had collected blood evidence—in the living room, kitchen, hallway, and bathroom.

Cox next asked her about collecting evidence the following day at Kim LeBlanc's apartment.

"I personally collected a Band-Aid wrapper, a piece of toilet paper in the bathroom trash, a cardboard contact lens box, two green rugs from the bathroom, a motorcycle helmet, and a stain on the bathroom floor," she said.

The Band-Aid wrapper and the toilet paper had tested TMB presumptive positive. The contact lens box had tested weak TMB positive. The motorcycle helmet had not been tested there. Three towels collected by Molina had tested positive. The floor stain had tested positive. And a piece of tissue paper by the bed later had tested presumptive positive.

"Could you explain to the jury what DNA is?" said Cox.

"DNA is a chemical found in our body. It is found in every nucleated cell in our body, meaning it's found almost anywhere in your body except for red blood cells. It's found in white blood cells but not red blood cells. It determines who we are. We inherit half of our DNA from our mother and half from our father. That's what makes us so unique. And we are, at the laboratory, able to look at sections of our DNA. It's called junk DNA. It doesn't mean anything. We can't tell if you have certain diseases, or we can't tell if you have blue eyes or brown hair. It's pieces of DNA that we all have in common, but yet different. And so, those are the pieces of DNA that we analyze in the laboratory for our testing purposes."

"Does every person have a unique configuration of the DNA?" said Cox.

"Yes, they do."

"Okay. Now, there are scientific tests that can distinguish differences between individuals based on their configuration of DNA?"

"That's correct."

"And, based on that, is it possible to collect a bloodstain from a crime scene and possibly connect it to a particular person, but in a preliminary step for that [to] exclude other people as possible donors of that stain?"

"Yes," she answered.

"Okay. Could you explain briefly the two different types of, or the different types of, DNA testing that your lab performs?"

"At our lab," said Hill, "we do two basic types of DNA tests. We do one test that's called the PCR test. And what that stands for is Preliminary Chain Reaction. And that's just a big word to say that the blood is copied. It is good for small bloodstains . . . It is put into an instrument that actually copies a specific section of your DNA. We're targeting a section of chromosome six. And that section is copied over and over, billions of times. And so that's what we actually analyze and type. And that's called your DQ-Alpha type. That's one type of test we do, is DQ-Alpha.

"Another type of PCR test we do, based on that same theory of the blood being copied over and over, is called D1S80. And that is on chromosome number one. And another test where the blood is copied over and over many times, and we're able to analyze your blood to your D1S80 type.

"A further discriminatory test is called RFLP. And this test looks at bigger sections of our DNA. Your DNA has to be in better condition. It can't be degraded. And you have to have a good bit of it to actually perform the tests, and the tests will work. This test, however, takes some time to do, whereas, the PCR test is a fast test. It can be done within a few days."

Hill then stated that, upon their return to the DPS lab, they had DQ-Alpha tested everything that had previously tested TMB positive.

Eventually, they had DQ-Alpha tested the blood samples of Thomas, LeBlanc, and Hartwell. On Thomas and Hartwell, they had also performed DIS80 and RFLP tests.

Thomas's DQ-Alpha type was 1.1, 1.3. His DIS80 type was 18, 24.

Regina's DQ-Alpha type was 2,3. Her DIS80 type was, like Thomas's, 18, 24.

LeBlanc's DQ-Alpha type was 1.1, 4.

Hill wrote all of that on the apartment diagram for the jurors.

Carpet bloodstains near the window and stains on the statue matched the DNA of Justin Thomas, she said. Blood on the foot portion of the black leather recliner matched that of Regina Hartwell. The stain on the arm of the recliner matched the DNA of Thomas. The blood on the top and side of the cube table belonged to Hartwell, as did a carpet stain near the end of the sofa.

In the hallway, one bloodstain matched the DNA of Thomas, another matched the DNA of Hartwell. In the bathroom, blood on the shower curtain rod matched Thomas's, blood on the shower curtain matched Hartwell's.

"Now," said Cox, "of all of the bloodstains recovered from that apartment that was tested, did any of the DQ-Alpha types of those bloodstains come back matching the DQ-Alpha type of Kim LeBlanc?"

"No."

"And how many separate stains were located that matched the DQ-Alpha type for Justin Thomas?"

"Five."

Six matched that of Regina Hartwell.

Hill then stated that the DQ-Alpha type and the DIS80 types are not as discriminatory as the RFLP test "because there are so many types in the population of these testing, and so we are one of those possible types. It's not picking you out from anyone else in the world. It's only picking you out from X-number of people."

"So really," responded Cox, "what is being said by your results is you cannot exclude Regina Hartwell as the donor of the blood samples that were found in the locations you indicated as matching Regina Hartwell's DQ-Alpha type?"

"That's correct."

"And the same goes for Justin Thomas," said Cox. "You cannot exclude Justin Thomas as the donor of the blood samples that match his DQ-Alpha type. Is that correct?"

"Right," answered Hill. "I can only say it's consistent with; it's not conclusively."

Court recessed until 1:35 p.m.

At 1:35 p.m., Jill Hill presented enlarged photographs of the DNA strips to the court and showed how the blood in the apartment samples matched the blood of Hartwell and Thomas.

She then discussed the DNA testing from Kim LeBlanc's apartment. The blood on the tissue paper found in the trash can by Kim's bed matched LeBlanc's. The blood on the toilet paper found in the bathroom matched Thomas's.

Hill next stated that she had performed a presumptive test on the lockblade knife, which had had a positive result. But further DNA testing had produced a negative result.

"Now," asked Cox, "if an object has been recovered from a fire and subjected to intense heat, would you expect to be able to get a DNA result on that?"

"Not always, no," she replied.

"Can intense heat degrade DNA?"

"Yes, it does."

She then testified that DQ-Alpha testing on the blood found in Kim LeBlanc's Jeep matched the blood type of Justin Thomas.

The witness was passed to the defense.

"One of the questions the prosecutor didn't ask you, but I'm going to," said Patrick Ganne, "is that in your report you talk about the proportion of how many people—"

"I can tell you, sir," Hill interrupted. "I have it."

For Regina Hartwell's DQ-Alpha type, 4.69 percent of Caucasians match it, 2.25 percent of Blacks, and 3.57 percent of Hispanics, said Hill.

When combined with her D1S80, approximately one in 119 Caucasians matches, one in 198 Hispanics, and one in 1,301 African-Americans, she said.

For Justin Thomas's DQ-Alpha match, 1.63 percent of Caucasians have the same, .55 percent of Blacks, and .82 percent of Hispanics. When combined with D1S8, one in 342 persons matches.

But Ganne then pointed out that that one-in-342 figure applied to only one piece of evidence—the statue—not all of the samples of blood evidence. Hill agreed.

He then focused on the knife.

"And you can't tell us whether it was human blood or any other kind of blood [that tested positive TMB presumptive]?"

"That's correct," replied Hill.

Ganne changed topics. "Have you told us, for example, have you presented any evidence that Justin Thomas was involved in the murder of Regina Hartwell?"

"I have told you that blood that is consistent with his blood was found in the apartment."

"Did you know, for example, or would it factor in your equation, that Justin Thomas lived in that apartment for a period of time?"

"That has no bearing on what I have to say," said Hill. "All I can say is that it's there."

"Does the fact that he's lived there give some explanation for it?" he continued.

"It could."

"It certainly . . . if a person claimed never to have been there, your testimony would cast a different light on it, would it not?"

"That's correct."

"Ms. Hill, as always it's always a pleasure to spend time with you. I thank you for your testimony." And Ganne passed the witness.

* * *

Gregg Cox looked at Jill Hill. "Now, earlier Mr. Ganne asked you some question about whether or not you could say that was human blood [on the knife]."

"Right."

"And you can't. Is that correct?"

"No."

"But is there any way you can say that there's no possibility that that was human blood?"

"No. I don't know."

"So it's possible it was."

"It's possible. I don't know."

He then returned to the DNA statistic of one in 342. "That basically means [if] you have 342 people, you are going to be able to eliminate 341 of them as the donor of the blood. But Justin Thomas, you could not eliminate. Is that correct?"

"That's correct."

At 2:25 p.m, the State rested its case.

I know white trash when I see it, thought Jeremy Barnes. He looked at Bonnie Thomas and her nephew Josh. Of course, Barnes was prejudiced. He knew it and he admitted it. He believed Regina was dead at the hands of their kinsman.

At 10 minutes after nine the following morning, the defense presented its first of only three witnesses—Justin Thomas's cousin Josh Mollett, a senior at Bowie High School in Austin.

Mollett stated that Justin came over to his house around eight a.m. on the day Regina Hartwell was murdered and that they spent the morning watching TV. Around 11:30 a.m., he drove Thomas over to Kim LeBlanc's apartment.

He also said he had met Kim and Regina a few times and

that they had acted like "friends or sisters." He was then asked
if he had ever overheard conversations about LeBlanc not
being able to make her Jeep payments.

"Uh, no," said Mollett.

Even with cross-examination by Gregg Cox, Josh Mollett
was on the stand for only five minutes.

"I need a clerk because his principal at school requires a
subpoena," said Ganne. "We call Bonnie Thomas."

Pat Ganne looked at Bonnie Thomas. It was tanned face to
tanned face. Beautiful blue eyes to beautiful blue eyes. They
were a team. Bonnie had bonded with Ganne's wife, K. C.
Anderson, Justin's first attorney.

Ganne smiled at Bonnie to reassure her. She was nervous
and did not want to be there. And that was obvious to the
courtroom. There wasn't a single flicker of joy in her face.

But why should there have been? Bonnie's nephew, the boy
who called her Momma B, who had once told her she was
more of a mom to him than his own mother had been, was on
trial for murder.

"Do you recall," said Ganne, "a particular incident, and help
us if you can, place it in time, when Justin injured his hand?"

"It was a Saturday or Sunday." Her voice was gravelly from
too many hard years. She wanted to look at Justin. She didn't.
"I want to say close to the Fourth of July. And he wanted to
get down and go out and see what was on the other side of the
river."

"Did he go over there for a particular purpose?"

"I don't think so. He just wanted to know what was on the
other side."

"Did you see him before he left?"

"Yeah."

"Did he have any type of injuries that you could see?"

"No."

"Did you see him when he came back?"

"Yes."

"And tell the jury what you saw"

She started to look straight at the jury. In any other situation, Bonnie Thomas would have. Bonnie Thomas was a straightforward type of woman.

"Well," she said, "we were very upset because he had, I don't know, fell across the fence or something, and he had a great big gash, and he was bleeding badly, and we wanted him to go to the doctor for stitches and he flat refused."

Ganne picked up the eight-foot length of chain. It rattled throughout the courtroom. He talked about Justin Thomas's father's broken truck that needed towing for repair. "Did you attempt to tow it with [your] tow bar?"

"Yes, sir," she answered.

"Were you successful?"

"No, sir."

"Was an alternative plan used, developed?"

"Well," said Bonnie, "not being able to use the tow bar, we just decided to get a chain and tow him in town with the chain."

"Was the obtaining of that chain a responsibility that was delegated to anyone?"

"Justin."

Ganne walked toward Bonnie with the bright, shiny chain in hand. "I'm going to show you what's been marked and introduced into evidence as State's Exhibit Number 52, and ask you if this looks familiar to you."

"That looks like the chain that we used to tow my brother's truck," she answered.

"And after you used it to tow your brother's truck, what was done with it?"

"The chain?"

"Yes, ma'am," he said politely.

"It was put in the back of my truck," said Bonnie.

"And it was left there?"

"Yes, sir."

"And it was still there when, in fact, it was taken from you?"

"Yes, sir," she answered.

"The garbage can—were you there when it was taken?"

"Yes, sir."

"And how was it being used at the time?"

"For our garbage."

"Was there, in fact, garbage in it?"

"I believe so, when they took it."

"And do you know what happened to the garbage?"

Bonnie shook her head, no.

"Was Justin assigned a responsibility of getting that?" said Ganne.

"Yes, sir," said Bonnie.

"That was part of the chores—"

"That his dad told him to go to town," Bonnie interrupted. "We were using a big box in the basement to put our garbage in and [it] just wasn't no good, so he told him to go get a garbage can for us."

"And is that when you piped in about the chain?"

"Yeah," she said.

"Who set up the chain the way it is? I notice it's just not a chain. It's got some other items on it." Ganne showed her the chain.

"Well," said Bonnie, "we had to put it through his bumper and put those nuts and bolts on there to hold it onto his bumper and the same to mine."

"Ms. Thomas," said Ganne, "I have no further questions. I think the prosecution may have some for you."

"May I have a glass of water, please?"

Judge Fuller smiled. "I wonder if it's today's or last week's," he joked.

* * *

Gail Van Winkle was erect, polite, businesslike. Her young, pale skin and bright, red lipstick were in direct odds to Bonnie's sun- and wind-weathered, natural face.

"Let me ask you some questions," said Van Winkle. "Did you see your brother's truck when it was towed?"

"Yes, I'm the one that helped tow it."

"And you see that this chain here has a padlock on it?"

"Yeah."

"Do you know where the key is to this padlock?"

"No, I have no idea."

"Have you seen this [padlock] before?"

"No."

"So when—do you know how this padlock got on this chain?"

"No. I have no idea. There was no padlock on that chain when we towed, I don't believe so, ma'am."

"When it was taken from your truck, it was on here, wasn't it?"

"I don't think so."

"So you're saying when the officer seized this, this padlock was not on this chain."

"I don't remember that lock being on that chain."

"Do you know why [Justin] would have bought cement?"

"No, ma'am."

"You did not ask him to buy cement."

"No, ma'am."

"And you didn't ask him to buy a padlock."

"No, ma'am."

"You don't have any idea why Justin Thomas would purchase that."

"No, ma'am."

Bonnie Thomas was on the stand for less than an hour.

CHAPTER 25

"What are you, crazy?" Regina Hartwell's friends taunted Melody Mann, Justin Thomas's new girlfriend. She sat there, her blue eyes focused on a paperback novel, her young, tanned, thin legs, sticking out of her short shorts. To Hartwell's friends, the curly, blonde-haired teenager looked as trashy as her novel.

"Your psycho boyfriend is going to go to prison."

Mann took a lot of verbal abuse, from Regina's friends, from a Christian, cussing mother, from an angry brother who had no qualms about telling their mother to "shut the fuck up." It was no wonder she was attracted to Justin Thomas, a man capable of extreme love and extreme anger.

Each day, Melody sat outside the courthouse, perched on a concrete wall, and hand signaled her love to Justin, as though talking in street-gang sign language. Melody Mann had had her own brushes with the law. Sitting in a courtroom, as she did that day, was not an unknown to her.

At 10:10 a.m., Justin Heith Thomas took the witness stand in front of a jury of his peers—twelve mostly highly educated men and women. It was his choice, and his choice only, to testify. Jim Sawyer questioned him.

"When did you first notice Kim LeBlanc?"

"She asked me a couple of questions [at the gym] about, you know, different lifts to improve certain strengths. I guess that would have been the first time. I don't know when that was."

"Were you attracted to her?"

"Oh, yeah," said Thomas. "I thought she was, you know, very pretty."

"Did you begin a sexual relationship with Kim LeBlanc that first night [y'all went out]?"

"Yes, sir, that first night."

"Was it a fairly intense physical relationship that you enjoyed with her?"

"Yes, sir."

"If we had an intensity scale," said Sawyer, "from, let's say, one to ten, where would that relationship lie in terms of physical intensity that you enjoyed with her?"

"Had to peak the scale—ten," Thomas said.

Melody Mann clutched her paperback novel.

"Was that a flattering relationship to you? Were you happy to be in this relationship?"

"Oh, yeah, I was."

"Had you dated a girl that was as pretty as she was?"

Bonnie held in her wallet a photo of Justin's ex-wife, Dawn, and their two children, the ex-wife who looked almost exactly like Kim LeBlanc.

"I didn't think—I didn't ever think so. I thought she—"

Melody Mann just sat there.

"When you met Regina three or four weeks after you knew Kim, was it clear to you what that relationship was?"

"Quite apparent, right away."

"Did they treat each other with affection even in your presence?"

"Yes," said Thomas, "they did. In fact, every time the three of us were together, Regina was usually in Kim's lap or Kim was usually holding Regina."

"Did you personally have any problem with the relationship between Regina Hartwell and Kim LeBlanc?"

"No."

Sawyer and Ganne had talked with Thomas about his testimony perhaps a half a dozen times.

"Now, you heard the testimony about the motor-scooter accident. Did you have an accident on that motor scooter?"

"Yes, sir."

"Can you recall for the jury about when it was you had it?"

"I believe it was . . . they had returned from the trip [to Cancun]. I can't recall [the] exact date, though."

Jeremy Barnes had testifed that the accident had been before the trip to Cancun. So had Kim LeBlanc.

"Whenever you were moving out of the apartment after the trip to Cancun, what was the relationship, to your understanding, what was the relationship between Kim and Regina?"

"Well," said Justin, "it was kind of messed up because, for a while there, Kim thought I was—[that] Regina and I were messing around, which wasn't the case." He didn't blink an eye. "They were arguing about money. And it didn't seem like it was going all that well between them, you know. But, like I said, a lot of times Regina would pull Kim to the side and they would talk."

"Was there ever a time when Kim LeBlanc told you that Regina was mistreating her or that she was being taken advantage of in such a way that she felt that you should go and kill her?"

"No."

"Was there ever a time when she looked at you and said you got to go bump her off?"

"I don't recall that. I recall her telling me—"

"At this time I'm going to object to hearsay," Gail Van Winkle interrupted. "Kim's statements are hearsay and that's not admissible."

"I'm sorry," Jim Sawyer said, then looked at Judge Fuller. "They're absolutely not hearsay. Kim's statements come in. She's an accomplice here. I'm sorry. They come in."

"Only if they can show somehow that it's a conspiracy to commit a murder between the defendant and Kim," argued Van Winkle. "If it's just a statement that she made out of court, then it's hearsay. If they're going to say it's [a] co-conspirator statement between the defendant and Kim LeBlanc in the furtherance of this murder, then I gather it's not hearsay."

"Kim, if Kim LeBlanc, God forbid, is in fact the murderer, . . ." said Sawyer sarcastically.

Judge Fuller soon sent the jury out of the courtroom.

"Let me speak directly to the record," said Sawyer. "This witness is the accomplice. If she is conspiring on her own to commit murder instead of [being] a patsy, then I think any statement—"

"How can you conspire with yourself?" asked Judge Fuller.

"Of course, you can conspire with yourself. If she has intent, then I think that the statements are admissible."

The attorneys argued, the Judge wisecracked, Thomas was

questioned out of the jury's presence, the attorneys argued
more, and the Judge listened. Sawyer was denied permission
to ask Thomas the questions about what LeBlanc said.

"So the jury can know, were you any kind of a cocaine
addict or drug addict at that time?"

"No, sir. I could do without it."

"Did you do drugs on a recreational basis?"

"Yes, sir, I did."

"Did you and Regina ever go into business as Kim described, you know, where you all went out and sold dope at
the 404 Club?"

"No, sir, we didn't."

"All right," said Sawyer. "Did Regina ever give you, you
know, large sums of money so that you could go out and buy
dope and front it out to drug dealers?"

"Not large sums," said Thomas. He was soft-spoken,
polite. "Just enough to party with at the time."

"She was only giving you money to buy dope to use herself?"

"For the three of us or the two of them."

"Did you . . . was there anything that had happened between you two or among the three of you, you know, that left
you with the feeling that you just had to do something dramatic, or mean, or harmful?"

"Not at all," said Thomas. "In fact, when they returned
[from Cancun], I bought them a pretty expensive gift as a ges-
ture of friendship 'cause, like I said, I thought her and I—"

"A gift for whom?"

"Regina."

"What was that gift?"

"A leather recliner."

Damn, thought Sawyer. *God damn.* This was the first that he'd heard that Thomas had purchased the recliner. And God knows how many times he'd told his client not to volunteer any information on the stand.

"All right," said Sawyer, staring his brown eyes on his client. "Is that, in fact, a leather recliner that we have seen in these photographs inside that apartment?"

"Yes, sir, it is."

"And that's a gift you paid for with your money?" Sawyer acted nonchalant.

"Yes, sir," said Thomas.

"Wasn't money that Regina gave you?"

"No, sir, it wasn't."

"All right. What happened that morning, the morning of the 29th?"

The jurors leaned in to listen intently.

"I got up pretty early. I couldn't sleep. We were doing drugs that night. I got up pretty early and I wanted to go out to my house. Kim was asleep, so I didn't want to wake her up. I walked over to my cousin Josh's."

"You heard Josh's testimony this morning, didn't you?"

"Yes, sir."

"Was he testifying truthfully to the jury about what you all did that morning?"

"Yes, sir."

"Did anything special happen that morning, you know, between you and Josh?"

"No. We wrestled around, you know, just b.s. like we normally do."

"All right. You remember when Kim was testifying to the

jury and she said that you had gathered your posse, I think she called it, at Jim's Frontier to discuss slaughtering Regina Hartwell." Sawyer had a knack for description. "Is that true?" And he loved that knack. Outside of court, he grinned and laughed when he referred to Kim LeBlanc as a "skinny-assed snitch, bitch and witch."

"No."

"All right. Did you ever go up there, you know, and visit anybody and say, 'We're going to go and kill this woman'?"

"No."

"And you heard her when she testified . . . to the jury that you all had conspired to get rid of the Jeep, of Regina's Jeep, after she had been killed. Is that true?"

"No, sir."

"And what vehicle was it that you were offering to sell or trying to sell at that time?"

"It was Kim's Jeep."

"Why were you trying to sell it?"

"She was having problems making the payments or something to do like that. Regina was offering to pay it off, but she didn't want to because she didn't want to be attached with Regina. She wanted to break things off. I was, you know, trying to help her out. I have a few friends that had Jeeps, were interested in Jeeps."

"Let's come back to the 29th. Josh dropped you at your place?"

"No, sir."

"Where did he leave you off?"

"At Kim's apartment."

"All right. What did you do?"

"I walked up to the door, and at that time I had a key. So I opened the door and went in, and when I went in Kim was real hysterical. She had come out of the shower. The water was still on. I asked her, 'What's wrong? What's wrong?' And she was just hysterical. And she got back into the shower. I didn't really pay it no attention because I just thought, well, she's geeking, man, she wants some more coke or something."

"You say 'she's geeking.' What does that mean?"

"That she's showing physical signs of a dependency," said Thomas.

"And then what happened?"

"And she told me that, uh, Regina was dead."

"What was your reaction to that?"

"I was like, 'What are you talking about? What do you mean Regina's dead?'"

"What happened next?"

"She said—"

"At this time, I object," said Van Winkle, "to statements that Kim made unless they're going to—they're in furtherance of a conspiracy, as hearsay."

"Maybe we should approach the bench," said Sawyer.

The opposing forces gathered in front of Judge Fuller.

"What I want to get to now," whispered Sawyer, "is about what had happened that morning prior to his arrival. Those are inculpatory. If you want the jury out while we argue this. But I don't think this is rocket science."

Several minutes later, Judge Fuller, overruled Van Winkle and allowed Sawyer his questions.

"And then what happened?"

"She asked for my help, and she begged for my help. Said she needed my help."

"Why?" asked Sawyer. "Help to do what?"

"I guess to try to, you know," Thomas tried to sound meek, "conceal the fact that what was done was done."

Sawyer looked straight at his big client. "Mr. Thomas, answer to the jury directly. What did she want you to do?"

"She wanted me to help her somehow get rid of, I guess, the body, [that was] what she was asking."

"Did you do it?"

"Yes, sir, I did."

"Did you leave the apartment—her apartment, Kim's?"

"We left together."

"Was it pretty soon after you had been dropped off by Josh?"

"It was a while because I tried after I got the explanation, well, after I, you know, started believing her, I was like, you know, 'Call the police. What are you talking about?' That's what I told her."

"You never did call the police, though, did you?"

"I couldn't convince her to, and I didn't, no."

"Did you all go over to Regina's apartment from Kim's place?"

"Yes, we did."

"Did you actually go into the apartment with her?"

"Yes, we did. Yes, I did."

"Just tell the jury where was Regina's body in the apartment as you recall when you walked in."

"She was lying face-up in the bathtub."

"What was your state of mind by the time you all got to your [father's] place?"

"Pretty much shocked."

"Were you scared?"

"Very scared."

"What was Kim, what was her demeanor like? What was she looking like?"

"She's pretty relaxed because she was on coke. So she was pretty relaxed."

"Did you go and buy this garbage can, and the chain, and that concrete to bury her in the river?"

"No, sir."

"Did you ever, even for a minute, contemplate chopping up this woman's body and putting it in the garbage can?"

"No, sir," said Thomas. "I didn't want to touch it."

Sawyer pulled out the bowie knife. "Before you saw it here in court, had you ever seen this knife before?"

"No, sir."

"This knife belong to you?"

"No, it doesn't."

"Did you know that this had been wrapped in cloth and put under Regina's body?"

"No, sir."

"Whenever you carried Regina's body down to the Jeep, did you know what it was that had killed her, that is, did you know whether she had been stabbed, or shot, or electrocuted, or what her manner of death was?"

"No. I mean, at first, she was in the bathtub and she was wet. So at first, you know, common sense, maybe, you know, she drowned."

"During this time, all the way up to the time that you actually got the body, had Kim ever said to you, 'I killed her'?"

"No, sir, she didn't."

* * *

Thomas then told of burning the body, of running to the
motel, of returning to his father's house for the Fourth of July
weekend, and that his aunt Bonnie Thomas had indeed told
the truth about how he cut his hand. Then he got up, walked
over to the jurors, spread his hands, and showed them his
long-since-healed wound.

Moments later, Jim Sawyer passed the witness.

Gail Van Winkle looked at her notes, and then looked at
Justin Heith Thomas. She always made lots of notes. "Write
everything down," her mother had taught her. Gail Van
Winkle even woke during the night to write things down;
she didn't want to forget anything.

"You recall the testimony that there was quite a bit of blood
in the apartment, Regina's apartment, that was found by the
DPS lab team. You recall that?"

"Yes, ma'am," said Thomas, "I do."

"You recall your blood being identified on the shower-
curtain rod."

"Yes, ma'am, I do."

"Okay. And various other parts of the house."

"Yes, ma'am."

"It's your testimony that you didn't have a cut on your hand
and that's not your blood from your wound."

"I believe," said Thomas, "that was there from when I got
in the accident on the scooter."

"Okay," said Van Winkle. "So it's your testimony you got a
scrape on your knee."

"It was more than a scrape," said Thomas.

"And the blood," she said, "ended up on the shower-curtain
rod in her bathroom. You dispute the testimony from the lab
tech that that's your blood."

"Oh, no."

"Okay. So your blood from a scooter accident appeared

on the shower-curtain rod in the bathroom where the body was found."

"That's where I washed my cuts," Thomas explained. "I took a shower and washed."

"You're saying after the scooter accident. How did you get blood on the palm of your hand? How did the blood get from your knee on a shower-curtain rod?"

"It was on my elbows," he said.

"Did you touch the shower-curtain rod with your elbow?"

"I imagine I did. I had to hold myself up to wash my knees."

"You're a tall man. A shower-curtain rod's generally over your head or at your face level. Is that not correct?"

"To keep balance," he said.

"So, with your elbow you balanced yourself?"

"No, no. I had washrags, too. I imagine I put a washrag up there. I was washing out wounds."

"So you would have wiped the shower-curtain rod with a bloody washcloth? Is that your testimony?"

"I could have," answered Thomas. "I don't know how it got there. I'm not saying I know how it got there."

"You were gushing blood from your scooter accident?"

"It wasn't gushing, but it was bleeding."

"Was it bleeding to the point where it would fling onto the walls?"

"Bleeding to the point where it would drop if I wasn't holding something over it."

"Drop how? Just onto the ground?"

"Yes, ma'am."

"Any idea how your blood was found on the walls in the hallway of Regina's apartment?"

"No, ma'am."

"Not from the scooter accident," Van Winkle said.

"I don't know how, ma'am."

"Would you be, I mean, it's not consistent with your injury is it?"

"Blood was dripping from my elbow and one of my knees."

"Dripping from your elbow?"

"Dripping like straight down, like, you know, it was forming up and after it collected, it would drip."

"So Kim's description of your scooter accident would, you obviously disagree with."

"Yes, ma'am."

"And you're saying it was pretty serious."

"Yes, ma'am."

"Did you get it treated by a doctor?"

"No, ma'am."

"But it was enough, it was bleeding where it got on other parts of the furniture as well. Is that right?"

"I presume," Thomas answered.

"Do you recall it bleeding onto the chair, the black leather chair?"

"Yes, ma'am."

"How did it get on the chair?"

"When I first came in, I sat down on the chair."

"Okay. And what part of your body touched the chair?"

"My elbows, my knee."

"So you had a bleeding elbow and knee and you wiped it on this nice, new, black leather—"

"No, I didn't wipe it on." Justin Thomas's father had always insisted that the boy be neat.

"You're saying it dripped."

"I sat down," he said.

"Did you see it drip off onto the leather chair?"

"No." He forgot the "ma'am."

"But that's your testimony as to how the blood got there on [the chair in] Regina's apartment."

"Yes, ma'am."

* * *

Gail Van Winkle had had only one night to prepare her cross-examination of Justin Thomas. Only the day before Gregg Cox and she had decided that she would question Thomas.

"Any reason you'd be standing by the window?"

"I don't recall."

"You have no idea how your blood got by the window on the carpet."

"That would be in front of the chair, not directly in front of the chair," Thomas replied.

"And do you have any idea how your blood got on the . . . there was a statue on the coffee table. Do you remember the coffee table, the blood that was there on the statue?"

"I was standing pretty much over the coffee table."

"So you were dripping onto the coffee table."

"Could have."

"Did you ever clean [the blood] up?"

"No. Regina said not to worry about it. 'Don't worry about it, Jay.'"

"Now you testified that you lived with Regina a couple of days before Kim and Regina went to Cancun."

"Yes, ma'am."

"And she let you stay in her apartment with her before she left."

"Couple of days prior to. Well, three of us stayed there."

"The three of you stayed there. And why did you not stay at Kim's apartment with Kim?"

"One or two nights we did."

"So you weren't living with Regina then, were you?"

"I had my stuff there, yeah, I was."

"And you were living there."

"I remember one night before they went to Cancun, we went and stayed at Kim's because she wanted to have sex and we obviously couldn't do that with Regina there."

"Would have been kind of awkward to stay at Regina's, wouldn't it, with Kim, when you had an apartment that was empty? Where did you sleep?"

"When?"

"At Regina's when Regina was there?"

"When she was there I slept on the couch."

"And you chose to do that rather than stay at Kim's."

"Well, Kim had a roommate at the time. We didn't . . . I don't think he liked me too much."

"Her roommate had his own room, didn't he?"

"No. It was a one-[bed]room apartment. Kim had the bedroom. He lived in the living room."

"But you had a place to go for privacy."

"Yes."

"But you chose to stay at Regina's rather than stay at Kim's."

"It's not like I stayed there every night," said Thomas. "I went back and forth."

"So you weren't living at Regina's."

"Yes, I was. That's where I resided."

"And your testimony is Regina had no problem with you and Kim staying at her one-bedroom apartment when you had a place to stay. That was the setup."

"Well, when we were there, we were usually up on drugs, and when they got tired is when either Kim would leave or I would leave with Kim."

"So you wouldn't spend the night."

"Not all the time."

"But you were living there."

"Yes."

"Now, when you cut your hand, you were at your, where you say you cut your hand, at your parents' place."

"Can I finish now?" asked Thomas.

"I'm asking you a question," said Van Winkle. "Do you want to continue an answer?"

"You didn't let me finish explaining how I got it."

"About what? How you got what?"

"How I cut my hand."

"Well, let me ask that question. I believe that was quite a few questions ago. You're saying that you have more explanation."

"You asked me to explain—you wanted to hear the whole thing and then you . . ."

"If you would like to continue to explain how you cut your hand, go ahead."

"Okay, I came back from across the river, and you have to jump a fence to get back into our property, and when I did that is when I snagged my hand."

"So you weren't mending a fence on your father's land."

"Not at that time, no, ma'am."

"And that's not how you got this wound."

Thomas looked at the prosecutor. "What do you mean?"

"You were not, at the time you got your wound, mending a fence."

"No, ma'am."

"Why did you tell Detective Carter that?"

"I couldn't really recollect. I was, like I said, I was pretty shocked at the time, plus I was pretty strung out."

"But you told Detective Carter that you did it mending a fence."

"I don't necessarily remember saying that, but I guess I could have."

"You didn't tell him the truth?"

"I don't remember what I said to Detective Carter that night."

"Now you heard testimony," said Van Winkle, "that there was—your blood was found in Kim's Jeep."

"Yes, ma'am."

"That had nothing to do with the scooter accident, did it?"

"No, ma'am."

"Kim didn't come pick you up after you had your scooter accident, did she?"

"One of them did," he said, "but I can't . . . I don't remember which one it was."

Van Winkle looked at Thomas. She was an intimidating woman. "One of them did?" she asked.

"They came and—"

"I thought you rode the scooter back to Regina's."

"I rode to the store, where I called them."

"And then how did you get the scooter back to Regina's apartment?"

"They came." Thomas was getting frustrated. "I started to make sure it was still working and they came." His frustration was showing.

"Well, now you're saying Regina and Kim came and picked you up?"

"Yes, ma'am."

"After you had the scooter accident."

"Yes, ma'am."

"Was it Regina who picked you up?" Van Winkle was relentless.

"Yes, ma'am."

"Well, the blood was found in Kim's Jeep."

"I believe they came in Kim's Jeep."

"You're saying Regina picked you up in Kim's Jeep."

"No, they. They were both together at the time."

"Now you're saying Kim picked you up in Kim's Jeep?"

"No. Kim and Regina both."

"They came—"

"Kim's Jeep," he said.

"Now they're in Kim's Jeep. So your testimony is that blood from the scooter accident was what was found in Kim's Jeep. Is that your testimony?"

"No. I believe it was from my hand."

Ganne and Sawyer sat stone-faced. It was a noticeable departure from their usual animation, nodding "yes" when they agreed with the testimony, grimacing the word "ridiculous" when they disagreed with the testimony.

CHAPTER 26

Gail Van Winkle glanced at her notes, then looked straight into Thomas's eyes. "Know anybody named Rochon in Moreno Valley?"

"Two or three," said Thomas.

"Named Rochon?"

"Yes, ma'am."

"In fact, you, I believe, have denied that you dealt drugs with Regina. Is that right?"

"Yes, ma'am."

"Did you get a shipment from Rochon out of California?"

"No, ma'am."

"You never did?"

"No, ma'am."

"Never got crystal meth from him?"

"Not shipments."

"Well, how would you get them from him from California?"

"When I had made a trip previously, I had brought a little back with me."

"He never sent you any by UPS."

"No, ma'am."

"You made a lot of phone calls back and forth to him in California."

"Yes, ma'am."

"And after this murder, [you] still did, right?"

"I can't say how many. I don't recall. I talked to a lot of people on the phone."

"Well, I believe you just testified that you did do a small amount of dealing of drugs."

"No," said Thomas. "I obtained small amounts. I never sold small amounts or large amounts."

"When you got drugs, when you came over, did you not supply Regina and Kim with drugs?"

"Once or twice."

"So is it your testimony you're not a drug dealer because you didn't sell it to them, you just gave it to them?"

"Well, as much as, they got it more than I got it. I was just able to get it when they weren't able to get it. The drug game isn't necessarily one hundred percent all the time. Sometimes you call people and they have it, sometimes you don't. When they didn't have it, I called friends and they would have it."

"You had connections."

"Yeah," answered Thomas, "I guess."

"Basically," said Van Winkle, "what you could get was crystal meth. Is that right?"

"Cocaine, marijuana."

"And crystal meth."

"Yes, ma'am."

"In fact, didn't you get Kim started on crystal meth?"

"I wouldn't say I got her started. I didn't forcibly do it."

"You made it available," said Van Winkle.

"Yes, ma'am."

"And you continued to give her drugs even though, as you described her, she was clearly addicted."

"After it was apparent that she was, I didn't. I quit giving [it to] her."

"You're saying you quit?"

"Giving her."

"So when was it apparent that she was an addict?"

"Pretty much right away. I mean, ..." His voice trailed off.

Van Winkle's adrenaline pumped, the way it always did during a trial, the way Thomas had told Kim his had when he had carried Regina's body to the tub.

"Right away she was an addict and then you quit having anything to do with getting her drugs. Is that what you're testifying to?"

"I guess, right before, right before Regina's death, murder, death."

"Now you're saying it was right before Regina's death that you quit giving her drugs."

"Well," stuttered Thomas, "I mean, she was using up until the time, but she really didn't. It really wasn't. I guess her demeanor, having to have the drugs, weren't as bad as before."

"Until right before Regina's death," quizzed Van Winkle. "Is that your testimony now?"

"Yes, ma'am."

Thomas admitted to going to Builders Square and buying cement, a trash can, a chain, and a padlock. Van Winkle asked him why he bought cement. "I don't know," he responded at first. Then he added, "You can see on the picture [of my father's house], there's a stairwell on the outside of the house. It's a three-level house. It's on stilts. The outside stairway is wood and it's separated from the house because the foundation at the bottom is sinking because the ground stays wet pretty much all the time."

"So where was the cement when the police came out to your house?"

"In one of the trailers," he said.

"So it wasn't where all the other items were . . ."

She didn't ask him why he was thinking about running around buying concrete and trash cans for his dad when he had a dead body sitting back home underneath a tin shed in the hot, summer sun of Texas.

"Didn't offend you to burn her body up," said Van Winkle.

"Yeah, it offended me to do what I was doing," said Thomas. "I cared a lot for Kim."

"Cared a lot for Kim. And you want this jury to believe, when she came in and told you about Regina, that you told her to call the police, turn herself in?"

"Now, how did your blood get in Kim's bathroom trash?"

"I don't know," said Thomas. "Maybe when I shaved. I don't know. From the scooter accident. I don't know."

"Scooter accident. Kim's apartment."

"Like I said," he responded, "I went back and forth."

"You went back and forth after the scooter accident."

"The whole time."

"So the scooter accident that happened in May, the tissue with your blood on it would still be in the trash can?"

"I'm saying I don't know, ma'am."

"And you would agree that you had a better motive to kill Regina than Kim [did]."

"No, ma'am, I don't agree."

"You didn't think Regina was going to turn you into the police?"

"I wasn't worried about that because I wasn't doing anything to be worried for that reason."

"You were a drug connection, weren't you?"

"Both of us were."

"Well, didn't she have information that she could tell the police that would get you in trouble?"

"I don't believe so."

"And didn't you tell Kim, just hours before you killed her, you weren't going to let anybody send you to prison?"

"No, ma'am, I did not."

"And you weren't thinking about that; you weren't scared about that."

"No, ma'am, I was not."

"Pass the witness," said Van Winkle.

"Nothing further. Thank you, Your Honor," said Sawyer. The defense rested.

The state briefly recalled Maximina Bautista, out of the presence of the jury, and again tried to enter her testimony. She was asked if she recognized in the courtroom the man she had seen with the very, very short hair at the Heritage Inn. No, she said, she didn't.

Gail Van Winkle stated that, outside the courtroom, Bautista had told her that she had recognized Justin Thomas. Van Winkle's plea was to no avail.

Anita Morales returned to the stand to rebut a question regarding whether she'd entered the courtroom and heard any testimony. She said she hadn't.

The jury was dismissed until the following morning.

On Wednesday, August 21, 1996, at 9:05 a.m. the charge against Justin Heith Thomas was read.

"Ladies and gentlemen of the jury," said Judge Fuller. "The

defendant, Justin Thomas, stands charged by indictment with the offense of Murder alleged to have been committed in Travis County, Texas, on or about the 29th day of June, 1995. To this offense the defendant has entered a plea of 'Not Guilty.'

"You are instructed that the law applicable to this case is as follows:

I.

"A person commits the offense of murder if he:

"(1) intentionally or knowingly causes the death of an individual; or

"(2) intends to cause serious bodily injury and commits an act clearly dangerous to human life that causes the death of an individual.

II.

"'Individual' means a human being who has been born and is alive.

"'Serious bodily injury' means bodily injury that creates a substantial risk of death or that causes death, serious permanent disfigurement, or protracted loss or impairment of the function of any bodily member or organ.

"'Deadly weapon' means anything that in the manner of its use or intended use is capable of causing death or serious bodily injury.

III.

"A person acts intentionally, or with intent, with respect to a result of his conduct when it is his conscious objective or desire to cause the result.

"A person acts knowingly, or with knowledge, with respect to a result of his conduct when he is aware that his conduct is reasonably certain to cause the result.

IV.

"You are further instructed that you may consider all relevant facts and circumstances surrounding the killing, if any, of Regina Hartwell, and the previous relationship existing between the accused and Regina Hartwell, together with all relevant facts and circumstances going to show the condition of the mind of the accused at the time of the offense alleged in the indictment.

V.

"Now bearing in mind the foregoing definitions and instructions, if you believe from the evidence beyond a reasonable doubt that on or about the 29th day of June, 1995, in the County of Travis, and State of Texas, as alleged in the indictment, the defendant, Justin Thomas, did then and there, intentionally or knowingly cause the death of an individual, Regina Hartwell, by stabbing Regina Hartwell with a knife, a deadly weapon; or

"if you believe from the evidence beyond a reasonable doubt that on or about the 29th day of June, 1995, in the County of Travis, and State of Texas, as alleged in the indictment, the defendant, Justin Thomas, did then and there, with intent to cause serious bodily injury to Regina Hartwell commit an act clearly dangerous to human life thereby causing the death of an individual, Regina Hartwell, by stabbing Regina Hartwell with a knife, a deadly weapon;

"then you will find the defendant guilty of Murder, and so say by your verdict; but if you do not so believe, or if you have a reasonable doubt thereof, you will acquit the defendant and say by your verdict 'Not Guilty.'

VI.

"A conviction cannot be had upon the testimony of an accomplice unless the jury first believe that the accomplice's evidence is true and that it shows the defendant is guilty of the offense charged against him, and even then you cannot convict unless the accomplice's testimony is corroborated by other evidence tending to connect the defendant with the offense charged, and the corroboration is not sufficient if it merely shows the commission of the offense, but it must tend to connect the defendant with its commission.

"You are further instructed that mere presence of the accused in the company of an accomplice witness shortly before or after the time of the offense, if any, is not, in itself, sufficient corroboration of the accomplice witness's testimony.

"You are charged that Kim LeBlanc was an accomplice if any offense was committed, and you are instructed that you cannot find the defendant guilty upon the testimony of Kim LeBlanc unless you first believe that the testimony of the said Kim LeBlanc is true and that it shows the defendant is guilty as charged in the indictment; and even then you cannot convict the defendant, Justin Thomas, unless you further believe that there is other evidence in this case, outside the evidence of said Kim LeBlanc, tending to connect the defendant with the commission of the offense charged in the indictment and then from all the evidence you must believe beyond a reasonable doubt that the defendant is guilty.

VII.

"In all criminal cases, the burden of proof is on the State. All persons are presumed innocent and no person may be convicted unless each element of the offense is proved beyond a reasonable doubt. The fact that the defendant has been arrested, confined, or indicted for, or otherwise charged with an offense gives rise to no inference of guilt at his trial. The law does not require the defendant to prove his innocence or produce any evidence at all. The presumption of innocence alone is sufficient to acquit the defendant unless the jurors are satisfied beyond a reasonable doubt of the defendant's guilt after a careful and impartial consideration of all the evidence in the case.

"The prosecution has the burden of proving the defendant

guilty and it must do so by proving each and every element of the offense charged beyond a reasonable doubt and if it fails to do so, you must acquit the defendant.

"It is not required that the prosecution prove guilt beyond all possible doubt; it is required that the prosecutor's proof excludes all 'reasonable doubt' concerning the defendant's guilt.

"A 'reasonable doubt' is a doubt based on reason and common sense after a careful and impartial consideration of all the evidence in the case. It is the kind of doubt that would make a reasonable person hesitate to act in the most important of his own affairs.

"Proof beyond a reasonable doubt, therefore, must be proof of such convincing character that you would be willing to rely and act upon it without hesitation in the most important of your own affairs.

"In the event you have a reasonable doubt as to the defendant's guilt after considering all the evidence before you, and these instructions, you will acquit the defendant and say by your verdict 'Not Guilty.'

"'Element of offense' means (a) the forbidden conduct; (b) the required culpability, and (c) the required result (if any). 'Conduct' means an act or omission and its accompanying mental state. 'Required culpability' means the mental state required by law such as intent, knowledge, recklessness or criminal negligence.

"You are further instructed as a part of the law in this case that the indictment against the defendant is not evidence in the case, and that the true and sole use of the indictment is to charge the offense, and to inform the defendant of the offense alleged against him.

"The reading of the indictment to the jury in the statement of the case of the state against the defendant cannot be considered as a fact or circumstance against the defendant in your deliberations.

"In deliberating on the cause you are not to refer to or

discuss any matter or issue not in evidence before you; and in determining the guilt or innocence of the defendant, you shall not discuss or consider the punishment, if any, which may be assessed against the defendant in the event he is found guilty beyond a reasonable doubt.

"You are charged that it is only from the witness stand that the jury is permitted to receive evidence regarding the case, or any witness therein, and no juror is permitted to communicate to any other juror anything he may have heard regarding the case or any witness therein, from any source other than the witness stand.

"You are instructed that your verdict must be unanimous and it must reflect the individual verdict of each individual juror, and not mere acquiescence in the conclusion of the other jurors.

"You are the exclusive judges of the facts proved, of the credibility of the witnesses and of the weight to be given to the testimony, but you are bound to receive the law from the Court, which is herein given [to] you, and be governed thereby.

"After reading the charge, you shall not be permitted to separate from each other, nor shall you talk with anyone not of your jury. After argument of counsel, you will retire and select one of your members as your foreperson. It is his or her duty to preside at your deliberations and to vote with you in arriving at a unanimous verdict. After you have arrived at your verdict, you may use one of the forms attached hereto by having your foreperson sign his or her name to the particular form that conforms to your verdict, but in no event shall he or she sign more than one such form.

"There's two possible forms. One is, 'We, the jury, find the defendant, Justin Thomas, guilty of Murder as alleged in the indictment.' And the other is, 'We, the jury, find the defendant, Justin Thomas, not guilty.'

"Respectfully submitted,
Larry Fuller,
Senior Appellate Judge

"State ready?"

* * *

The jurors heard closing arguments.

Gail Van Winkle stood, her business suit buttoned tight. She'd barely touched food in days, always unable to eat during a trial.

". . . I want to talk to you a little bit about Kim LeBlanc," Van Winkle said. "Now I do not expect anyone of you to like Kim. I don't expect you to relate to her. I don't even expect you to sympathize with her. She did some very bad things. She was involved in murder. She helped dispose of the body. When she got up here and she testified, she seemed detached at times. I don't know why. I submit that she has gone through rehab. She is no longer living the life of a drug addict that she used to be. Maybe that's how she copes with her past. Maybe that's how she deals with her responsibility, the part that she played in her friend's death. I don't know. It doesn't really matter. Because we'll deal with Kim LeBlanc later."

"There have been no deals made with Kim LeBlanc other than what Mr. Cox told you . . . No deals have been made," Van Winkle emphasized.

"In fact, you tell us at the end of this trial what you think should happen to Kim LeBlanc. You tell us. But don't let your dislike for Kim LeBlanc, or your inability to understand or relate to Kim LeBlanc, distract you from the truth. Don't let your dislike for Kim let the defendant, a murderer, go free. We'll deal with her later. Focus on what the defendant did. Focus on the evidence."

Patrick Ganne faced the jurors, his suit sharp. "Now I've always been taught that it's inappropriate to talk about the dead," he said, seriously. "But let's review just exactly who Regina

Hartwell was. A young woman with more money than she needed, more money for her own good, who hung around Club 404, wherever that is," his tone self-righteous, "somewhere in the downtown business district, and went out, preyed on young freshman girls who came to school here at the University. Right?

"Something else I want you to know," said Ganne. His blue eyes were dramatically sad. "Mr. Sawyer and I both have nineteen-year-old daughters. You know, and parents are always the last to know. But I think, I think that a woman who gets on the stand and tells you that at the age of fourteen she acquired the knowledge of the power of her sexuality, that's scary. That is scary. Kim LeBlanc is a con artist, she's a user, and she's only got one thing left to do to walk out of this deal, [and that] is to con you. She's gotten past Mr. Cox."

"You've got the hardest job of any jury I've ever addressed," said Ganne, "because a person is dead. And I believe it's through the exercise of bad, immature judgment [that] a young prosecutor decided to go with a pretty girl and blame it on this big hulk over there." He pointed to Thomas. "When the weight of the evidence, the weight of the evidence, goes the other way. It's not even a weight. It's a bulk."

"I don't have anything else to say to you. I thank you for your attention. It's been tedious. This has taken a lot longer than I thought it would. On behalf of Justin Thomas, his family, I thank you for your attention. I ask you . . . no, I don't ask, I demand, society demands, the community demands that you do the right thing, that you be repulsed by what ha happened, that you consider the evidence, that you follow the instructions of Judge Fuller, and render the only verdict that can possibly be rendered in this case, and that is acquit Justin Thomas of committing that murder, even though you know," and he repeated for emphasis, "even though you know that he's up to his neck."

Court recessed for ten minutes before Jim Sawyer began his closing arguments.

As if meditating and concentrating, Sawyer looked down at his polished cowboy boots, then up at the jurors. "Many years ago now, many years ago when I was around six, a very wise, old man said, 'Be careful of the lions you meet. They'll fool you with the truth.' I had no idea what he meant. That old man never learned to speak English, never drove a car, never flew a plane. I'm fifty-one. I'm beginning to do that. That old man was my grandfather. I tell you that so you can appreciate the source."

"What's the first thing, from all the evidence before us? The first thing we absolutely know is that Regina Hartwell did nothing to deserve in any way, to invoke, to ask for the crime committed against her. The woman didn't do anything. Her weakness, if it was a weakness, is that she gave. Her weakness, if it was a weakness, is that she cared. Her weakness, if it was a weakness, is that she loved somebody. And whether you love wisely or foolishly, that's a real emotion. And I think there's no doubt in what you heard that, for whatever reason, she loved and cared for Kim LeBlanc.

"The converse I think was never true. Ms. LeBlanc with Ms. Hartwell did what she had been doing for all of her short life. What did we hear her say? What did we hear? . . .

"We heard her say sex is power. Sex is power. Sat right here and looked at you and told you so. And she began exercising that power when she was fourteen years old. She gave you one brief burst of tears. Remember? 'Oh, how can you do this to me?'" he mockingly said, like a schoolboy taunting a girl. "And then didn't cry again once about the fact that if she would have you believe her stepfather systematically raped her for four years. And she did nothing about it. Knowing what you have learned of her, learned of her here, tell me what you think she really was for four years. Do you think it was a relationship in which Ms. LeBlanc took?"

Sawyers's walnut brown eyes pierced the jurors. "You know, if Ms. LeBlanc, if she was less attractive, if she was bigger, [she] wouldn't cause as great a problem as I think she does. You know, Mr. Ganne told you a few minutes ago we both have daughters. You know, he might have gone on to say we suffered from a bias, one that will probably die out when men my age are gone. But, you know, what that bias is is one that says surely, 'Please, God, little, attractive girls don't commit horrible, brutal crimes. Please don't let that be true.' Surely not. And we have here, the first man around the corner. What a choice, huh? Whether by design or accident, whether she knew where she was going, could you get a better picture of beauty and the beast?" He looked at Thomas. "Could you? Great big, old, ugly boy, six feet four, 230 pounds.

"You know," said Sawyer, "my grandfather also told me once, 'Truth is not complicated. People are. Truth sits there all by itself.'"

Justin Thomas sat there looking like a handsome University of Texas football player.

Gregg Cox's shoulders were erect. He knew his game plan. "Now, the defense," said Cox, "and Mr. Ganne and Mr. Sawyer are very good lawyers. They're very articulate. They're very dramatic, theatrical with their closing arguments. But sometimes you have to wonder, were they in the same court-room as you? They're spinmasters. They like to put their little spin on the evidence.

"I believe it was Mr. Sawyer that said the weight of the evidence, the bulk of the evidence, points to Ms. LeBlanc in this case. Use your common sense. Does it?

"They said that they were going to show you that there was some kind of secret deal in exchange for her testimony. And because they weren't able to show that there was a deal, they attack me personally. They say I'm immature, that I have no experience at these things, and that I was conned by someone. Ladies and gentlemen, just you recall the evidence."

At 11:17 a.m., on Wednesday, August 21, 1996, the jury retired to deliberate.

CHAPTER 27

The jurors stood in their tiny, fourth-floor jury room. Wire mesh covered the windows that viewed Austin. It was hot. They stared quietly at each other. Their task before them was daunting. A young man's future was on the line.

Juror Greg Ledenbach watched and worried about doing the right thing. He was a high-tech, California bigwig with Austin's Sematech consortium. Only a year earlier had he moved to Austin. Never before had he served on a jury.

Ledenbach hadn't wanted to serve, but he felt it was his civic duty. A devout Catholic with three children to be a role model for, it wasn't in Ledenbach's moral structure to lie his way out of jury duty. He felt that the United States had the best justice system in the world, and he had to serve his duty if he expected others to serve their duty.

There he was in that Austin jury room on a hot, August day listening to a tale about lesbians and drugs and murder. "Beyond a reasonable doubt," he soon discovered, was not as easy as it seemed on TV, especially when he was responsible for someone's life, perhaps for the rest of that person's life.

* * *

"I believe," said one male juror, "that as we've gotten to know one another over this past week, that no one is going to be offended if I ask this. So, I'm going to ask: Do you mind if we pray together before we start this?"

Everyone agreed, and the juror led them in prayer.

Ledenbach was selected as foreman.

The twelve jurors then sat down to their deliberation; their minds reeled with testimony and closing arguments. They had been impressed with the prosecution's systematic, undramatic closing.

They had not been impressed by the defense's. In fact, some considered Ganne's and Sawyer's theatrical antics offensive. Like Kim LeBlanc, many of the jurors didn't understand Sawyer's perceived need to question LeBlanc, push LeBlanc, seemingly exploit LeBlanc and her alleged victimization by her stepfather.

They also didn't like the defense team's constant attack on Cox, particularly his youth and alleged inexperience. In fact, it turned the jurors off.

In contrast, the jurors respected Cox for refusing to drop down to the defense's street-fighting, mudslinging attorney-against-attorney tactics. They also admired the way Cox and Van Winkle had been professional, courteous, and respectful to the witnesses, even the witnesses for the defense. They were downright impressed by Gregg Cox and Gail Van Winkle.

"Does anybody feel like they've solidly made up their mind?" said Ledenbach.

Six jurors raised their hands, yes. Six raised their hands, undecided.

"We're going to have to discuss this and figure it out. If you believe he's guilty, why? What makes you believe he's guilty? If you don't believe beyond a reasonable doubt that he's guilty, why? What do you need to see or what do we need to discuss to make you make up your mind? And those of you who believe beyond a reasonable doubt that he is guilty, what would make you have doubt?"

Jeremy Barnes had cleaned up blood and it had been no big deal. That just plain shocked the jury. There was a lot of blood, enough to stain the carpet padding, and Barnes had thought it was from a nosebleed. *That much blood doesn't come from a nosebleed,* thought Ledenbach.

But Dr. Bayardo had said that most of the bleeding had been internal. *You can't not believe that guy.* His testimony and the autopsy photos had caused many a juror a sleepless night.

After seeing the police photo of Kim LeBlanc, juror Sheral Cole had thought the defense's argument that LeBlanc had manipulated Justin Thomas into murdering Regina Hartwell for Kim was hogwash.

Cole, a young attorney with flawless, smooth skin and a big smile, couldn't even talk her husband, who loved her dearly, into taking out the trash, so how could Kim LeBlanc have talked Justin Thomas into murdering Regina Hartwell?

When Kim LeBlanc took the witness stand, Sheral Cole had been shocked, as were all the jurors.

LeBlanc looked like the kind of girl Greg Ledenbach would agree to let his son go out with. Ledenbach couldn't believe that the Kim in the police photo and the one sitting in the witness chair were the same person. It made him realize the havoc drugs can wreak on the body.

But not Sheral Cole. Kim LeBlanc, thought Cole, was beautiful, the way Elizabeth Taylor is beautiful. Sheral began to "get" the defense's argument. Maybe Kim had talked Justin into murdering Regina. Who couldn't be captivated by such beauty?

In fact, Cole, the mother of two babies, had shivered and

shaken in her juror's chair when Kim had announced that she worked with children. Sheral Cole didn't buy it. Not one bit. She didn't buy it that Kim LeBlanc hadn't been in Regina Hartwell's apartment during the murder. She didn't buy it that Kim LeBlanc had been home sleeping or taking a shower. She didn't buy it because she didn't believe that someone would participate that much in a cover-up if she didn't have something to cover up. Sheral Cole believed one hundred percent that Kim LeBlanc had been in Regina Hartwell's apartment during the murder.

"I want to know whether or not the chain was used to tow a car. The reason for buying that chain is plausible," said one juror.

Four notes were sent to Judge Fuller. The jurors asked for a flip chart, the witness list, part of Jeremy Barnes's testimony, and portions of Justin Thomas's testimony. They asked for all of the evidence to be brought to the jury room. The photos of Regina's charred-to-a-black-crisp body. The knife. The trash can. The chain.

The jurors looked at and studied the chain. It was bright and shiny. It wasn't scratched up. Many of the jurors had towed cars before. Their chains, while towing, dragged on the ground and after towing, were dirty and scratched. The Thomas chain, after allegedly used for towing, was brand, spanking new—pristine condition. The jurors concluded it hadn't been used to tow anything.

That chain, and its simultaneous purchase with the trash can, also made them conclude that the can had been bought to use for the sole purpose of body disposal, not normal household-garbage disposal.

They discussed the theory of Thomas throwing the can filled with Hartwell's body in the river behind his father's home. The river there is shallow enough to walk across, they noted. Thomas had indeed walked across it. That meant, if he had thrown the can in the river, the can would have been visible. "That's kind of stupid," they reasoned. "But on the other hand, committing murder is stupid."

"We've never committed murder. So we can't say this is how we'd feel, but we kind of expect that you'd be rather irrational. So stupid things can seem rational in that case. So that's totally plausible that that's what they were going to do."

"So why didn't they do that?" asked Ledenbach. "Why did they burn her?"

"I think he panicked."

They recalled the length of the knife blade. The wound was longer than the knife found under Hartwell's body. It would need force to stab that deep. Someone very strong wielded that knife. They looked at LeBlanc's photo. The young person in it didn't look strong enough to stab Hartwell. If Ledenbach had passed on the street the Kim LeBlanc in that police photo, he wouldn't have had any interest in being anywhere near her. She was so emaciated that she looked like she might die.

It didn't bother the jurors that the knife hadn't burned, that it only had one small, blackened area on its handle. Not charred like the body. Simply blackened. They reasoned that, since it had been wedged under the body and wrapped in blue cloth, it hadn't gotten enough air to burn.

The jury continued to talk. They wanted to make sure they didn't miss anything, that they didn't misunderstand anything. They talked. They clarified. "How did you perceive that witness? Did you believe him?" They asked those questions back and forth, constantly. "What did you think?"

The facts weren't what impressed the jurors about Anita Morales. It was Anita Morales herself. Her body language added to her credibility. Anita seemed like she'd really lost a friend whom she had loved. It touched them.

Bonnie Thomas's coarseness, even if it was well-mannered coarseness, turned them off. Ledenbach thought Bonnie Thomas looked like she'd led a hard life—hard like an under-nourished, backwoods Appalachian woman. But that didn't mean he trusted her. He didn't. Ledenbach certainly didn't believe that Bonnie Thomas didn't do drugs with Justin and Kim. That made him believe Kim's testimony more.

They all felt the same thing. They all agreed.

To them, when Thomas took the stand, he seemed to say, "Well, I'm a really good farm boy and all this stuff is really ridiculous and I can pull the wool over your eyes and just listen to me how truthful I am." To them, he seemed to say, "If you believe this stuff, you've gotta be dumb."

They thought Thomas had told them what he believed they wanted to hear. It didn't matter if his testimony was consistent or inconsistent—they were still going to believe what he said. He contradicted the testimony of other witnesses. He even contradicted the statements of his own attorneys. The jurors noted that.

The young Texas Aggie juror, not much older than Thomas himself, picked up on what his fellow jurors didn't notice, what Ganne and Sawyer acted as though they didn't notice, and what the prosecutors didn't seem to notice.

He noted the contradictory testimony regarding the date of the scooter accident and the date Justin Thomas had given the black leather recliner to Regina Hartwell.

That's when the jurors sent the fourth note to Judge Fuller requesting "Jeremy's testimony of when scotter [sic] accident happened," and "Justin's testimony regarding when scotter [sic] accident happened." That portion of the note was written in one juror's handwriting. The last portion was written by another juror. "Justin's testimony regarding purchase of chair for Regina."

Time and again, Justin Thomas had blown it with the jurors.

The blood evidence, tied to the defendant's own testimony, contributed to the verdict.

The reading of the verdict was postponed until 2:15 p.m., until Ganne and Sawyer could be retrieved from lunch.

"We, the jury, find the defendant, Justin Thomas, guilty of Murder as alleged in the indictment."

Just three hours after the jury had begun its deliberations, Justin Thomas heard his conviction. Mark Hartwell wept. Melody Mann, Thomas's teenaged girlfriend, broke down. Regina's friends watched, and they felt guilty themselves. Jeremy Barnes walked over to hug and hold Melody. He knew what it was like to lose someone you love, no matter how good or bad they were.

On Friday, August 23, 1996, two days after the guilty verdict had been read, the jurors finally returned to the courtroom for the penalty phase of the trial. It had been postponed at the defense's request—they wanted to study the audio tape of Dorothy Brown's statement to the Riverside County, California authorities. Brown was the state's key penalty-phase witness.

Dorothy Brown stepped up to the witness stand. She was overweight and wore a sundress that was too tight, with straps too loose. They fell off of her shoulders. She had long, greasy, blonde hair. It wasn't natural blonde. She wore flip-flops on her feet.

A former speed freak, she looked, to put it in Texas terms, like she'd been rode hard and put up wet.

Dorothy Brown told her story about watching Thomas murder Rafael Noriega. Thomas smiled a few times. Dorothy looked scared. She focused her gaze on her questioner, with one, sole glance at the jurors.

Bonnie Thomas thought Dorothy Brown had been so geeked

out on drugs that September night in California that there was
no telling whom she thought she had seen pull the trigger on
the gun that had murdered Rafael.

Jeremy Barnes thought Dorothy Brown looked like an
Amazon.

Greg Ledenbach thought she was absolutely believable. She
had no reason to lie. She had nothing to gain. He understood
why she had told a slightly different story earlier to the police.
But he didn't see that those same reasons applied in 1996.

Kim LeBlanc stepped up to the stand one last time.
"Did [Justin Thomas] tell you why this murder [of Noriega]
had occurred?"

"He told me it was because he thought Rafa might have
been a narc."

Once again, the jurors were back in the jury room. Unmit-
igated relief relayed from face to face. Their guilty verdict
had not been a mistake. There wasn't any room left for any
nagging doubt. They were totally convinced, no shadow of a
doubt, that Justin Thomas was guilty of the murder of Regina
Hartwell, and even that Justin Thomas was guilty of the
murder of Rafael Noriega.

They believed Thomas had had the exact same reason for
murdering Noriega as he did for murdering Regina. They had
not overlooked anything in the trial evidence and testimony.
Even though there was no evidence that said he had done it,
there was no evidence, either, that said he hadn't done it.

Based on Justin Thomas's testimony alone, Sheral Cole
wanted to give him the electric chair, but that wasn't a possibility. The state hadn't sought the death penalty. Jurors are much
less likely to convict if the possibility of death is involved.

In less than an hour, the jurors assessed punishment.

* * *

Kim LeBlanc went to listen. She walked into the courtroom. She sat down next to Anita Morales. Regina's friends stared.

"I'm sorry," Kim said to Anita. "I was shocked when you talked to me the other day. That's why I didn't say anything. I didn't know what to say. You threw me off guard. But thank you for saying that. You know, I'm doing better now."

Kim continued to talk about herself. Then she looked around the courtroom.

"Justin's such an asshole," she said. "What do you think will happen to him?"

Morales was in shock. To her, it seemed that LeBlanc spoke as if she'd never had anything to do with Justin Thomas.

"Who's that?" asked Kim, leaning close to Anita.

"Dorothy Brown."

"Oh, that's Justin's ex-girlfriend," Kim said.

"We, the jury, having found the defendant, Justin Thomas, guilty of the offense of Murder, assess his punishment at confinement in the Institutional Division of the Texas Department of Criminal Justice for life."

It was the maximum possible sentence—life in prison with parole possible after thirty years.

Judge Fuller asked the jurors if they wanted to talk to the prosecutors and defense attorneys. "Yes," they said, "we have some questions."

They all had the same question. "Why did Justin testify?"

"Because it's his right, and he wanted to," Sawyer and Ganne answered. They also told the jurors that they had pleaded with him not to testify, but that Thomas had insisted.

From that, Ledenbach surmised that Thomas had believed

that, if he testified, he could convince the jurors that he was innocent.

"Why didn't Justin's father testify?" Ledenbach asked, stepping onto an item that all the jurors had wondered about. They'd guessed that Justin must have been guilty if his own father hadn't supported him.

"We couldn't put him on the stand because if Gregg Cox had asked him, 'Did you do drugs with Justin?' he would have had to say, 'Yes,'" Sawyer answered.

"Why did we have such a highly educated jury?"

"Because it's a very technical case. We wanted jurors who would understand the DNA evidence and take it for its scientific value," said Cox.

"Yes," agreed Sawyer, "it was a very technical case, and we wanted jurors who would listen to the facts."

The meeting with jurors and lawyers lasted fifteen minutes. Their question for Cox and Van Winkle was, "What are you going to do about Kim LeBlanc?"

Even though Greg Ledenbach believed Kim, he also believed that she should be indicted—that Regina Hartwell's murder wouldn't be closed until Kim LeBlanc went to trial.

Regina Hartwell's murder will never be completely closed. It still affects lives.

Within two months of his son's conviction, Jim Thomas attempted suicide, now a pattern on both sides of Justin's family.

He was found lying in his dream home, near death from an overdose of pills. Helicopters rushed to the Garfield house and flew Jim to the hospital. He lived, and signed himself into Pavilion Hospital—for treatment for depression and alcoholism. Jim Thomas had realized that Regina Hartwell hadn't been his son's first murder, and he couldn't live with that knowledge.

Jim told Bonnie, "If this had been your son, I wouldn't have stayed the way you did for Justin."

Bonnie's heart ached.

Kim LeBlanc's plea to the Regina Hartwell murder charge was postponed more than twenty times. The following Memorial Day weekend, nine months after she had testified against her former lover at the murder trial of Regina Hartwell, Kim LeBlanc wed. She married a slim, young, blond boy with an appearance similar to Tim Gray, her best friend. They live in Houston, home to Kim's natural father and Regina's father.

Mark Hartwell, according to Regina's friends, has "made a three-sixty." He is loving, kind, and tender toward them; he wants to be a father to them. They all love him.

Cathy LeBlanc, Kim's mother, remarried. Prior to the wedding, she expressed that she felt guilty that she wasn't a strong person, still replaying the words of Ken LeBlanc.

Judy Thomas, Justin's mother, began psychological therapy.

On June 11, 1997, John C. Carsey, Kim LeBlanc's high-powered attorney, filed motion after motion in Travis County, Texas. The motions were to suppress Kim's hidden videotape questioning by the Austin Police Department.

The next month, Justin Thomas wrote his father, who by then no longer communicated with his son, and asked for $20,000 for a defense attorney.

Days later, and just weeks after the second anniversary of Regina Hartwell's murder, Jim Thomas committed suicide. He used one of Justin's guns.

He couldn't be there for his son like Bonnie was.

On October 13, 1997, District Judge Bob Perkins ruled that the police videotape of Kim LeBlanc was inadmissible. She had, indeed, asked for an attorney seven times. The police, according to Carsey's motion, violated LeBlanc's rights according to the Fifth and Fourteenth Amendments of the U.S. Constitution.

On November 3, 1997, the state dropped the murder charge against Kim LeBlanc due to insufficient evidence.

But Regina Hartwell's burned-to-a-crisp corpse will never be dropped from the jurors' minds. That image of a blackened monkey carved out of hard lava just won't leave.

"Regina wanted so much to protect Kim and keep her safe. Now Kim is clean, getting her life together, and going to school. And to me, it cost Regina her life. But if Regina were here now, she'd say, 'That's the way I want it' because she cared that much about Kim," said Anita Morales.

"And you know what? The drama queen that Regina was, I don't think she would have wanted to go out any other way but this dramatically. That was Regina."

AUTHOR'S NOTE

I am constantly asked why I wrote this book. My answer is always the same. Because it's the story of abuse—be it alcohol, drug, sexual, physical or emotional—and how it destroys lives unless admitted and faced.

Three people in this story were involved in alcohol, drug, sexual, physical and/or emotional abuse. One is dead. One is serving a life sentence in prison. One eventually admitted and faced her abuses and is sober and a functioning member of society.

I wrote this book because on the surface I have nothing in common with these people, but scratch below the surface and my friends, my family, my society and myself have too much in common with Kim, Regina and Justin.

Regina, you are not forgotten. You are still affecting lives. Thank God, there are steps to a life as beautiful as your smile.

Thanks goes to Deborah Hamilton-Lynne who brought me this story, Gregg Cox who gave me an interview before there was a book deal, Monica Harris who picked up on the idea, Paul Dinas who bought it, Jane Dystel who closed it, and Karen Haas who edited it.

Thanks also to Gail Van Winkle, Sgt. David Carter, Joel Silva, K.C. Anderson, Patrick Ganne, Jim Sawyer, Bonnie Thomas, John Carsey, Sheral Cole, Greg Ledenbach, Tommy Swate and, yes, Justin Thomas. Justin, you are always in my thoughts and prayers.

A special thanks to Regina's friends—Ynema Mangum (and Sheila), "Pam Carson," Amy Seymoure, "Sam," "Kyle Blake," "Brad Wilson," and "Mike White."

A very special and heartfelt thanks goes to Jeremy Barnes and, particularly, "Anita Morales." I couldn't have written this book without you both.

I also could not have written it without my friends—Deb, Beth Martin Brown, Kathy Greenwood, Susie Craig, Kathe Williams, Jane Emily, Frank Campbell, Cynthia Clawson, Patti Berry and the Austin Writers' League. Thanks, too, to my heroes Ben Masselink, of the University of Southern California Masters of Professional Writing program, and George Holmes.

But most of all thanks to my family—Mommie, Siba, Jeane, Robert, Townie, Kathy, and Lavonia. You've given me support that only God knows. I guess that means we're stuck with each other.

POSTSCRIPT: THE SECOND TRIAL

Justin Thomas sat in his Texas prison whites, the only apparel he'd worn since his conviction for murdering Regina Hartwell more than three years earlier. His short-sleeved pullover tunic of heavy cotton revealed the ever-increasing number of tattoos on his lean torso. The matching buttonless, zipperless, and belt-less pants covered his hard, tattooed legs. The date was January 26, 2000, the start of a new century, a time when some thought life would end and others hoped for a new beginning.

"Specifically," Thomas questioned, "what does your office intend for me?" He coolly watched Martin Silva, an investigator with the Riverside County, California, District Attorney's Office.

Justin Thomas was one of those who hoped for a new beginning. "I wanna be with my kids, you know what I'm saying? I got something out there." He really believed this. "I got goals I wanna obtain, man." But Justin Thomas's life before Regina Hartwell was about to come back to get him—

first creating a new beginning, then, seven years later, a whole new ending.

Martin Silva had flown from California to Texas to interview Thomas about the murder of Rafael "Rafa" Noriega, the very same Rafa whom Dorothy Brown had accused Thomas of killing. "Well," Silva said, audibly exhaling, "we're—we're probably gonna, we're probably gonna see if there's enough to, uh, if—if—if there's gonna be enough to charge you."

"Charge me?"

In fact, on June 30, 1999, Riverside, California, authorities had issued a warrant for the arrest of Thomas for the murder of Noriega. The warrant carried the added weight of serious felony because a firearm had been used, special circumstances—there had been a robbery during commission of the murder—as well the burden of a previous conviction, the murder of Regina Hartwell.

Silva didn't tell Thomas that. What he said was "There's a lot of finger-pointing. . . ." Then he mentioned the name Kelly Smith. "You don't remember Kelly Smith? . . . Man! It's the kid that drove up there with you guys. With you an-an-and Dorothy."

"Drove up where?" Thomas tried to sound innocent.

"Up to the egg ranch—the skinny kid."

"Skinny kid?" Thomas replied. There was a sly grin on his face. Thomas insisted that he was in Texas at the time of Rafael Noriega's murder—with his father and grandmother, trying to kick his crystal meth habit so that he could repair his failing marriage to his then-wife, Dawn. He also swore he was in the military when Noriega disappeared.

Neither was true.

He further insisted that he didn't have anything to hide, though he was nervous. "Because I got screwed over in this case . . . by trying to help Kim out, you know what I'm saying? And I know how easy it is—"

Silva laughed.

"—for the DA's office to manipulate the law, man, you know what I'm saying?"

"Well, I—"

"Goddamn! . . . You know what I'm saying? But . . . it keeps popping up."

The Noriega case had popped up in 1994, 1996, and 1998. By then, Thomas had thought there wasn't enough evidence to corroborate Brown's story and believed the case against him had been dropped.

"You just can't make things disappear," Silva said.

And they didn't. On June 13, 2000, nearly one year after the California warrant had been issued, Thomas stood in a Riverside County courtroom. He'd been extradited from Texas to the "Golden State" to face the Noriega murder charges. Thomas pleaded not guilty and was held without bail.

On July 5, 2000, five years to the day that he was incarcerated for Regina Hartwell's murder, Thomas's first California public defender asked to be removed from the case. Pete Scalisi, a veteran defender in capital murder cases, replaced him. On December 7, 2001, the state of California announced its intention to seek the death penalty. That began a nonstop series of postponements that would take Thomas through more than a dozen judges, two district attorneys, as well as three prosecutors. Twice, Deputy District Attorney Chuck Hughes took over the prosecution. He became obsessed with putting Thomas on death row.

Thomas was equally obsessed with fighting his Texas conviction. On December 22, 2006, more than ten years after he'd been pronounced guilty in Austin, the California court allowed Thomas to sit as co-counsel on his Texas case, as he hoped for an appeal, still claiming he did not kill Regina Hartwell. By the beginning of 2007, Thomas wanted to fire his attorneys and be his own lawyer on the California case too. On February 23, 2007, the court granted Thomas's motion—Scalisi and Darryl Exum, who had since joined the

California defense team, were relegated to the role of standby counsel.

Approximately two weeks later, the court deposited tax-payer money in Thomas's trust account so that he could buy a phone card. The card was only supposed to pay for phone calls that would help him prepare for his defense. Thomas used them for other purposes. He was becoming an old pro at manipulating the judicial system for his benefit.

By August 2007, after sitting in the Riverside County jail for more than seven years, the longest time of any inmate in the jail's history, Thomas told reporters from the *Riverside Press-Enterprise* that he spent his time studying the law and he'd just received a stack of legal manuals, which the court had purchased for him. Right about that same time, Thomas relinquished his role as attorney.

But the morning of October 3, 2007, the day his trial was to begin, the defense asked to withdraw as counsel. They were in constant conflict with their client. Their motion was denied. The case was moved a final time to Judge Terrence R. Boren, a cold case strike force judge from Marin County, California. The following week, the prosecution presented Judge Boren with a motion to have Thomas appear in restraints in front of the jury every day of the trial. Hughes wanted the defendant in restraints because of his reputed Mexican Mafia connections.

On October 29, 2007, fifteen years after Rafael Noriega's decomposing body had been discovered, opening arguments began in *The People of the State of California* v. *Justin Heath Thomas,* now spelled "Heath" rather than "Heith." (Thomas had thought his name was spelled one way; his birth certificate spelled it another.)

Not wearing restraints, Thomas sat before the jury; his hair hung past his shoulders and was styled in two huge poof balls. Thomas's attorneys had asked him to cut his hair or tie it into a ponytail to be tucked neatly inside his shirt so that he'd look more acceptable to the jury. They wanted to keep him out of the death chamber. Thomas had strategically disobeyed their desires. He had his own plan. Thus, with his hair combed in rebellious poofs, he listened for thirty-four minutes as Deputy District Attorney Chuck Hughes presented his opening arguments. Hughes's case strategy was to retry the Texas case.

The defense declined to make an opening statement.

The prosecution began its case in chief by providing the jury with color photographs of a wooden pallet with dust-coated shoes protruding from it and of Noriega's decomposed body, which lay partially covered by desert rocks and dirt. Hughes also showed the jurors a photograph of a watch, a bracelet, and a cross on a chain. He added a color photograph of four bags containing a white substance—drugs.

He next showed the jurors a sealed bag, which was then unsealed. A .45-caliber casing rolled out. Whereas Regina Hartwell had been stabbed, Rafael Noriega had been shot—as many as five times. And whereas Regina Hartwell's body had been burned, no one could confirm that Noriega's had been burned. His body was decomposed too badly. Those were things Thomas's defense attorneys wanted the jury to understand.

To end that first day of prosecutorial testimony, Deputy District Attorney V. Hightower stepped into the witness-box. Hughes read aloud the Texas prosecutor's questions that Dorothy Brown had been asked in 1996. Hightower read the Texas answers. Dorothy Brown was unavailable to testify in this trial. She'd been killed in a police shoot-out in Orange County, California, in 2004. Hughes also read the Texas defense team's questions to Brown because Justin Thomas's California attorneys refused to participate in the prosecution's courtroom re-creation.

* * *

The following morning, Hughes began retrying the Texas case. The date was October 30, 2007, four days before Justin Thomas's 36th birthday and four days before the tenth anniversary of the day the state of Texas dropped its murder charges against Kim LeBlanc. Hughes called Kim LeBlanc to the stand.

For LeBlanc, Thomas wore his hair down and free, like romance novel cover model Fabio. Thomas was leaner than he'd been in 1995. His brow was a bit more prominent. Squiggles of wrinkles lined his forehead. Gray circles aged his eyes. Still, he was handsome for a man who had spent thirteen years incarcerated, eleven of those in administrative segregation.

The pretty, petite, blond cheerleader had grown into a slightly chubby, married thirty-one-year-old with long, warm brown hair highlighted with blond. Justin Thomas thought she looked stunning. He'd always told her she'd look beautiful with long hair, and what he saw on that witness stand confirmed his every belief. She was sworn in as Kimberley Reeder. She tossed her highlighted locks flirtatiously. He fell in love all over again, in love before the prosecutor had even asked Kim LeBlanc Reeder if someone had admitted to her that he had killed Regina Hartwell.

"Justin Thomas," she answered. Just like in Texas, Kim LeBlanc Reeder had been granted immunity from prosecution in return for her testimony against Thomas. Gregg Cox had facilitated the California immunity agreement. LeBlanc Reeder pointed to her former lover. "He's wearing a green blouse with burgundy tie."

Thomas, whose upper body was now covered in even more tattoos—one depicting a skull full of nails, others showing fanged demons, as well as women with long, flowing tresses—was still loving Kim LeBlanc.

"He told you that he killed Rafa in California?"

"Right."

"And why did he say he killed Rafa?"

"Because he was a narc."

It was the same reason Kim LeBlanc had given for Regina Hartwell's murder in Texas. And from then on, Hughes focused his questioning of Kim LeBlanc Reeder on Austin, Texas, July 1994 to July 1995, events that happened nearly two years and more after the murder of Rafael Noriega.

He placed a photograph of Regina Hartwell on the Elmo projector that sat between the defense and prosecution's tables. The Elmo beamed the image over the five courtroom televisions. LeBlanc Reeder turned to her right and stared at the photograph on a small black Panasonic TV. She had no reaction to the picture of Regina.

Hughes placed a photograph of the young LeBlanc on the Elmo. She looked at it on the TV screen and turned away. It was the same black-eyed, red-nosed, sickly photo the police had taken of her on July 5, 1995. She began to cry. "I need a break."

As Kim LeBlanc Reeder exited the courtroom for her requested recess, others in the room focused on the fact that she hadn't reacted at all, not one iota, to the picture of her dead friend, Regina Hartwell. But she had wept over her own wasted image.

After court reconvened, Chuck Hughes asked LeBlanc Reeder if she had an idea what Justin Thomas planned to do to Regina Hartwell. She believed he was going to kill her, she said. She swore she didn't want Regina murdered; she just wanted more drugs. Likewise, she didn't phone the police because she wanted to get high. "Even though I knew it was going to cost her her life."

Hughes took her through the disposal of Hartwell's body. For the most part, LeBlanc Reeder answered every detailed question, including her belief that Jim Thomas, Justin's father, new that Regina Hartwell's dead body was in her Jeep.

Then, under Hughes's questioning, she reported that the last time she used drugs was on July 5, 1995, the day the Austin police had picked her up for questioning. After completing rehab, she "went back to college, joined the army, got out of the army, figured out what I wanted to be, finished my degree, and now I'm a research scientist."

"What subject do you research?" Hughes said.

"Cancer," she replied.

Justin Thomas sat up straighter. He was so proud of Kim. He'd dated a girl who had become a cancer research scientist.

She was a mother too.

On Halloween, 2007, the young mother endured a four-hour cross-examination by Pete Scalisi. Would you have testified against Mr. Thomas without immunity?" Scalisi asked regarding the Regina Hartwell murder trial.

LeBlanc Reeder said she didn't know. "I was pretty scared." She later added, "I would have been incriminating myself for murder."

Scalisi asked if on the very first night she'd met Regina Hartwell, had she thought Hartwell was attracted to her in a romantic, sexual way?

"I did."

"And were you interested in her in that way?"

"Yes." LeBlanc Reeder said she, too, was attracted to Hartwell.

"In a physical sense?" Scalisi queried.

"In a physical sense."

"Were you having some sex with her?"

"We were having some intimate time, yes." At Scalisi's goading, Kim LeBlanc Reeder stated that in August of 199- she and Regina Hartwell began having intimate time together twice a week, which he called "some kind of sexual activity," and she agreed.

Scalisi asked LeBlanc Reeder if she recalled being asked about her sex life with Regina Hartwell during the Texas trial—"when you testified under oath."

"I don't remember."

"Would it refresh your recollection if I showed you your testimony?" He showed her page 117, line ten, of the Texas trial transcript, where she talked about touching Regina Hartwell's private parts with a vibrator a week and a half before Hartwell was murdered.

LeBlanc Reeder read the lines and then stated in the California courtroom, "It says right here, 'Did you have sex with her?'"

"What did you say?" Scalisi responded.

"I said that I did not. But I didn't have sex with her," LeBlanc Reeder protested. "But we did kiss. We did touch each other, but we didn't have sex."

"Earlier today, did you tell the jury twice a week you would sleep with her and have sex, some kind of sexual relations?"

"We would mess around. We would kiss. We would touch each other. We would do things, but I don't remember exactly if we—I don't remember what we did sexually. Obviously, it was intimate."

Scalisi asked her what she was thinking when he'd used the word "sex."

"Well, we were—we touched each other. We were—I mean, we're two women."

Indeed, Scalisi believed he was catching LeBlanc Reeder in frequent lies.

She turned and looked at the jury. "It's very possible that a year after getting clean that I remembered something differently than I do thirteen years later at thirty-one. I mean, I really am trying to do the best I can to remember."

Scalisi baited her about not phoning Hartwell and warning her that Thomas was going to kill her, despite believing that's exactly what was about to happen. "So, to you, it didn't matter if she lived or died?"

"It didn't matter."

He questioned her about her unsubstantiated alibi that she was alone in her apartment, sleeping, when Regina Hartwell was stabbed to death. Scalisi looked into LeBlanc Reeder's eyes and plainly stated, "Did you kill Ms. Hartwell?"

"No."

He asked her if she'd gone to Hartwell's apartment between the time Regina was murdered and the time Kim went there to meet Anita Morales and Jeremy Barnes and helped file the missing person report. LeBlanc Reeder hesitated before answering, "I don't think so."

He quizzed her about her hesitation. "Let's put it this way," Scalisi said, "you can't say for certain that you didn't?"

"No, I can't for certain." She also stated that she didn't know whether or not she'd been videotaped while being interviewed at the Austin Police Department.

Chuck Hughes had that videotape of the July 5, 1995, interview. Gregg Cox had provided it, as well as all of his work product, to Hughes. Cox, too, wanted Thomas to get the death penalty.

"Did you tell the police in that interview, that statement, that you wanted Regina Hartwell dead?"

"I don't remember if I said that or not."

"Do you think you said that?"

"I could have said that. Is it written down in there?" she inquired.

"Basically, yes," Scalisi responded. He later asked her if she had fallen in love with Justin Thomas.

"I did."

A smile crept across Thomas's face.

"He took care of you and was protective of you?"

"He was protective."

Thomas again sat up straighter.

Scalisi asked Kim LeBlanc Reeder if she'd ever been in jail for the murder of Regina Hartwell, other than being questioned by the police on July 5, 1995.

"I was sitting in that holding cell probably for five hours max," she responded.

He looked at the jury to note their reaction. "Why did they drop the charge against you?"

". . . Asking for the lawyer and not getting it was the loophole," she stated.

Several of the jurors looked away from her. Some in the courtroom thought she was cold and calculating, but Pete Scalisi savored every admission Kim LeBlanc Reeder had made, from the fact that she and Regina Hartwell had been sexual partners to the fact that she would have been incriminating herself for murder if she'd testified in Texas without immunity. She'd even testified that she hadn't known Regina Hartwell had been in love with her.

The following day, the jurors listened to investigator Martin Silva's audiotaped 2000 interview with Justin Thomas, during which Silva outlined Kelly Smith's story.

"And you tell me where he's full of shit," Silva said to Thomas. Smith was at Dorothy Brown's house when Thomas and Noriega agreed to meet that night to trade marijuana for crystal meth. Smith and Brown then followed Thomas to the ranch. "And he doesn't really know what happens up there, but there's some gunshots that go off and then eventually . . . he goes up there after that. . . ."

Thomas audibly chuckled on the tape.

"Now he says he doesn't see what happens to the guy. He doesn't see a body, doesn't see anything. . . . You tell him [to] take the car back to the house, and he's going, 'No, no, no,' and you said . . . you better take the car back to the house." Terrified, Smith jumped into Noriega's vehicle, drove one hundred yards, stopped, jumped out, and ran to a friend's house. There he told the friend everything that had happened. Silva found the friend in Tennessee, and he confirmed Smith's story.

Silva then recounted Dorothy Brown's story for Thomas, including Thomas yelling, "Yoo-hoo," as he rode in the truck bed with Noriega's dead body, and looked into the duffel bag full of drugs.

Thomas laughed.

"Of course, she claims, you know, 'I didn't know anything was gonna happen.' You know, 'I didn't have nothing to do with it. . . .' I mean, she just tries to minimize . . . as much as possible." But she, too, had told a friend what happened, and that friend had corroborated her story. Still, Silva wanted to know Thomas's side of the story.

"Two things I can tell you from jump," Thomas answered. First, he and Noriega had never met at night. Second, they'd always met in public places. Plus, Dorothy Brown and her friends had planned on "jacking" Thomas for his drugs. "I know you don't know about that."

"Right, I don't," Silva said.

"You're in front of these dudes, you know, who wanna fuck you over and take your shit, you know what I'm saying, and you kill and you don't even know it."

Court didn't resume until six days later, on November 7, 2007, when Anita Morales, now an officer with the Travis County Sheriff's Department, Jeremy Barnes, Terry Duval, the volunteer firefighter, and John Barton, from the Bastrop County Sheriff's Department, all testified.

Again, court recessed for a week. But on November 13, 2007, Chuck Hughes was wrapping up his "Texas trial" by calling Austin witnesses Mark Gilchrest, Don Nelson, Gary Molina, Texas Ranger Rock Wardlow, and Travis County coroner Roberto Bayardo, M.D. All provided the same photographic evidence and testimony that they had in 1996, all about the murder of Regina Hartwell, nothing concerning the murder of Rafael Noriega.

Ninety-five percent of the State's case, defense attorney Scalisi declared that day, was the Texas case, not the California case. The only evidence the State presented that connected Justin Thomas to the murder of Rafael Noriega was that of the dead Dorothy Brown. Kelly Smith never set foot in the courtroom. Scalisi was ticked. Per capita, Riverside prosecuted more death penalty cases and got more death penalty convictions than any other county in the state of California, often on cases with weak evidence. In other words, Riverside was the Houston, Texas, of California.

Still, under normal circumstances, Scalisi believed, *The People of the State of California* v. *Justin Heath Thomas* would not have been a death penalty case because it was the trial of one drug dealer killing another drug dealer. But because of Thomas's conviction in Texas, because he didn't get the death penalty for murdering Regina Hartwell, California intended on doing what Texas hadn't done—kill Justin Thomas.

The day before the Thomas trial officially began, the *Riverside Press-Enterprise* ran a story announcing that the district attorney's office would be giving 5 percent raises to the salaries of its attorneys who prosecuted death penalty cases. This "new approach" to "show appreciation and support" for its death penalty prosecutors was also intended "to keep those talented lawyers in the courtroom." That, too, ticked off Scalisi—Hughes didn't need to be handling this case. He'd been promoted already.

On November 14, 2007, after the People called Texan Michael Mihills, former classmate of Kim LeBlanc Reeder and a member of Justin Thomas's posse that had met with him at Jim's restaurant the night before Hartwell's murder, the People rested. Jurors were dismissed until November 27, 2007. Thanksgiving was coming up.

* * *

On November 26, 2007, S. Alex Stalcup, M.D., an addiction medicine expert who had interviewed Justin Thomas in 2004, sent a letter to Pete Scalisi addressing Thomas's lifelong problems with violence, the effects of fetal alcohol syndrome on Thomas's brain development as a child, and Scalisi's concerns over Thomas's "disruptive" trial behavior. Thomas talked in court when he wasn't supposed to, sometimes showed up in his jail clothes rather than street clothes, and snickered inappropriately.

Thomas's difficulties were "the result of genetic loading for addiction and mental illness" due "in part" to "his mother's daily drunkenness and her continuous use of cannabis (marijuana)" during her pregnancy with Justin, as well as her "continuing alcoholism and depression during his infancy, which severely damaged the essential maternal-infant bond with Justin," Stalcup believed. That, combined with Justin's own early drug addiction, "yielded a brain condition termed 'hypofrontality,'" which impaired Justin's judgment abilities and impulse control.

Stalcup stated that the symptoms of hypofrontality were obvious in Thomas: *Fidgeting and lack of concentration, bizarre and inappropriate facial expressions, disregard for the effect of his appearance on observers, casual indifference and inappropriate behavior.*

He wrote: *Having interviewed about 50 defendants in homicide cases, I recognize the damage done by early drug exposure.* For the last decade, Stalcup had served as medical director at the New Leaf Treatment Center in Lafayette, California. In 1998, he'd begun a research study on methamphetamine addicts. As part of that study, he'd done physical and neurological examinations on people who had been meth addicts for six to twenty-five years. *In all the interviews that I have conducted, Mr. Thomas started using drugs at the earli*

est age, by far, with a predictable tragic outcome for him.
Indeed, Stalcup referred to Justin Thomas as a "textbook case."

The next day, Justin Thomas was back to wanting to represent himself, and the defense presented its case. Scalisi called one witness, Special Investigator Martin Silva.

"Now Kelly seems to think that he saw maybe two people firing at each other," Silva said to Thomas back in 2000. "Now, you know, if that's the case, you know, this guy tried to shoot you first or whatever, I mean, that's important. . . . Whether you went up there and just ambushed the guy or whether you went up there and, you know, he—he tried to shoot you. . . ."

Thomas's attorneys had urged their client to plead self-defense.

"Like why did it happen?" Silva asked. "Did you get attacked?" Time and again, Silva offered Thomas a self-defense out. "Maybe this guy was after you, or, I mean, if there's a reason for this to happen . . ."

Time and again, Thomas had refused self-defense.

"You meet with him all the time, and then *boom*! All of a sudden you kill him? I mean, you know, that doesn't sound right. Something had to, you know, something had to trigger something. . . . Whose fault was it, you know?"

Silva was on the stand for less than an hour, after which the defense rested.

At 3:56 P.M., the jury retired to commence deliberations. Four minutes later, they recessed for the day. For three days, the jury mulled the evidence, before adjourning for the weekend. They returned on December 3. And on December 4, 2007, while the jury still wondered what they were going to do about Justin Thomas, the Office of the District Attorney, County of Riverside, issued a press release announcing the promotion of Chief Deputy District Attorney Chuck Hughes to Assistant District Attorney. It was his third promotion in three years.

Two days later, on December 6, 2007, in the jury's seventh day of deliberation, at 3:33 P.M., they returned a verdict. Justin Thomas was found guilty on all counts. He made faces, snickered, and even downright laughed.

On December 10, 2007, dressed in his orange jail clothes and surrounded by five deputies, Thomas was disruptive in the courtroom again. He talked throughout the proceedings. He made a speech to the judge announcing one more time that he wanted to serve as his own attorney. The judge questioned Thomas's understanding. Thomas assured Judge Boren that he did understand what he was doing—he was going to get a lot more financial resources for his defense.

Thomas spent the next day listening to Riverside County sheriff's deputies Thomas Montez and Dirk Webb tell the jurors how Thomas had been found with shanks, and then to the testimony of Dawn Thomas Bothof, his ex-wife.

When she'd walked into the courtroom, her long, brown hair flowing over her shoulders and gleaming, even in the green glare of the courtroom lighting, Justin Thomas fell in love all over again. Just as he had with Kim LeBlanc Reeder. And just like Kim had, Dawn appeared to have turned her life around. She was working as a real estate agent with a nationally known firm.

Dawn Bothof looked over at Justin Thomas. She hadn't seen him since 1994. Their divorce hadn't been finalized until 1998, two years after he'd been convicted for the murder of Regina Hartwell. But when she testified that he'd been captain of his high school football team, he thought he saw pride on her face, as if she still loved him.

"How do you feel about Mr. Thomas today?"

"Just disgusted," Bothof answered. "I mean, there's being

scared, disgusted, angry, embarrassed." Also just like LeBlanc Reeder, she didn't want to be in that courtroom.

"You're afraid that he'll somehow hurt you?"

"Yes." She recalled an argument that had ended with Thomas firing a shotgun, the blast exploding past their son and her and into a wall. She recounted a night when Thomas left the house in a drunken rage, threatening to kill a bouncer, only to return many hours later, threw Dawn on the bed, climbed on top of her, wrapped one hand around her neck, and choked her. "I was blacking out." She thought she was going to die.

Her sister ran into the room and yelled, "Stop! What are you doing?"

"And then he just, kind of, like, stopped. It was like he— like he just changed, like a different person." Bothof and her sister ran out the door and raced to a friend's house. When they eventually returned home, they found six-four Justin Thomas on the toilet, his head down, the gun propped against it, a slimy substance running from his noggin to his lap. "I thought he was dead." He was only feeling guilty.

They took the gun from him, loaded him in the back of his truck, and drove him to his uncle's ranch. But Thomas jumped out of the truck, crying that people were after him, watching him. "They're out here." He pounded on the window and then was gone. "He probably stayed the night in the dirt in the hills somewhere. . . ."

There were "many times" that Thomas said he knew how to kill people and where to dump their bodies. "He even showed me where he would dump bodies." She described the hills behind the ranch. "And he said nobody would find any bodies there. There's tons of bodies out there."

"Did he actually say he dumped a body out there, or he was talking theoretically?"

"He would say that and take it back. He did it. I did it. 'Oh, I'm just trying to scare you.' Stuff like that."

"Was there a time after he came back from Texas where he said to you that 'I've done it before. I can do it to you'?"

"Yes."

"Referring to killing?"

"Uh-huh."

She recalled the Valentine's Day fight in Hawaii, the result, she said, of telling Thomas that she was leaving him. "He got hysterical. Got a knife." For the next three days, she said, he held their son and her hostage, while on their couch, threatening to kill her with the knife if she took away their son.

"He didn't leave the couch for three days?" Hughes asked.

"Well, he went to the bathroom."

"Why didn't you leave while he was in the bathroom?"

"It was right by the door."

"Did you see him sleep at all?"

"No. He was accustomed to not sleeping." But she sneaked a call to 911. And as Thomas raised the knife to stab her, and Dawn cried, "Let me go, let me go," the police stared through the glass of the front door. Thomas suddenly stabbed at the cast on his leg, trying to get it off. A cop drew his weapon and yelled, "Stop. Stop. Right now." He tapped on the window. Thomas stopped.

Dawn had been pregnant at the time. "That's why I left. . . . While I was staying with him, he kicked me in the stomach and threw me down to the ground and stuff like that."

On cross-examination by Darryl Exum, Bothof admitted she'd started some of the fights with Thomas, though never the physical aspects. However, she had slapped her current husband, the police had been called, and she'd been arrested for assault.

As she walked out of the courtroom, Justin Thomas turned to her and said, "You know, Dawn, I'm sorry. I'm sorry." He then tried to ask her about their son. But that didn't go well, and he immediately fell out of love. In fact, he became so upset that he started talking to himself—though Justin Thomas talking to himself wasn't unusual.

Despite his client being inconsolably distraught, Darryl Exum had to board a jet for an emergency trip to the East Coast. Exum's mother had fallen seriously ill. As his jet lifted off the ground, Exum thought the defense case was going to proceed without him. Instead, it was postponed until he could return. Chuck Hughes feared that Thomas might later charge ineffective assistance if Exum wasn't there. Pete Scalisi agreed.

But the fact that court hadn't proceeded as Exum had expected, along with the fact that Thomas was demanding that he testify first in his defense, had destroyed Exum's tactical plan. So when court reconvened on Monday morning, December 17, 2007, Exum begged for a one-day postponement to prepare for direct examination.

He argued that he had to "make sure" his "client's rights are protected." Additionally, if Thomas chose to testify about certain things that his attorneys opposed, which Exum expected him to, he and Scalisi needed to make sure they weren't involved in such: "I'm trying to save my client's life. . . ."

But Thomas wanted to proceed. Chuck Hughes wanted to proceed.

Judge Boren gave Exum thirty minutes to talk with Thomas and prepare.

When the jury slipped into their chairs, Justin Thomas already sat in the witness-box. Exum quickly directed the testimony to Thomas's childhood, revealing that Jim Thomas had given his son drugs before Justin was seven years old, due to that Justin was snorting methamphetamines and cocaine by the age of nine or ten, and by age fourteen, he was injecting speed with his father's help.

Suddenly Exum stopped to emphasize to Thomas that this was a death penalty case, while stressing to the jury that

Thomas was testifying against the recommendation of both of his attorneys. He asked Thomas to tell the jurors why he was testifying.

"We didn't talk about that, Darryl."

"I understand I didn't ask you, but could you tell the jury?"

"When it comes time to read them this"—Thomas gestured toward a piece of paper—"yeah, I'll tell them."

"Justin, you're not answering my questions. Is that correct?"

"No, I'm not answering that."

With the judge's permission, Exum led his client. "Justin, it's correct you told Mr. Scalisi and myself that you want this jury to give you a death verdict. Is that a correct statement, or is that incorrect?"

"It's worded incorrect."

"You want the jury to come back with a finding of death. You don't necessarily want to get death, but you want the jury to come back with a finding of death?"

"That's correct."

"Now, you understand—and you don't want me to, but you understand I'm not going to do that, ask the jury to give you death, correct?"

"I understand."

"And that's against what you want?"

"Yeah, that's very against what I need."

Exum pointed out that Thomas didn't want to answer any questions about his drug use because his client didn't "want this jury to know the truth about those things."

"You make it sound like I'm trying to hide or manipulate their mind. I'm not. I'm not trying to do that," Thomas testified.

"No, but . . . you have said to me and Mr. Scalisi that you don't want this jury to have that kind of information because that might be the kind of information that might make them think you should get life without parole."

"Yeah."

And with that, Exum returned to Thomas's drug use, with

Thomas begrudgingly admitting that by the time he was thirteen years old, he was using LSD "weekly at times." Exum then asked Thomas for details of when he first injected drugs.

"You keep asking me things that I know we didn't talk about, Darryl."

"I understand," the attorney responded. "But I still want you to answer these questions for the jury. Will you do that?"

"No."

However, Thomas eventually admitted that he shot drugs before he was sixteen years old.

"Where did you get the needle?"

Thomas laughed. "I don't remember." Thomas reluctantly provided the details of how he injected meth at age fourteen. "I was scared, so I needed my dad's help. . . . [Pops] instructed me on how to do it right, and not to use no one else's needle, don't share needles, how to clean it."

"Anything else? Did he hold your arm?"

"How to tie off. How to pop the vein. How to hit the vein."

Exum insinuated that there were times when Jim Thomas wanted his son to do drugs.

"I guess it would be fair to say," Justin Thomas agreed.

Exum displayed childhood photos to the jury: Justin with his father, Justin as a baby holding a ball, Justin at eight years old—an age when he was doing drugs. He noted that Thomas had made good grades in school, as long as he paid attention, which wasn't something Justin was very good at.

"Let's talk about a typical time when you got drinks."

"The adults aren't paying attention, and me, being the demon seed that I was, tried to talk my cousins into getting a couple of snorts of whatever they had to feel so good."

"Why did you say you were a 'demon seed'?"

Thomas laughed once again.

"Aren't you just saying that because you want the jury to think that?"

"No," he said. "I mean, it's pretty true."

"Right. But you want the jury to think that, don't you?"

Thomas was silent. "Aren't all young boys at that age referred to as 'demon seeds'?"

"My question is this, Justin, you want the jury to think that you were a demon seed, right? You want the jury to think you've been bad your whole life, right?"

"What I want is for them not to do me any favors."

"And not doing you any favors means you want a death finding from them?"

"Yes."

"And you know to get a death verdict from them they've got to think you're bad?"

"Yes."

Court clerk Heather Chavez had thought Thomas was bad. That's why one day in court when the lights had gone out due to a blackout, she'd run, in panic, in fear of Justin Thomas. When she'd returned to the courtroom, Thomas had looked at her and said, "You scared of the dark?"

"Fuck you," she'd responded.

But in the weeks of the trial, they'd chatted. She'd gotten to know him. She no longer feared him. In fact, she admired the way he read and constantly studied. Every day he studied. Every day he meditated. Every day he did calisthenics.

"I don't want to manipulate them into anything," Thomas responded. "If they think that, they need to come to that their own conclusion."

"Is it the reason you're testifying so that they will give you that verdict, but you don't want them to feel bad about doing it? Is that fair?"

"That's fair."

"That's one of the reasons why you don't want me to call any witnesses?"

"It's not important. It has no bearing to the case."

"I'll ask it differently. You don't want me to call witnesses in this case. Why is that?"

"Because I know, genuinely, they don't care, and, genuinely, I don't care."

"What is your understanding of why I would call those kind of people?"

"To bring out the good character and the good things I've done throughout my life."

"Why would you not want the jury to know about that?"

"It doesn't suit my best interest."

"What is this best interest that you keep talking about?"

"I feel if I answer that that I'll be manipulating them or they'll think I'm trying to. I'm not trying to do that. I'm trying to give them the facts as they know it and ease their minds and hearts."

Exum asked Thomas to help the jury understand why he wanted the death penalty.

"No," he flatly stated.

"Even if the judge orders you to answer, you're not going to answer?"

"No."

"Is it your feeling, Justin, that you want this jury to say if he doesn't care, why should we care? I mean, isn't that part of it?"

"In essence, but it's not the context of my argument."

"Because, isn't it true that you—I mean, it's true that you believe if they don't care, it will be easier for them to have a finding . . ."

"Yes."

"Of death?"

"Right."

Exum asked Thomas to recall his laughter at the guilty verdict. Thomas laughed again at the memory. "Wasn't that a manipulation?" Exum asked.

"How?" Thomas questioned.

Exum repeated, "Wasn't that a manipulation?"

"No, it was a reaction," Thomas proclaimed.

"Was it funny?"

"Given the way the system works in this county, yes, it was funny. It was something I knew . . . was coming."

"Didn't you think that by laughing they would think that you didn't care? That you were making a mockery of what they did?"

"What I think of this whole thing has been a mockery of what it's supposed to be."

"But isn't that the real reason why you wanted to testify first, to discount all the witnesses, to discount all other evidence?"

"The reason was to try to let them see from my viewpoint, stand in my shoes. I know that can hardly be done, but for them to understand the reason why I think the way I think, why I would like to have [it] happen the way I would like to have it happen."

"I just want to ask you—"

"Yes. I'm not suicidal. I don't want aided suicide. But in the best interest of my future, how things turned out, to impose a death sentence is in my best interest, I believe. I don't need to go any further than that because then that's where I believe I will be—or they might feel me trying to manipulate them into something, and I don't want to do that."

"But there's a reason why you want a death sentence and it's not to die?"

"Right."

"Can you tell the jury that reason now?"

"Why?"

"Because I'm asking you."

"Then I don't get what I want—I don't get what I need, excuse me. And I seen how you twisted everything to get happen what you want happen. You've outmaneuvered me again."

"Isn't what you're talking about is there's been things you wanted me to do in this case and I haven't done them?"

"Several. Several. Yes."

"And I told you that my job as your lawyer is to tell this jury why your life should be spared, correct?"

"Yeah, that's your job."

"You told me not to do that. Would that be fair?"

"Yes."

"Why?"

Thomas's laughter filled the courtroom. "If the jury returns a sentence of life without, I won't be afforded the—"

Scalisi objected, and was overruled.

"The attention, scrutiny, and resources that I would with the death penalty that I think I deserve because of the prejudicial, biased rulings, lack of funds to adequately investigate and prepare the whole case. I mean, for seven years this case has went in one direction that I've not wanted it to, and I've asked, begged, and pleaded with you and Mr. Scalisi and investigators numerous times to proceed with the strategy that I was asking and that didn't happen."

Exum noted that Thomas's strategy would have led to the death penalty.

"It wouldn't have, had we done it my way from the beginning," Thomas replied, "but now—"

It would, Exum agreed.

And Thomas began arguing with his attorney, saying they were off track, complaining that they hadn't discussed this or his answers. "This is another thing that I've been pointing out to everybody from the beginning, man. You guys just—"

"I know," Exum stated. "Strike that. I'm sorry." He asked if the defense attorneys' strategy had been to get life without parole.

"What happened to a strategy of not guilty?" Thomas complained.

They returned to drugs, with Thomas stating that from ages seven to nine, he took drugs because he "wanted to get where they would take me."

Exum asked why.

"I guess I thought it was better than where I was at."

They talked about Thomas's days as a football star, with Thomas stating that football was the best thing that ever happened to him. Among other things, it reduced his drug use.

Exum pulled out and displayed Thomas's many football awards, from junior varsity to varsity, from California to Oregon, emphasizing that Thomas's play sent his teams to championships. He brought out Thomas's team pictures. He noted that in high school Thomas was six feet three inches tall and 245 pounds, thirty pounds heavier than Thomas's prison weight. He mentioned Thomas's drug dealing in high school, but quickly moved to Thomas playing semipro football.

"I got all the rookie awards that season, defensive player of the year, rookie of the year. . . ." After his second year, he was asked to try out for an American Football Conference team. But drugs, which he was using to give him a football speed edge, destroyed his dreams. He was a meth addict at age twenty.

When Exum showed a photo of Thomas at age nineteen with his mother, Thomas laughed. At that age, he was smoking marijuana primarily and used meth only once or twice a month when he needed to stay up to make his drug rounds, he said.

Exum noted that he and Scalisi had tried to get Thomas to have an MRI to examine his brain for damage. Thomas had refused the scan "because I don't feel that I'm brain damaged or predisposed to the drug use or abuse in my life." He told the jury, "I chose the path that I lived and I'm here because of it." He'd refused other medical evaluations after one expert had ruled he had an addictive personality. Thomas stated that such tests weren't in his best interest "if that's used to show the jury that life without is a better sentence."

Exum mentioned the testimony of the jail deputy who had found a shank in Thomas's boxer shorts and asked Thomas how many times he'd been stabbed.

"Seventeen stabbings and twelve lacerations on four different occasions." The scars lined and dotted his neck, chest, and arms.

He asked why Thomas had warned the deputy about the shank in his boxers.

"Because I didn't want him to get hurt." But Thomas did say if he needed to defend himself, he "most definitely" would stab someone.

Exum asked his client to explain how he got stabbed.

"The path you choose when you're inside, if you choose to get involved in politics, if you choose to get involved in drugs, anything that has to do with power inside." With a glint in his hazel eyes, Justin Thomas loved to hint that he was involved in jail politics.

"And from time to time, you've had people who—who are close to you like that, who have done injury to you. Would that be fair to say?" Exum asked.

Thomas again sat silently in the witness chair.

Exum repeated his question.

"I'm not going to answer that."

"Justin, there was something else that you've been telling me for the past couple of days that you wanted to say to the jury, and I'm going to give you that chance to say it now."

Thomas wanted to know if he could recite it. "That's just the easiest way. I don't want to get tongue-tied." So in his Hispanic rapper voice that he'd adopted in jail, Justin Thomas began to recite a poem he'd composed.

"'To give you all peace of mind and lighten the heavy burden on your hearts and your spirits, know that the path that I've chosen for myself in the past thirteen years that I've been locked up, either sentence is a sentence of death. If you found the elements to find me guilty, then you've also found the elements to impose the death sentence.

"'For those who love me, hold on if you must, but the spirit of the warrior is not geared to indulging or complaining, nor is he geared to winning or losing. The spirit of the warrior is geared only to the struggle, and he knows every struggle is a warrior's last battle on earth. A warrior allows his spirit to flow free and clear. He dreams of beautiful things and wages his battle, knowing his will is impeccable. He embraces death as part of the struggle. For those who hate me, a warrior laughs and laughs and laughs.'"

Darryl Exum had to turn this around. "Correct me if I'm wrong, you're basically telling the jury that it's not because you've been using drugs since you were seven years old? . . . It's not because of anything related to how you were born? . . . It's not because of anything related to your brain? . . . It's because of the path you chose?"

"The path I chose."

"Not because your father gave you cocaine when you were eight years old, right?"

"That's what I'm saying."

"It's not because you got your first taste of alcohol when you were three years old, right?"

"I believe in my heart, no," Thomas stated. "It's not."

"Does shooting up have anything to do with it when you were fourteen?"

"No. If I was an addict, as much drugs as I've had in my lifetime in one time, many times I could have ODed if I was an addict. An addict has to use it. They don't have control over it. I've stopped my use."

Exum asked Thomas if he could have chosen to stop when he was a free man, walking the streets.

"I believe so."

"But you didn't choose to stop, did you?"

"Didn't want to."

"Right. Because your father wanted you to keep doing it, for one. Would that be fair?"

"No, that's not fair."

Exum quoted Thomas: "'I think he wanted me to do it.'"

"I don't remember saying that."

"I'm asking you," Exum persisted.

"You're very sagacious," Thomas responded. "You probably did get that out of me, but I don't remember that."

"Do you think that's true?"

"On some level, he wanted me to."

"Yeah. Showed you how to tie off your arm?"

"Looking back now," Exum said, "you think the drugs had an effect on you?"

"Throughout my whole life," Thomas stated.

And if they'd had an effect on him, was he truly sure he'd chosen his path? Exum wondered.

"Yes," Thomas stated.

"You, the kid who between seven and thirteen took at least four different kinds of drugs and drank, right? I mean, is that a fair characterization?"

"That's fair, but I'm not looking for an excuse or a reason."

"It's not an excuse?" the defense attorney questioned.

"It's not an excuse. It's not a predisposition."

"It could be a reason," Exum argued.

"No."

"If it's a reason, then this jury might have a reason not to give you death?"

"Exactly."

Chuck Hughes looked at Justin Thomas and greeted him.

"Good afternoon, Mr. Hughes," Thomas responded.

"Let's not dance around it," Hughes said. "You want the death penalty, not because you want to die, but because you want lawyers for the rest of your life. Is that right?"

"Not the rest of my life," Thomas replied. "Just as long as it takes to prove the injustice I've suffered the past thirteen years."

"You think you'll get better appellate work if you get the death penalty. Is that right?"

"Yes."

"That's why you want the death penalty. Isn't that right?"

"Yes."

He asked about Thomas's spirit of the warrior philosophy, declaring it was a "prison thing," more specifically a Mexican prison-gang philosophy.

Thomas repeatedly denied being a prison gang member, despite his tattoos to the contrary, which Hughes emphasized were prison tattoos and were gang-based. Scalisi repeatedly objected to such references. But, indeed, Thomas's favorite tattoo read *SUR 13* (Sur short for *Surenos,* Spanish for Southerner, 13 for the thirteenth letter in the alphabet—M), which could indicate membership in or affiliation with the Southern California Mexican Mafia. Hughes insinuated that Thomas had been a prison gang member in Texas, too. A tattoo across Thomas's shoulders, one he'd had while imprisoned in Texas, read *Sureños,* another indication he might be affiliated with the Mexican Mafia.

Thomas's responses hinted that the prosecutor might be correct.

Hughes referred to letters the defendant had written while in Texas stating that "people who break down in a fight are hos," and "what you do to hos is you make them commit sexual acts and make them clean your cell" and make them pay protection.

"I didn't force it from them," Thomas responded. "They voluntarily gave it. They wanted my protection."

Thomas had been in many prison fights, Hughes argued. Though Thomas may or may not have actually started them, he'd frequently egged them on. While incarcerated in Texas, he'd bragged to his family that he'd won six fights, lost one, and had one draw.

Thomas admitted he'd been in three fights since arriving

in Riverside, but he argued he'd never stabbed anyone with his shanks.

Hughes countered that Thomas didn't have to stab anyone himself because he had others who would do it for him. "Don't you run the jail?"

"No, sir."

"Didn't you on March 9, 2004, tell Correctional Deputy Galindo that you run the jail?"

Thomas again denied that.

But Hughes insisted that on March 9, 2004, after Deputy Galindo had handed the inmate his *Maxim* magazine and Thomas had complained about the disappearance of other magazines, Thomas had told the deputy, "Don't you know who I am? I am 'Russo.' I'm running things here and that's no secret."

Thomas denied saying such a thing, but stated that he was called "Russian," not "Russo," a moniker he'd picked up in Texas.

Hughes asked him if he was a "shot caller" in jail, a title often associated with the Mexican Mafia. Thomas hesitated before answering, "No, sir." Hughes jumped on that hesitation.

"Well, I mean, it just doesn't make sense to me. I wouldn't gain any ground for me to put it out there like that," Thomas stated. "In fact, it would do the opposite. It would draw too much attention to someone if they were, so that doesn't make any sense." He then asked the prosecutor if that was the only instance he had on him.

"No," Hughes said.

"Pray tell," Thomas returned. "Go on. If there's more, let me see it, because that's news to me."

"The way it works is I'll ask the questions. And cover the areas that I need to cover."

"Okay. I'm sorry."

Hughes argued that Thomas had lied on the witness stand in Texas. Sometimes Thomas denied that and sometimes he admitted it. "So the truth is," Hughes demanded, "you're willing to lie to a jury to try to avoid a murder conviction. Isn't that right?"

"I've already been convicted," Thomas stated. "What am I trying to get away from?"

"And I'm talking to you about under what circumstances you're willing to lie to a jury." He asked if Rafael Noriega had been his drug supplier.

"I won't answer that."

"You already admitted it to Martin Silva on tape, didn't you?"

"Okay," Thomas responded. "But I won't admit to it on the stand." A rule of the Mexican Mafia was don't be rat.

Hughes pointed out that Dorothy Brown had testified that Noriega was Thomas's supplier. "Was she telling the truth?"

"That's your assumption," Thomas answered.

"Was it accurate?" Hughes repeated.

"I don't want to answer that."

"Well, with me, that's not an option you have."

"I'm not answering you, Mr. Hughes."

Judge Boren ordered Thomas to answer.

"I do not want to answer that question, Your Honor."

"I understand that you don't want to, but I'm ordering you to."

Hughes decided to simply rephrase his question. "You're not going to deny that it was accurate, are you?"

Thomas didn't respond.

"Are you refusing to answer any further questions?"

"In regard to him, yes, sir."

"Now, you said you stopped using drugs from time to time. Is that right?"

"Yes, sir."

Hughes glared at Thomas. "I'm sorry. Something funny? I just saw you smile, maybe a laugh. Did I miss something?"

"I smile quite often, Mr. Hughes."

"I didn't miss anything?"

"No, sir."

Hughes emphasized that the real reason Thomas didn't want the jail deputy to get injured on the shank hidden in Thomas's boxers was because an injured deputy would only make Thomas's jail life worse. He stated that despite the fact that Thomas hadn't used meth since July 5, 1995, he had used inhalants while incarcerated.

"Paint thinner," Thomas clarified.

Repeatedly Hughes stressed—and Thomas agreed—that Thomas had chosen not to use. For Thomas, drugs weren't a need, an obsession, a craving. They were a choice, just as his entire life had been. "The path you've chosen?"

"Yes, sir."

"The warrior spirit you've adopted?"

"Yes, sir."

"No other reason than that?"

"No, sir."

Darryl Exum stood. "Now, we've all heard it's true, you know, law of the jungle in prison. Somebody's going to get you or you're going to have to get somebody. Is it really like that?"

"Yes, sir."

"Okay. In prison, do you do your best to protect yourself?"

"Yes, sir, every day."

"Okay. Why? Why don't you just let somebody kill you?"

Thomas laughed.

"I'm not trying to be silly," Exum insisted.

"No, I know what you're trying to do again."

"Sorry," the attorney said.

"What was your question again?"

"Why don't you just let somebody kill you?"

"I don't want to die.

* * *

The following day, against Justin Thomas's wishes, Darryl Exum called S. Alex Stalcup, M.D., to the stand. On September 14, 2004, Stalcup had written a letter to Pete Scalisi outlining the doctor's previous February 2004 visit with Justin Thomas. *Addiction is predominantly an inherited disease; approximately 70 percent of addicts have a family history of addiction with 2 generations,* he wrote.

Judy Thomas had smoked marijuana and gotten drunk every single day of her pregnancy with Justin, according to Justin's uncle Andy Anchondo. According to Dr. Stalcup, fetal alcohol syndrome damaged Justin Thomas's brain, impaired his reasoning abilities, logic, memory of good and bad consequences, self-worth, appreciation of right and wrong, and impulse control. Judy Thomas's continued substance abuse after Justin's birth, combined with her depression, as well as Jim Thomas's addictions and depressions, caused a serious attachment disorder. *Apart from the toxic results of alcohol and drug use during pregnancy, attachment disorder is an ominous predictor of subsequent maladaptive behavior in later years,* Stalcup wrote.

Thomas had told Stalcup he "got overboard into drugs" his senior year in high school, after suffering a football injury that prevented him from playing: "I got introduced to meth on a grand scale, pounds of it. . . . I was using a lot, and had trouble because I was using as much as I was dealing; it was hard to stay ahead of my debts." When playing semipro ball, "it got me," Thomas said. "I used until my nose was raw. I started smoking it until I lost my voice. I shot up until I lost my veins, then I rotated them." Justin Thomas was injecting seven to fourteen grams of speed into his body every single day. He was going two or three weeks without sleep. Twice, he was robbed. He was making drug deals with people he didn't know, moving pounds of meth. He described himself as a "gold mine" for Rafael Noriega.

"Then I got behind. It was 'pay up or else.' I thought everyone was out to get me. 'What the hell do I do now?' I always had weapons. There was a legitimate threat. I believed it, took it all serious. My death was imminent if they found me."

As a result of his own—yet inherited—drug abuse, Justin Thomas became severely mentally ill, suffering methamphetamine toxic psychosis, Stalcup said. The doctor referred to meth toxic psychosis as "a deadly psychotic behavior." It worsened Thomas's already pitiable reasoning abilities and impulse control. *Consequently, in a threatening environment Mr. Thomas would be at extremely high risk for displaying paranoid, impulsive behavior,* Stalcup penned.

Thomas told Stalcup, "I lost my mind, for months. I had the TV telling me things; I got paranoid. I got suspicious of friends. I saw rocks and bushes move. I'd shoot at things I thought were video cameras. . . . My dad taught me that there was a separate reality and only the select few could tap into it. I thought I was tapped into it. I had guardian angels, eyes, telling me what was what. I believed what they told me."

In 2007, Stalcup summed up: "In my opinion, to understand Mr. Thomas, it is necessary to place his behavior in the broad context of his strong genetic predisposition to addiction and mental illness, fetal alcohol exposure, attachment disorder, and uniquely early onset drug addiction. Mr. Thomas suffered all of these injuries before he had any consciousness of what was occurring. He has no responsibility for his genetic heritage and fetal damage; nor is he responsible for the injury done to him by his alcoholic and drug-addicted parents, who gave him addicting drugs throughout childhood. . . . This is the patho-physiologic basis for the poor judgment and impaired ability to inhibit impulses exhibited prominently and consistently by Justin Thomas."

At 2:29 P.M. on December 19, 2007, the jurors began deliberating the life-or-death fate of Justin Thomas. By noon on

December 21, 2007, they declared they were at an impasse. Further deliberation most likely would not be helpful, the foreman told the judge. The defense asked for a mistrial. The prosecution asked for further deliberation. Court was adjourned until January 3, 2008.

On January 3, 2008, the jurors required a mere two hours to reach their decision. At 3:27 P.M., court clerk Heather Chavez tried to read the verdict. She couldn't. Her tears wouldn't let her. Judge Boren read, "'We, the jury, in the above entitled action, fix the penalty for the murder of Rafael Noriega, in count one, as death.'"

Justin Thomas gave Heather Chavez a thumbs-up.

The women jurors cried too, but the panel believed Justin Heath Thomas showed no remorse at all.

Thomas believed his California death penalty conviction would allow him the funds to research his appeal in Texas. But his appeal time in Texas had long since run out. His only hope was a federal appeal based on new evidence proving his innocence. Such evidence didn't seem to exist. Still, Thomas had hope. That hope included freedom and spending time at a brothel, followed by taking time to adjust to freedom. After all, routine, he knew, was what had kept him alive in prison. And he must maintain routine to stay alive in the world. Justin Thomas believed he could have that routine by starting an Internet porn business. He'd be good at that, he thought with a grin.

Thanks to death, life was beginning, at least in Justin Thomas's brain.

MORE MUST-READ TRUE CRIME
FROM PINNACLE